CLEMATIS & CLIMBERS

Collins *practical gardener*

CLEMATIS & CLIMBERS

JOHN FELTWELL

First published in 2003 by HarperCollins*Publishers*

77–85 Fulham Palace Road, London, W6 8JB

The Collins website address is:

www.collins.co.uk

Cover photography by Tim Sandall

Photographic props: Coolings Nurseries, Rushmore Hill, Knockholt, Kent, TN14 7NN, www.coolings.co.uk

Design and editorial: Focus Publishing, Sevenoaks, Kent

Project editor: Guy Croton

Editor: Vanessa Townsend

Project co-ordinator: Caroline Watson

Design & illustration: David Etherington

For HarperCollins

Managing Editor: Angela Newton

Art Direction: Luke Griffin

Editor: Alastair Laing

A CIP catalogue record for this book is available from the British Library

ISBN 0007146523

Colour reproduction by Colourscan

Printed and bound in Great Britain by The Bath Press Ltd

Contents

Introduction

Climbers have to get up to get on. In their elevated part of the horticultural world, it is a life and death struggle to get high enough to find the light they need to grow new leaves, produce flowers and then set seed. The higher a climbing plant grows, the better able it is to disperse seeds – the key to successful survival. We, as gardeners, can encourage this natural process with careful planting and consistent care, whilst enjoying the flowers and foliage of these incredibly rewarding plants in so many different ways.

Planning for the growth of climbers is important, as some are so vigorous that they cannot be recommended for small patio or courtyard gardens. Fortunately, many smaller, less vigorous varieties are widely available, so it is fair to say that this category of plants truly offers something for everyone.

Many clematis and other climbing plants produce magnificent flowers, but there are also varieties that are often excellent for their foliage instead, especially evergreen varieties such as Cissus and Hedera, which can be grown to cover up unsightly backdrops and walls. These plants are also excellent for growing over fences, up trees, trellis and against buildings and sheds. Some climbers are also good at trailing, and will therefore grace hanging baskets or can be grown at the top of walls to trail downwards. Many climbing plants prefer the twilight world of shady gardens and are excellent choices for ground cover, while others produce dramatic fruits.

Clematis 'Blekitny Aniol'

Cucumis – the common gourd – growing on an arch

Clematis are amongst the most popular plants in the world. Their diversity is enormous and there are many to choose from to meet the structural and colour needs of the garden. There are herbaceous clematis that die down each year, small alpine varieties with cream flowers, and lots to choose from at mid-height for the herbaceous border. There are many more for trellis, tripods and walls and for growing through trees and hedgerows.

Amongst the most popular and vigorous climbers suitable for larger gardens are the Montana clematis, the ivies and Virginia creepers. There are also the tropical varieties that are popularly grown in conservatories, greenhouses and as house plants, or outside in warmer climates. These include bougainvilleas, streptosolens, tecomas and mandevillas.

As a general rule, it is a good idea to choose species of clematis and other climbers as opposed to hybrids and varieties, since the former always have a natural tendency to be hardier and thus more able to fight off disease. It is also advisable to read the sales label attached to a plant so that it can be checked for suitability for your garden. Choose wisely and buy well, and these magnificent plants will give you endless pleasure.

How to Use This Book

This book is divided into three parts. The opening chapters guide you through all areas of garden practice, from assessing your site, through planting and general care to propagation techniques. A comprehensive plant directory follows, with individual entries on over 250 of the most commonly available clematis and climbing plants. These are listed in alphabetical order, with separate chapters devoted respectively to clematis varieties and an extensive range of other climbers. The final section of the book covers plant problems. Troubleshooting pages allow you to diagnose the likely cause of any problems, and a directory of pests and diseases offers advice on how to solve them.

latin name of the plant genus, followed by its **common name**

detailed descriptions give specific advice on care for each plant, including pruning and pests and diseases

alphabetical tabs on the side of the page, colour-coded to help you quickly find the plant you want

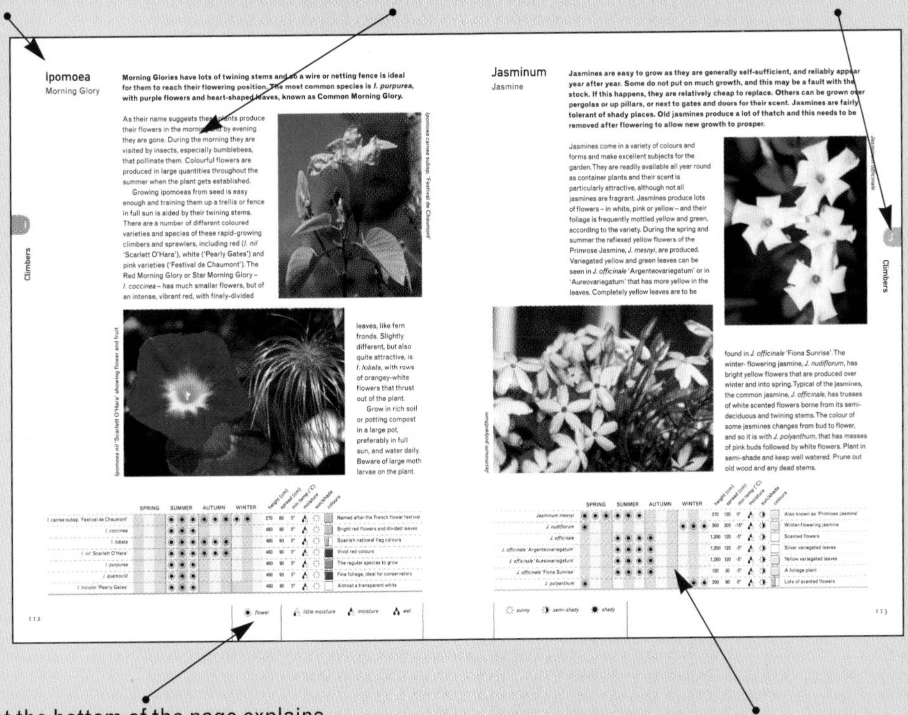

Ipomoea
Morning Glory

Morning Glories have lots of twining stems and so a wire or netting fence is ideal for them to reach their flowering position. The most common species is *I. purpurea*, with purple flowers and heart-shaped leaves, known as Common Morning Glory.

As their name suggests these plants produce their flowers in the morning and by evening they are gone. During the morning they are visited by insects, especially bumblebees, that pollinate them. Colourful flowers are produced in large quantities throughout the summer when the plant gets established.

Growing ipomoeas from seed is easy enough and training them up a trellis or fence in full sun is aided by their twining stems. There are a number of different coloured varieties and species of these rapid-growing climbers and sprawlers, including red (*I. nil* 'Scarlett O'Hara'), white ('Pearly Gates') and pink varieties ('Festival de Chaumont'). The Red Morning Glory or Star Morning Glory – *I. coccinea* – has much smaller flowers, but of an intense, vibrant red, with finely-divided leaves, like fern fronds. Slightly different, but also quite attractive, is *I. lobata*, with rows of orangey-white flowers that thrust out of the plant.

Grow in rich soil or potting compost in a large pot, preferably in full sun, and water daily. Beware of large moth larvae on the plant.

Ipomoea carnea subsp. 'Festival de Chaumont'

Ipomoea nil 'Scarlett O'Hara' showing flower and fruit

	SPRING	SUMMER	AUTUMN	WINTER	height (cm)	spread (cm)	min temp (°C)	moisture	sun/shade	colours	
I. carnea subsp. 'Festival de Chaumont'		● ● ●	● ● ●	● ●	270	80	5°				Named after the French flower festival
I. coccinea		● ● ●			460	90	5°				Bright red flowers and divided leaves
I. lobata		● ● ●	● ● ●		460	90	5°				Spanish national flag colours
I. nil 'Scarlett O'Hara'		● ● ●	● ● ●		460	90	5°				Vivid red colours
I. purpurea		● ● ●			460	90	5°				The regular species to grow
I. quamoclit		● ● ●			460	90	5°				Fine foliage, ideal for conservatory
I. tricolor 'Pearly Gates'		● ● ●			460	90	5°				Almost a transparent white

● flower   little moisture   moisture   wet

112

Climbers

Jasminum
Jasmine

Jasmines are easy to grow as they are generally self-sufficient, and reliably appear year after year. Some do not put on much growth, and this may be a fault with the stock. If this happens, they are relatively cheap to replace. Others can be grown over pergolas or up pillars, or next to gates and doors for their scent. Jasmines are fairly tolerant of shady places. Old jasmines produce a lot of thatch and this needs to be removed after flowering to allow new growth to prosper.

Jasmines come in a variety of colours and forms and make excellent subjects for the garden. They are readily available all year round as container plants and their scent is particularly attractive, although not all jasmines are fragrant. Jasmines produce lots of flowers – in white, pink or yellow – and their foliage is frequently mottled yellow and green, according to the variety. During the spring and summer the reflexed yellow flowers of the Primrose Jasmine, *J. mesnyi*, are produced. Variegated yellow and green leaves can be seen in *J. officinale* 'Argenteovariegatum' or in 'Aureovariegatum' that has more yellow in the leaves. Completely yellow leaves are to be found in *J. officinale* 'Fiona Sunrise'. The winter- flowering jasmine, *J. nudiflorum*, has bright yellow flowers that are produced over winter and into spring. Typical of the jasmines, the common jasmine, *J. officinale*, has trusses of white scented flowers borne from its semi-deciduous and twining stems. The colour of some jasmines changes from bud to flower, and so it is with *J. polyanthum*, that has masses of pink buds followed by white flowers. Plant in semi-shade and keep well watered. Prune out old wood and any dead stems.

Jasminum officinale

Jasminum polyanthum

	SPRING	SUMMER	AUTUMN	WINTER	height (cm)	spread (cm)	min temp (°C)	moisture	sun/shade	colours	
Jasminum mesnyi	● ● ●	● ● ●			370	120	0°				Also known as 'Primrose Jasmine'
J. nudiflorum	●			● ● ●	300	300	-15°				Winter-flowering jasmine
J. officinale		● ● ●	●		1,200	120	-5°				Scented flowers
J. officinale 'Argenteovariegatum'		● ● ●	●		1,200	120	-5°				Silver variegated leaves
J. officinale 'Aureovariegatum'		● ● ●	●		1,200	120	-5°				Yellow variegated leaves
J. officinale 'Fiona Sunrise'		● ● ●	●		120	30	-5°				A foliage plant
J. polyanthum	●			● ●	300	90	0°				Lots of scented flowers

sunny   semi-shady   shady

113

a key at the bottom of the page explains what each symbol means

variety charts list recommended varieties for most genera of climber and species of clematis that feature more than one variety. These display key information to help you choose your ideal plant, showing:

- when the plant is in flower during the year
- the height and spread after optimum growth
- the water and light requirements
- the principle colour of the flowers (or foliage)
- additional comments from the author

Assessing Your Garden

Your garden offers great opportunities for growing clematis and climbers, whatever its size or shape. However, before rushing in with a spade and an armful of new climbers, make a note of where the sunny areas are, which parts of the garden or patio see more shade and at what times of the day, which borders retain water and which are free-draining. This exercise will help you choose the right plants for your particular garden area (see opposite page).

In a small courtyard garden, you can use climbing plants as trailers in hanging baskets or in window boxes. For the summer season, sub-tropical exotic climbers can be experimented with – for instance allamandas, aristolochias, rhodochitons and tecomarias.

Colourful annual climbers, such as nasturtiums, can really brighten up a dull patio. They can also be planted among runner beans to add a touch of colour. Old varieties of climbing vegetables and decorative gourds are now freely available by mail order, and you can have great fun with these around the garden. Why not cover up the side of a dull-looking shed with these or some of the other vigorous growing climbers you will find in this book?

Clematis montana 'Tetrarose' in full bloom

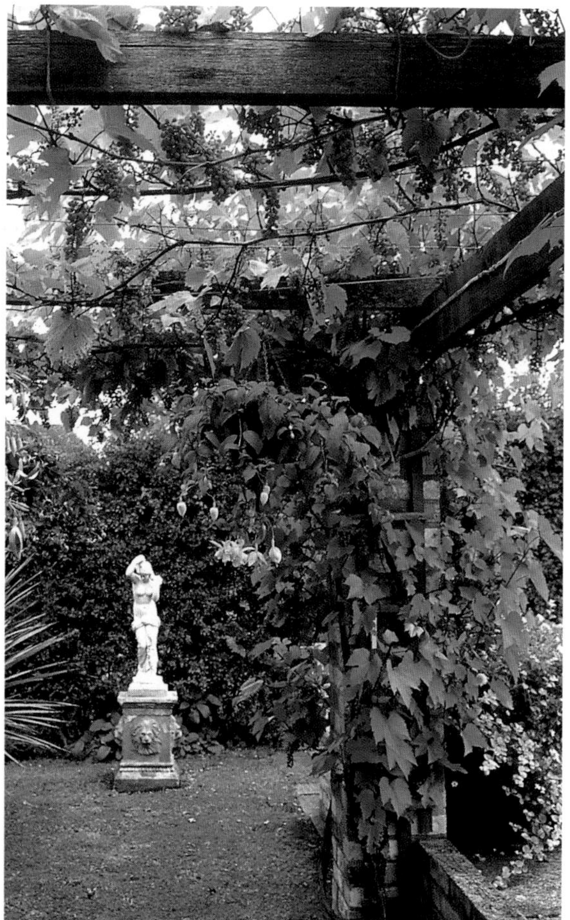
Pergolas offer infinite possibilities for climbers

In a busy herbaceous border, introduce a climber to scramble through the foliage as if it had been there all the time. While a border is developing and buds are popping, try experimenting with climbers or scramblers to make interesting colour combinations. Evergreen shrubs make an ideal backdrop to a colourful rambler.

If your garden does not have a tree as its centrepiece, a wigwam or pyramid can be used instead to great effect. You can grow at least four climbers around such a structure – hybrid clematis are ideal. For a garden with a pergola, the opportunities to decorate the pillars and crossbars with climbers are almost infinite. Climbing roses and honeysuckles do well, interspersed with hybrid clematis.

Around the outside of the house is a good place for Virginia creepers, climbing hydrangea, climbing roses and ivies. These are also excellent for a long vista, where you can break up the horizon, creating a more enclosed space. Due to the fact that they are evergreen, ivies offer particularly good value as year-round climbers.

Specific Conditions

Each garden is different, with its own specific, prevailing conditions to take into account. The illustration below is a representation of a 'typical' garden, comprising a number of different elements which usually feature in most gardens.

Of course, your own garden may look very different from the one illustrated here, but you will almost certainly need to take the same factors into account when assessing the suitability of your garden for the cultivation of clematis and climbers. Remember that it is always easier to work with conditions as you find them. Don't try too hard to fight Nature, because Nature usually wins in the end. That said, with a few slight changes to your garden, you can improve considerably your plants' chances of growing, without too much effort and expense.

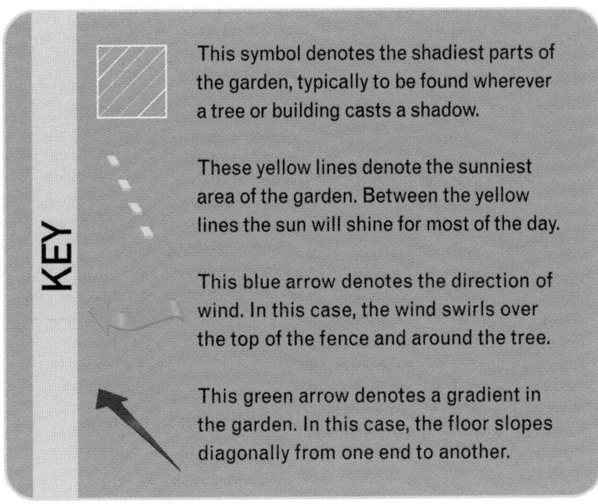

moderate breeze – do not plant susceptible climbers in this area

free-draining area due to gradient

sunny, fenced corner, ideal for putting up a trellis or wire netting support for sun-loving climbers

shaded area in the afternoons – suitable for shade-tolerant climbers

put trellis up to brighten up an otherwise dull shed

established evergreen shrub – ideal for growing a rambler through – but prone to damp, so plant tolerant climbers

shaded area in the mornings

suitable for semi-shade-tolerant climbers

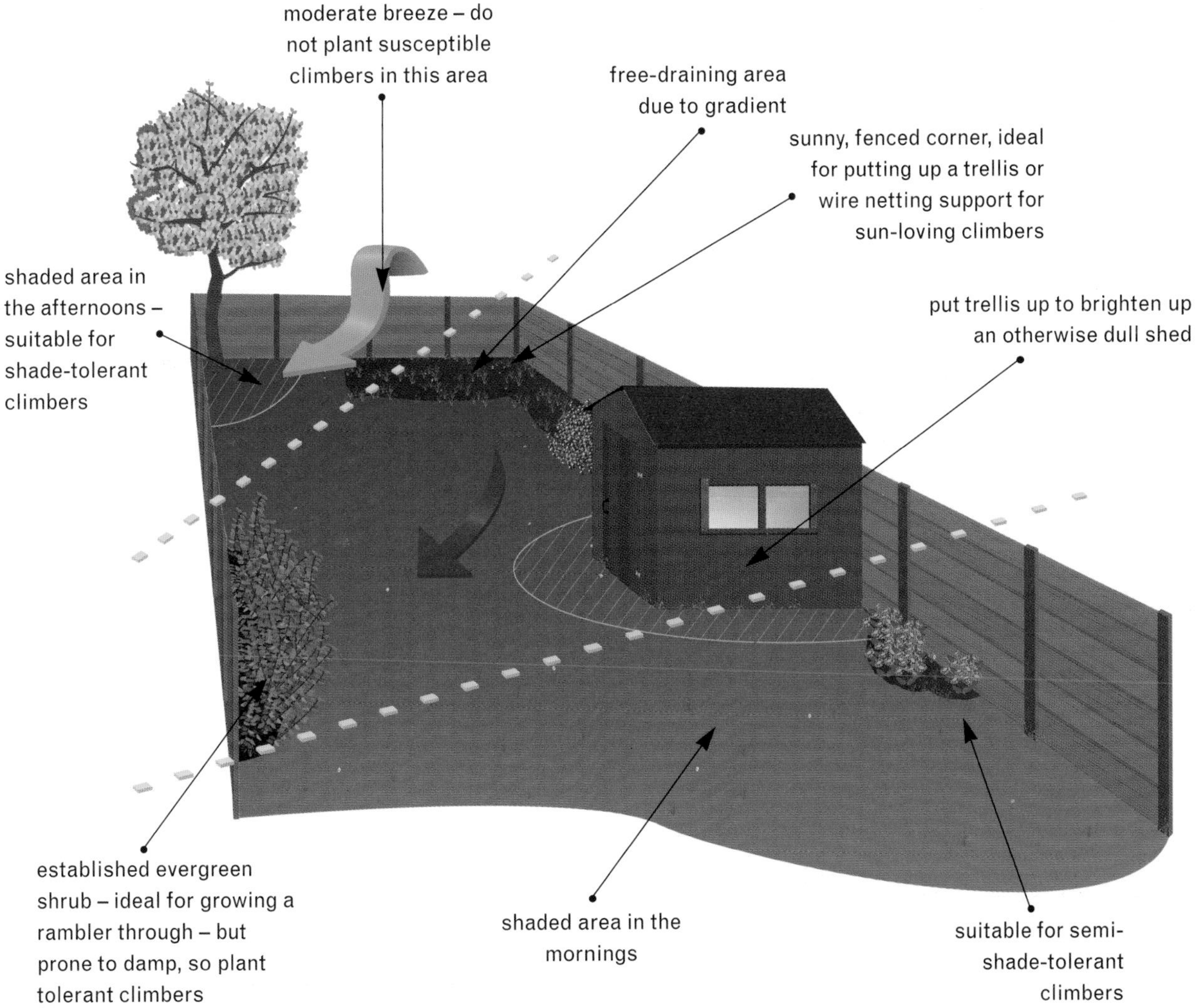

Choosing & Buying Plants

What is the plant for?

When you are choosing plants there are a number of factors to be taken into consideration. What you have in mind for the plant – ie. where you want to position it, the conditions you have in your garden, how large you want the plant to grow and how much time you can afford to spend looking after it – should determine the type of plant you are looking for and your ultimate choice.

You can either choose to buy plants by mail order or visit a nursery or garden centre. Visiting a nursery does at least give you the chance to inspect all the plants on display and buy the specimen that is in the best condition and which most closely suits your requirements. If it is an instant effect that you're after, then a plant smothered with lots of buds should do the job nicely; if, however, the plant is required as part of a long-term planting scheme, then a more critical eye is needed.

Clematis flammula spilling out of an urn in a botanic garden

Checking for a healthy rootball

There are several key indicators that will tell you instantly whether a plant is in good condition or not and a healthy rootball is certainly one of the most important. Look for a pot-grown climber that sits well in its container; neither so tight that it has become pot bound and stunted, nor so loose that it comes right out of the pot when lifted. The roots should not be growing too far outside the confines of the pot and nor should they be waterlogged and soggy. Another sign of neglect to watch out for is stems that have not been tied in. Also, reject any plant where the surface of the pot is covered in green moss, which might indicate that it has been sitting in a damp place for a while. A healthy rootball is easy enough to check for before you commit yourself to buying the plant and will provide you with a good indication of the overall health of the plant.

A healthy, well-formed rootball

soil	Clematis prefer to be grown in well-drained, fertile, humus-rich soil
site	Sun or partial shade in a sheltered position is favoured by most clematis
watering	Clematis should be kept well watered and never allowed to dry out
general care	Mulch with manure in late winter. Feed regularly with fertilizers. Provide support and prune heavy top growth
pests & diseases	Clematis wilt may be a problem. Watch out for aphids and whitefly, and spray at the first sign

Avoid plants like this *Clematis armandii* that has diseased leaves

TIP

When choosing a clematis or other climbing plant, look closely at the leaves – they are full of clues. Small, pale green leaves indicate a lack of feeding; no leaves on the stem suggests that the plant has been allowed to dry out frequently; few leaves at the top of the plant indicate that it has probably been in the pot too long.

A robust plant

A robust plant should have a well balanced shape and should look generally healthy, with a range of shoots arising all around the plant. It need not necessarily be the tallest of the bunch, with lead shoots going out in all directions, so do not be afraid to reject such a plant in favour of checking out another garden centre that might have better, fresher stock. The plant should not necessarily have flowers at this stage, though some climbers do flower precociously. However, if this is the case beware, as this may be an indication that the plant has invested all its energy into flowering at the expense of making sufficient root growth.

Checking for pests and diseases

The health of a plant is of paramount importance if you are to ensure that it becomes well established in your garden. As mentioned on the previous page, while mail order can be a convenient and time-saving way of buying plants, the downside is that inspection is out of the question. Visiting several nurseries or garden centres to assess the quality of the stock is the safest bet.

The plant you choose should be disease-free – as far as it is possible to inspect it – and should have no obvious pests adhering to it, no cut or partially eaten leaves or nibbled stems, and no white grubs in the root-ball. Discard any specimens that have slugs around their roots, around the pot or in the soil. The colour of the leaves should be impeccable, with no visible discolorations, dead ends or dead pieces.

Check that the roots of the plant are not exposed, as if they are this will often suggest that the plant has not been planted properly. Any signs of damage at root level also mean that disease could set in. Similarly, dirty pots or potting mixture that is full of weeds or algae can lead to problems later on.

Additionally, sparseness of leaves, spindly stems and flowers solely at the top of the plant usually indicate that a plant is probably potbound.

Clematis montana and *Laburnum* in a springtime display

Planting

Soak before planting

All potted plants need to be soaked thoroughly for at least ten minutes before they are planted. Plunge the entire rootball into a bucket of water, leaving it in its pot so that the compost does not disperse. This will give you time to prepare the hole in which to plant your clematis or climber, or to prepare a container for it. The roots of the plant need to be well watered so that it can get off to a good start as soon as it is has been put in the ground. You cannot simply rely on sufficient water permeating through the soil or compost after planting.

Preparing the hole

The hole that you dig for your plant needs to be at least three times the size of the rootball to be accommodated. In the case of clematis, as a rule the deeper the hole you dig the better. The hole can be up to even a metre (3ft) deep. Arrange a few dead sticks or small stones at the bottom of the hole, to assist drainage. This is particularly important in clay soil, which does not drain well. If too much water remains in the hole, it will rot the roots of the plant. The hole then needs to be filled with water so that all the surrounding soil is thoroughly permeated with moisture. Place the plant in the hole and then firm all around it with compost.

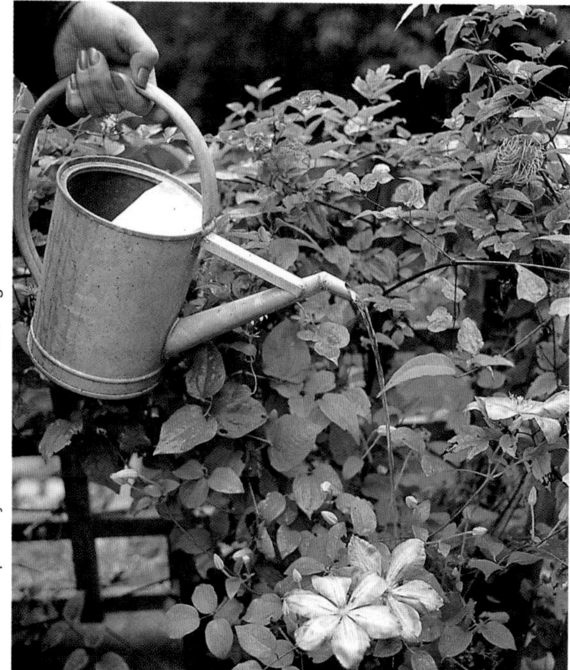

Clematis especially thrive on lots of watering

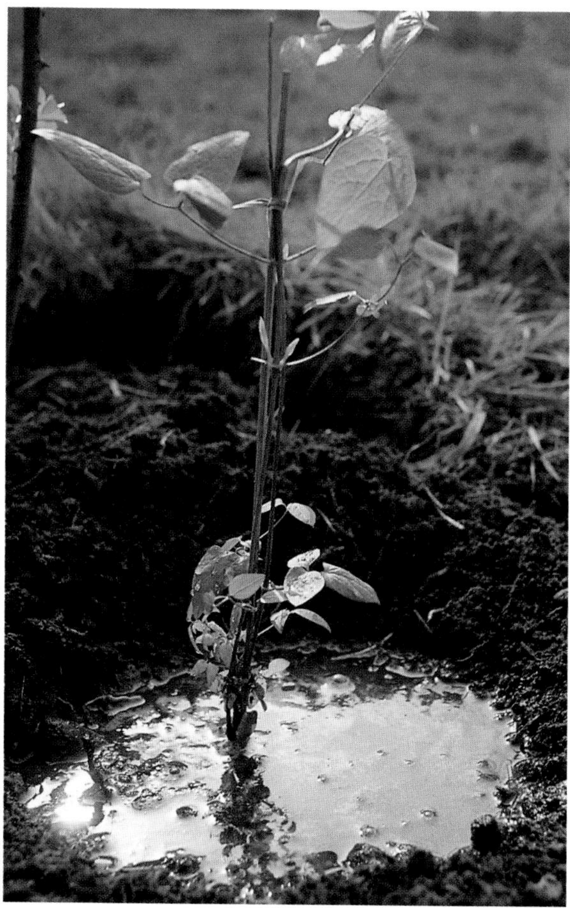

A small trench dug around the plant helps trap water

A depression needs to be made all the way around the climber so that when it is subsequently watered the water does not run off away from the plant. The depression should be in the form of a funnel directing water to the centre of the plant. Clematis thrive on lots of water, so give them plenty in the morning and evening. However, avoid overwatering during hot sunny weather, since the sudden application of cold water on warm root hairs can have a disastrous effect.

TIP

Clematis and climbers will grow in many soil types, providing there is an adequate supply of water and nutrients. With clay soil, add composted bark or straw manure to open the soil and increase the amount of air in it. If the soil is dry and sandy, adding copious amounts of manure or compost will help improve its water-retaining capabilities.

Planting onto a Tripod

There is no end to the immense choice of support systems available for climbers. These include ready-made structures bought directly from the garden centre, the types you self-assemble at home or a frame that is designed and put together at home for the gardener's particular individual purpose. A climber planted in a container can either be positioned against a wall with trellis or other support for it to clamber up, or else given its own support to climb within the pot. The climber can then be placed wherever is desired in the garden and need not be confined to a wall area. The ideal growing aid to use in a container is a tripod, as a climbing plant can be easily trained to grow up within and around the vertical struts that form the structure.

In the example shown, a ready-made hazel stick tripod is used for training ivy up and out of a pot. Make sure that the pot used is large enough to accommodate the dimensions of the tripod. First of all, put pieces of broken pot into the base of the pot for drainage, followed by some compost. Carefully transfer the plant out of its original container, wearing gloves to protect the plant, and introduce it to the new pot [A]. Once the plant is in its new home, fit the tripod firmly into the pot. Gently tease out the ivy stems and ease them through the hazel tripod [B], being careful not to break any on the way through the uprights. Tie up the ivy stems to the tripod using raffia or any type of loose twine [C].

Once the plant has become established on the tripod, regular trimming will keep it the desired shape or you can allow it to spread freely, depending on the look required for the patio or area of the garden.

Different shaped pots or containers can be used for training climbers. For example, if you want to use a square tub, then the best support to use would be a pyramid trellis. These can be bought in one piece or come in separate parts, allowing the climber to be eased through the trellis after each section has been put in place as you construct the pyramid. Whatever shape you choose, the plant will enjoy scrambling up and through it, bringing a little visual delight to your garden or patio.

A

B

C

A

B

C

Planting onto Canes

As an alternative to buying a ready-made tripod, you can use everyday bamboo canes to train a climber in a pot or container.

Carefully select a potted plant with established growth and good potential. Take the plant out of its pot and, retaining as much of the rootball as possible, carefully introduce it to the new pot [A], retaining the plant's original cane support for the time being. Once the plant is potted, water in thoroughly [B]. Allow for the plant to take up most of the water before putting in the new canes. Take the plant's original cane support away (re-use it if it is a similar height to the others) and arrange the canes around the plant. Tie up the stems using raffia or any type of loose twine [C].

Care & Maintenance

All plants need a little care and attention if they are to thrive. Simple maintenance, as outlined here, will help to ensure a fantastic garden all-year round.

TIP The picture below shows wire that is biting into an established vine. In this case, the fact that the wire support is embedded in the stem does not cause too much of a problem; however, to prevent growing stems becoming constricted and causing stems to die back, as a rule fix up plastic-coated wire, which in addition will not rust.

Tying Up and Support

Vine eyes and wire lattice

Vine eyes are the most practical means for securing a climber's support on walls. They are long lasting (as long as you choose the galvanized variety), and they can support a lot of weight. They will also help thwart the effects of wind and storm damage to any plant attached to them. Remember that many climbers are extremely vigorous and will ride roughshod over any short-term measures to tie them up – leading instead to damage to both plants and masonry.

When planning the spread of climbers it is best to anticipate the area to be covered and put in enough vine eyes accordingly. Vine eyes can be driven or screwed directly into brickwork, mortar and masonry. Hold the vine eye steady and hammer, or screw it, into the wall. (If you have a traditional-shaped vine eye – a long, round-headed shape – leave about 5cm (2in) of the vine eye showing on the outside.) Thread wire through the eye and twist until taut, taking the wire across and linking up with the other vine eyes. This lattice of wire attached to vine eyes will provide a supporting framework strong enough for most climbers. The next step is to tie in the stems to the wire.

Traditional vine eyes

A vine eye with a training wire attached

Wires biting into an established vine

Tying in

There are many different products available for tying climbing stems to wire or trellis structures. Always check that the plant has not outgrown its ties each year or that the product used has not rotted and come away from its support.

String is the most useful method for tying up leading shoots of climbers, and for tying in pruned wands of climbers after fruiting. Other materials may be appropriate, depending on the nature of the climber, the amount of wind damage expected and the desired look for display plants. For example, you can buy different coloured string to camouflage the ties and hide their obtrusiveness.

Raffia and twines are useful for soft stems, and wire loops can be put on woody stems, so long as the stems are not permitted to grow into the wood. Paper-covered twist ties are ideal when planting up a clematis in a pot, for example, as the delicate stems are gently held in place by these ties and can be easily removed once the plant has taken hold and established itself.

Netting and wire netting

For self-attaching climbers, an open net can be fixed to a wall and the plant encouraged to climb up it. There are many different types of netting available, invariably made of plastic, and in various colours. The problem with nets is that they can look awful until they are obscured with plants – and also, if you have a climber that needs to be cut down at the end of the season, untangling it from the netting holes can be tiresome. But as a quick and easy means of providing support, they have their merits.

Plastic netting is generally quite floppy and therefore needs to be well secured to a wall or fence to prevent it falling down or blowing over in the wind, taking your climber with it. To make the actual netting seem less obvious to the eye before the plant covers it, try buying a plastic netting in a colour that blends in with the background surface. For example, if your wall is painted white, don't fix up black netting! Work with the material that you have to make the most of your support system.

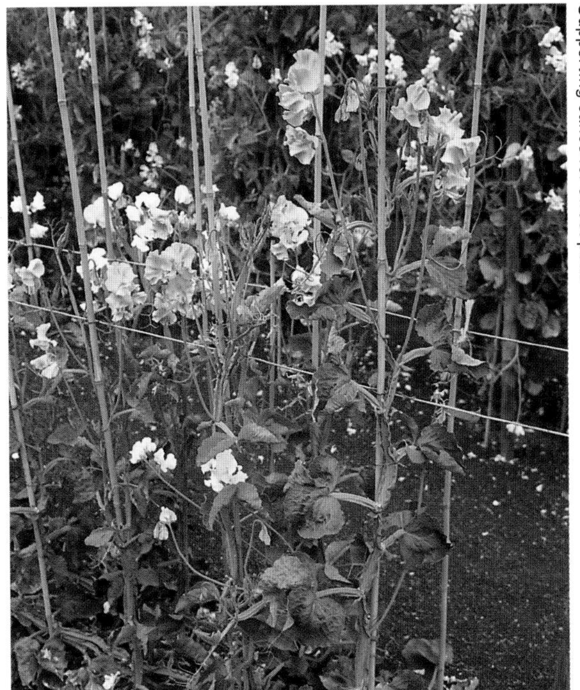

Supporting canes for sweet peas

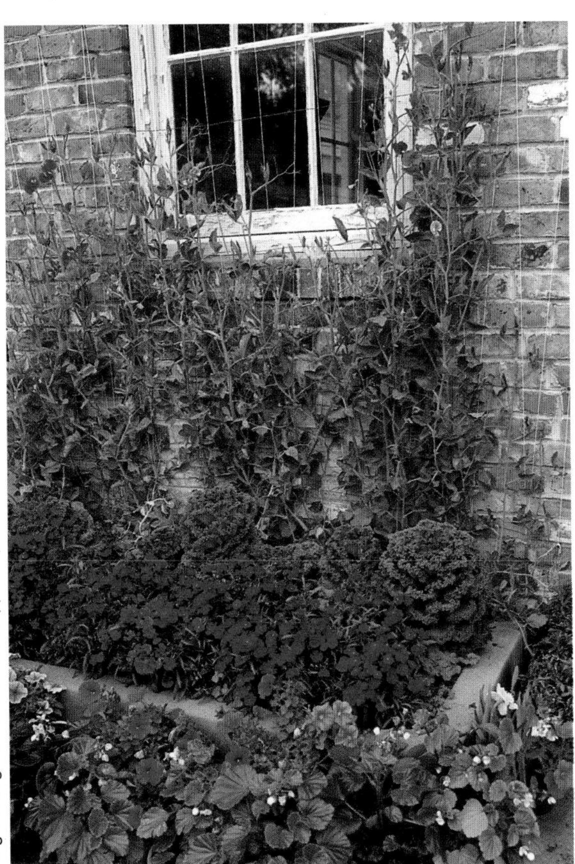

String netting makes a useful support up walls

Natural supports

Natural products look so much better as supports for climbers. Young shoots of a variety of plants can be used, ranging from hazel and willow to bamboo canes. These can be used singly or in a woven fashion to support climbers on their way up. They might be used as temporary support to get the climber into a hedgerow or tree branch, for instance, which will then take over the support role.

The more divided foliage of broom and hazel, cut in winter to avoid leaves forming, can be used to make small wigwams for shorter climbers on which to scramble. Larger supporting structures made of natural materials set the scene for a grand display of climbers in the garden. Supports can be made out of rustic wood in any shape or structure, such as a trellis, an arbour or a gazebo. Even before the plant scrambles up it, the structure can look attractive and dynamic in its own right, introducing a real focal point for the garden.

An old stone wall that has seen better days can be attractively disguised by climbing plants. If the climber needs help to cling on before scrambling up and covering the whole area, unobtrusive wall attachments such as vine eyes will hide the fact that any support has been provided at all.

Pruning

Clematis

Whatever the species or cultivar, clematis are pruned in three different ways.

Group 1 plants are those clematis that flower in the spring on last year's stems, so do not cut any old stems out. These include the alpinas and macropetalas, which are generally easy to contain and do not tend to spread all over the place. Occasionally, some will flower twice in one season if lightly pruned after the first flowering. For their early years, many Group 1 clematis often do not need any pruning at all.

Lightly pruning a clematis

Group 2 clematis – such as *Clematis* 'Marie Boisselot' – flower in early summer, also on last year's growth, so you should only cut these plants back in early spring before new growth begins, in this way leaving next year's crop of flowers unaffected. Remove all dead wood and leaves (see right), and even cut down to ground level if there are unsightly pieces of main stem.

Group 3 clematis are those that flower in late summer or early autumn on the current year's growth, so beware of taking away any new growth from these plants once they have begun sprouting new stems. Some are vigorous growers, however, such as the 'Jackmanii' clematis, and these can be pruned back to a pair of good buds on old stems, about 30cm (12in) above ground level.

A word of caution: beware of the apparently 'dead' stems of clematis, particularly in Groups 1 and 2. These should not be pruned as they are usually alive and will break readily, losing you at least one year's growth. The key is to wait until the plant sprouts and to tie the clematis up to avoid accidents and wind damage.

TIP

Although the very thought of pruning can instill fear into the heart of many a gardener, the basic rule is not to panic. Quite often, the worst that can happen if you do make a mistake is that the plant will flower later than it should. When pruning back a really overgrown specimen, you may need to cut it back hard and start again.

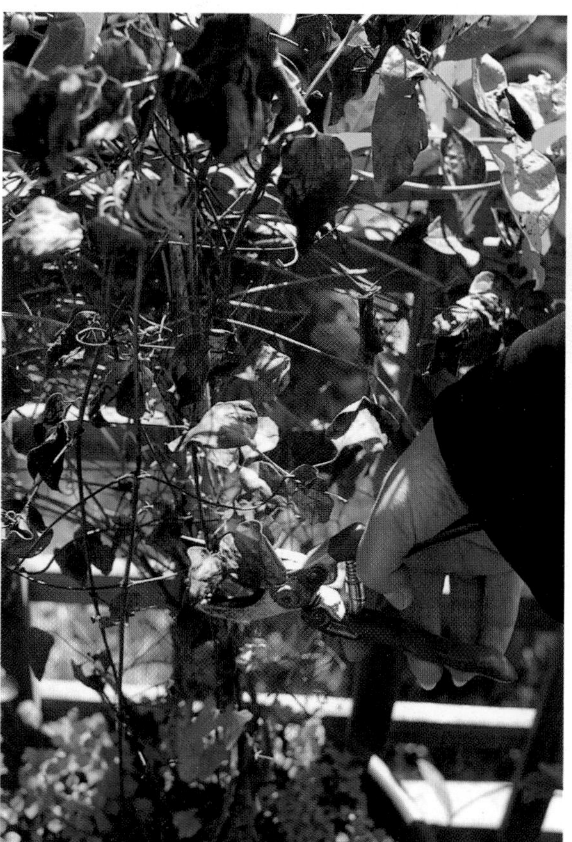

Pruning dead wood and leaves

Other climbers

For almost all established climbers, routine pruning is essential in successfully training a plant to promote vigorous, healthy growth and build a strong framework on which to grow.

It is important to separate the new wood from the old in climbers and rambling roses. Rambling roses flower only on new wood, and so all old wood needs to be pruned out. Climbing roses flower just the once in summer on the old wood of their long stems. They often do not need to be pruned in their first year during establishment. Thereafter they can be trained and pruned to maintain their shape.

Some other climbers like wisteria also benefit from a good prune. They can be sawn back in winter to their thick woody stems (thicker than a man's arm if it is an established specimen), and still they will sprout as if nothing has happened. In late summer, prune back the vigorous, leafy shoots, which will encourage more new buds to sprout the following year. Climbers that leave a thatch of dead material as they die back – such as the solanums, lathryus and tropaeolums – need to be cut back to ground level and the dead thatch burnt. Vitis can be pruned back to the first two buds on woody growth.

This shed is in danger of collapse under the weight of an overgrown *Humulus lupulus*...

...so a thorough pruning will benefit both the plant and its supporting structure

TIP

Using the correct tools for pruning is essential. A sharp pair of secateurs is the best piece of equipment for most pruning tasks, although for more drastic cutting back, long-handled loppers, gardening shears or even a handsaw – in the case of established wisteria – can all have their uses.

The only regime some climbers need is to be pruned back to keep them from straying too far beyond their allotted space, such as Parthenocissus, Hedera and Actinidia. The first two genera of climbers can be pruned and trained to fit defined areas of walls; ivy can be clipped to make intricate patterns and knots along walls.

Climbing honeysuckles can be pruned back severely if they have developed into a mass of tangled stems that bear flowers only at the top of the plant, making the rest of the honeysuckle look extremely shabby. Don't be too shy with the pruning – use shears for speed to remove dead material.

Feeding

All flowering plants benefit from regular feeding during the growing season, and clematis and other climbers are no exception. A regular feed using any one of a number of products currently on the market should help to ensure healthy, strong foliage and an abundance of flowers throughout the spring and summer months.

Applying feed

Fertilizers are available in either liquid, powder or granular form. All fertilizers will contain at least one of the three major elements required by plants for healthy growth: nitrogen for leaf and stem growth, potash to help fruit and flower formation, and phosphate to encourage a strong, healthy root system. 'Straight' fertilizers contain one element only and the purpose of these is generally either to encourage one particular function of plant growth or to correct a particular deficiency. 'Compound' fertilizers, on the other hand, contain all three elements and are generally sufficient for most plants' needs. When buying general purpose compound fertilizers, look on the bag for the three numbers that will tell you the content: for example 7.5.7 means that it contains 7 parts of nitrogen, 5 of phosphate and 7 of potash.

Liquid fertilizers have one advantage over solids in that they are instantly available to the plants. The main disadvantage is that they don't stay in the soil very long and so have to be used regularly. The easiest way to apply it is to use a watering can. Measure the correct amount into the cap of the fertilizer bottle [A]. Do not exceed the dosage as you may scorch the plant. Pour the liquid into the watering can and dilute with water [B]. Water in thoroughly around the roots of the plant [C].

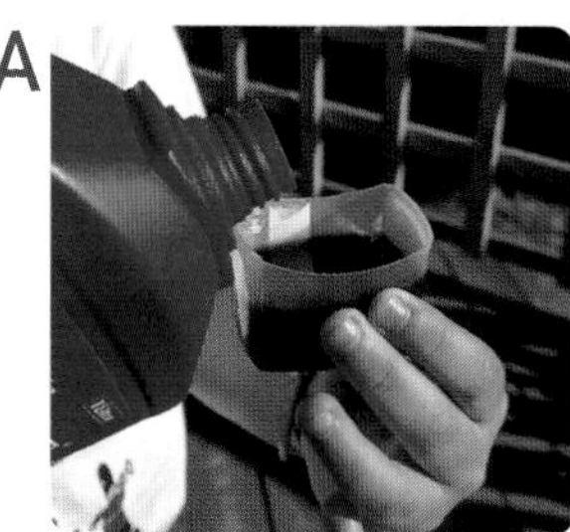

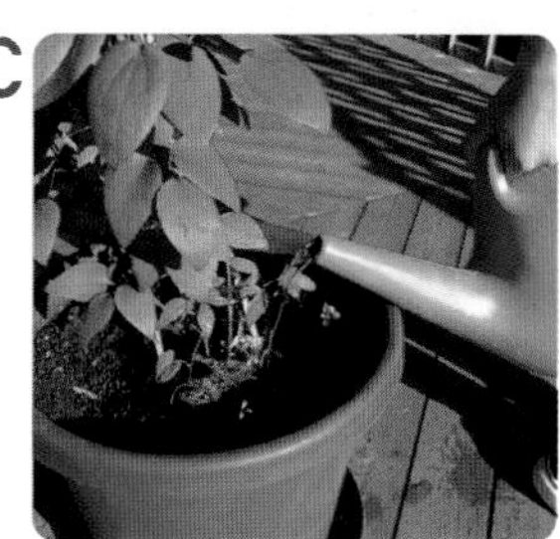

ALTERNATIVE COMPOUND FERTILIZERS	
There are numerous organic and artificial fertilizers on the market, all suited to a particular purpose. The following are a small selection of the most popular.	
Organic	Blood, fish and bone meal: a popular organic compound fertilizer that contains all three major nutrients. Simply sprinkle around the roots of the plant and then mix into the soil using a trowel or fork. Regular applications will help to maintain nutrient levels. Chicken manure concentrate: an organic compound fertilizer available in either powder or pellet form, the latter providing a useful slow- release action.
Artificial	Growmore: one of the most popular artificial compound fertilizers. Its effects are rapid and it is particularly suitable for use on vegetables and as a lawn feed. Rose fertilizer: one of several specialized compound fertilizers which can be used to feed all flowering plants, as well as fruit trees and bushes during the spring and summer.

Slow-release pellets

Slightly easier are the slow release pellets (see below) that are just thrown onto the surface around the plant, releasing essential nutrients to the plant each time it is watered or rained upon. Controlled release fertilizers comprise a compound fertilizer that has been pelleted and then coated in resin. The resin dissolves slowly, allowing the feed to be released over a long period, thus enabling the gardener to feed perhaps just once or twice a season.

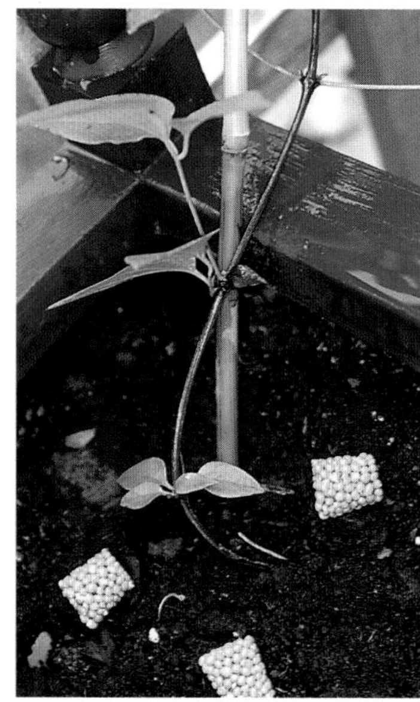

Propagating from Seeds

Collecting the seeds of climbers requires good timing. Seeds should not be collected too early when they won't have matured and hardened off, or too late, when they have started to rot or disperse from the plant. Keep an eye out for the state of maturity of the fruits, and whether they are showing signs of drying out and dispersing their seeds. Sometimes you may have to pick the ripe fruit to dry it out indoors. Hang the fruits up or lay the seeds on a tray for them to dry, before you are caught out by a damp autumn. The seeds should be fully dried, and any with imperfections – for instance, signs of weevil beetle attack – should be destroyed. Collect the seeds in a small paper bag, label it in pencil with the species and date, and then store it away from mice in a cool, dry place. Use the seeds within a year.

Sowing the seeds of clematis and climbers is very straightforward. They can be grown in small pots or trays filled with special compost for seeding [A]. The pot should be filled to 1cm (½in) beneath the rim, with the growing medium then lightly pressed down and watered. When the water has drained away, sprinkle on the seeds [B], and either finely cover them with more special seeding compost or gently insert the seeds a few millimetres (less than quarter of an inch) below the surface of the growing medium. Keep the surface of the compost moist at all times [C], but do not overwater or allow the pot or tray to become waterlogged, as this will damage the seeds.

The pots and trays should be kept in a warm place – on a windowsill or in a proprietary germinating box/chamber with a plastic cover and gentle undertray heating. Humidity is kept high in these boxes, but beware of the increased chance of fungal spores, such as mildew attacking the young and vulnerable plants.

A

B

C

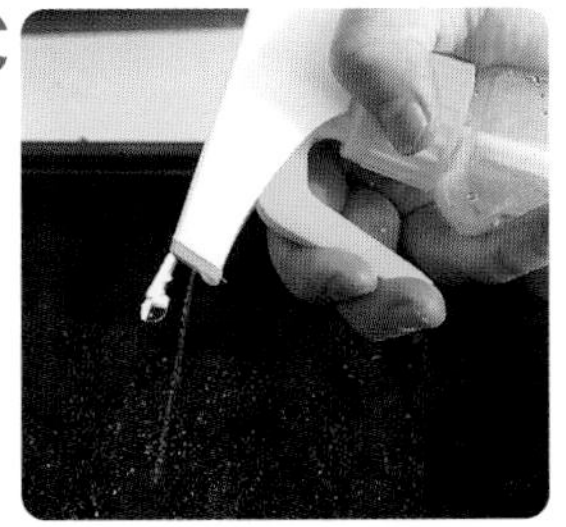

A tray of germinating clematis seeds

TIP

Growing from seed can be an extremely rewarding experience. To achieve the very best results, try to ensure the conditions and equipment used are clean. Dirt or residual rotting debris that comes into contact with the seeds can cause disease and pest infestation, which will stifle the plant at germination.

When the seedlings have at least one pair of leaves, they can be pricked out into small pots of compost and grown on. Repeat this process when the seedlings have at least doubled in size, each time using larger pots. Wait until the young plant has consolidated its roots within the pot, and then it can be taken out of the pot with its adhering rootball and planted directly into a hole dug especially for it. If you have previously staked the plant, then the stake can go straight into the hole at the same time as the rootball, and will then be ready in place when the time comes to tie up the climber.

Features of Climbers

Climbers have a number of attractive features and, as such, may be grown for differing qualities. Flowers are an obvious attraction, but many climbers also have distinctive foliage or may even produce fruits.

Leaves

The great advantage of gardening with climbers is their ability to climb surfaces and to produce masses of leaves. This often reflects their natural habitats, where they have to grow fast to find the sunshine in the shady places in which they germinate. Producing leaves is a means to grow, for the leaves are in effect solar panels that absorb the sun's energy and this energy is then converted into growth. Leaf production is fast and prolific in many climbers, flowering being reserved for much later on.

The leaves of many climbers are themselves of great attraction in the garden and are often the whole reason for growing these plants – the flowers being less conspicuous. Spectacular autumnal colours, as seen in plants such as Parthenocissus (the Virginia creeper) or Celastrus, make leafy climbers worthwhile. Climbers that smother walls with foliage are good value, especially where they are evergreen, such as ivy or *Ficus pumila*. Fun and variety can be had with deciduous climbers such as the white, pink and green leaves of *Actinidia kolmokita*. Where leaves and flowers come together and complement each other, this is the perfect combination, such as is found in the climber *Dregea*.

There is a great variety of different coloured leaves among climbers, ranging from the variegated leaves of jasmines and bougainvillea, to the bright yellow leaves of ivies and hops, and even to the plum red colours of vine leaves.

Ficus pumila 'Variegata'

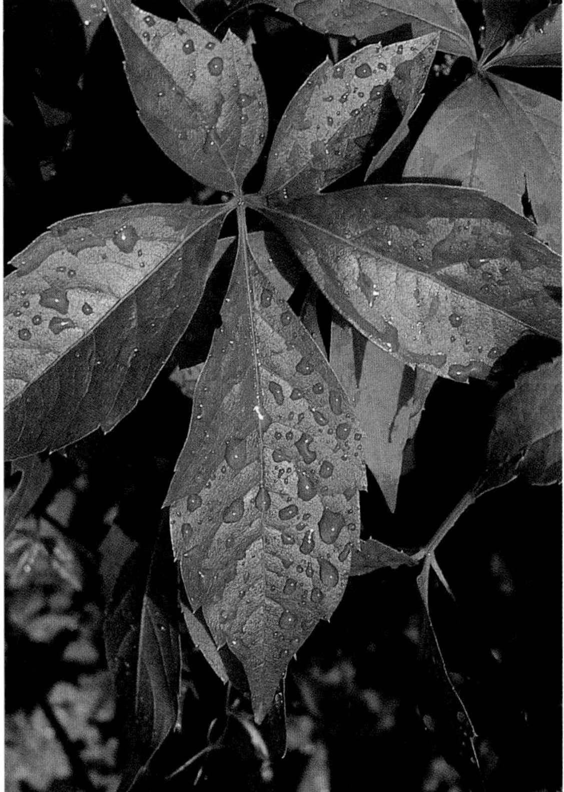

Parthenocissus (Virginia creeper)

Flowers

A few climbers, especially those that flower in the spring, produce flowers before their leaves have come out. This is to take advantage of the pollinating insects that awaken from hibernation and then immediately visit the first flowers of spring. The opportunistic Wisteria is a particularly good example of this kind of plant: its intertwining stems break out in flower at the onset of spring to catch the early insects. It is a high-risk strategy since a late frost can kill flowers overnight, but the payoff for successful pollination is fruit production.

The mass of flowers produced by many climbers makes gardening with this type of plant so worthwhile. Dazzling displays of sweet peas, mandevillas, morning glories and nasturtiums all attest to the floriferous powers of climbers that are commonly grown in gardens and on patios. The shape and size of flowers produced by climbers is seemingly boundless.

The purpose of flowers in most colourful climbers is to attract insects, so the flowers are a reflection of the attracting powers of the plant in association with a particular group of insects, such as bumblebees, honeybees and flies. Some climbers produce wonderfully scented flowers to attract insects, such as honeysuckle. Others, such as bougainvillea and clematis, have scentless yet vividly coloured bracts, and tiny, inconspicuous cream flowers.

Once established, flowering climbers trained up a pergola, archway or all over a wall can add the most amazing splash of dynamic colour to any garden or patio and become a real focal point. Rich scent is often an attractive added bonus.

TIP

Nasturtiums (*Tropaeolum spp.*) produce abundant foliage and are versatile flowering subjects as well, climbing up pillars or splaying over the sides of hanging baskets and window boxes. They can climb trellis, shin up other plants, scramble over just about anything or smother the ground with their excellent array of brightly coloured flowers.

Clematis 'Princess of Wales'

Ipomoea quamoclit

Fruits

Fruits of climbers either contain a single seed or many different seeds. In any case they are all produced after germination, when the flower ovary swells to produce a casing that envelops the seed. In many cases the surround is colourful and edible, and is a lure to birds. Birds – and to a lesser extent reptiles, such as lizards – eat the fruits and either pass the seeds out of their gut or flick them away while eating. The dispersal of seeds by birds is a good thing for all climbers.

Look out for the fruits of wisteria that are produced at the end of summer; being a member of the pea family, they are produced like runner beans, the seeds neatly arranged along the long pod. Other leguminous climbers left to 'go to seed' produce long pods in a similar manner. Sweet peas are another good example.

Passion flower fruits showing seeds

The fruits of a purple-leaved grape vine contain seeds

TIP

The Vine group, which include grapes, kiwi fruits and passion fruits, requires warm, sheltered positions for its fruits to ripen. In cool areas, ensure that the plants are given a sheltered environment or grow them in a conservatory or greenhouse. Prune stems back after fruiting each year to encourage new shoots to grow.

Climbers of the *Vitis* (vine) family produce fruits (grapes), which in some species are edible or can be used to make wine. The ornamental vines are cultivated for both their foliage and fruits. They are normally grown over a trellis, pergola or fence, or trained against a wall.

Passion flowers (*Passiflora spp.*), produce not only stunning flowers but ovoid- to spherical-shaped, fleshy fruits of various colours, which are variable in size and are often edible. The fruits generally mature to an orange-yellow or deep purple colour in the autumn. Birds and other wildlife visitors are good dispersers of the fruits. *Passiflora edulis*, otherwise known as Passion fruit, produces fruits that can be harvested for human consumption. Pick the fruits when they begin to change colour from green to either purple or yellow. The fruits can grow as large as 7cm (3in) in diameter. The two species of Passion fruit most commonly grown are the yellow-fruited *P. edulis* f. *flavicarpa* and the purple-fruited *P. edulis*.

Seeds

Seeds are produced in large quantities by clematis, each with a long tail or 'pappus' of hairs that carries it gently in the wind to be dispersed well away from the parent plant.

Inspect the fruit of Old Man's beard, *Clematis vitalba*, whose millions of tailed seeds resemble long facial hair when grouped together while still attached to their fruits. Unlike those climbers that have edible lures, clematis have evolved seeds for wind dispersal, which does not involve the bright colours needed to attract birds.

When roses 'set seed' they have several seeds within each hip, each protected by a covering of tiny hairs. Some climbers are grown for their bright autumnal fruits, such as *Rose filipes* 'Kiftsgate'. When birds eat the fruits, they fly off and inevitably pass the seeds out in a different place. Decorative fruits with seeds include the Heart Seed or Balloon Vine (*Cardiospermum spp.*) and the Butterfly Vine (*Stigmaphyllum spp.*) that has wings just like those of a butterfly.

Although the majority of climbers' fruits and seeds are of no great interest to the gardener, there are a few that are exploited in the garden and commercially, such as Cucurbita, Ficus, Humulus, Lathyrus, Passiflora, Phaseolus and Vitis. They have merits that surpass their food appeal. Try growing a selection of these up walls, over arches or over pergolas. Climbing crops in the garden are now a popular and well-established feature.

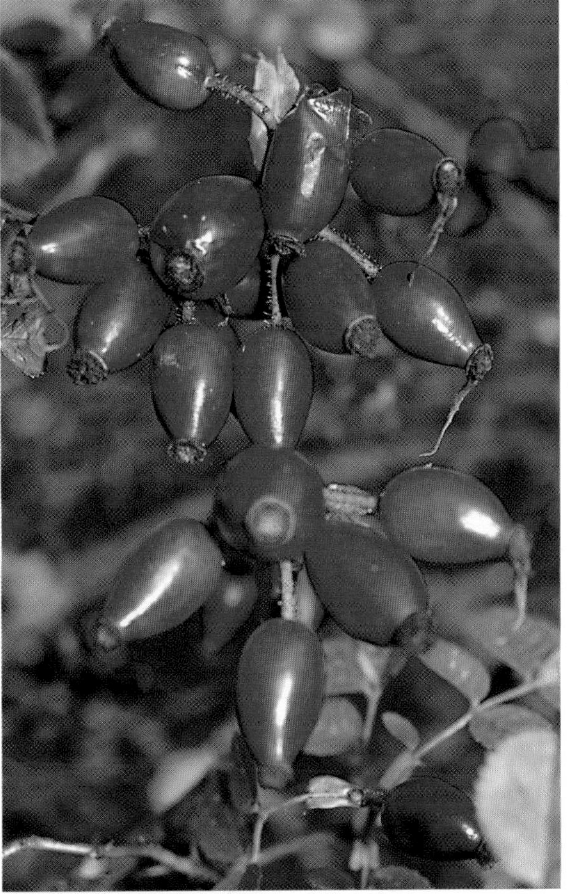

The red hips or fruits of wild rose contain many seeds

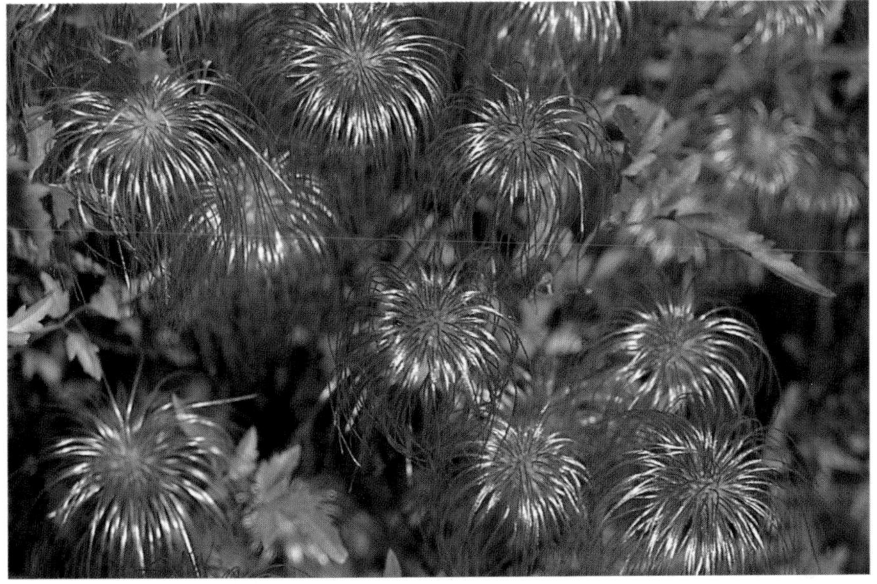

Seed heads of *Clematis tangutica*

Some climbers such as the hop (Humulus) exist as single sex plants. In the garden centre it is not always possible to know which sex you are buying. Not until they are mature do you find Humulus with hop fruits in the female, or garlands of male flowers that produce nothing but pollen. The female flowers of *Humulus lupulus* are used in brewing.

Climbing Methods

Twining leaf-stalks

Successful climbing in clematis is achieved by having highly versatile leaf-stalks that seek out and hug the contours of their host plant. The stalk bends round the host and allows the rest of the plant to press on upwards to find further footholds. A mass of leaf-stalks reinforces the attachment to the host, consolidating the clematis' pre-eminent position as the king of twiners.

Coiled tendrils of a passiflora

Tendrils can also twirl in the opposite direction (as shown in the photograph below), in this way making the union between plant and support that much more reliable.

Climbing stems

Some plants use their growing stems to find support, and this can be a very effective and fast way of securing their position before moving on and upwards. They do this by having a long growing stem that moves around in a circular manner (time-lapse photography can really show this to good effect) until it catches a support. Then it starts to twine around the support, before moving on to find further supports.

In most climbing plants, the leading stem rotates in a clockwise direction as the plant grows. However, some climbers, such as the Akebia, twist themselves around in an anticlockwise direction. It is impossible to train a climber that twists in one particular direction to wind itself around in the opposite direction. Plants will often die rather than deviate from their natural orientation. Sometimes, climbing stems will entwine around each other to form a dense framework that is strong and solid, helping to support the entire plant.

Twining tendrils

Passion flowers make headway up walls and trellises by having twining tendrils. These are very effective for a variety of reasons. They arise from nodes on the stem and actively seek out places on which to cling onto nearby support, usually other stems of the same plant. When they find a support, they twirl around like a spring. This 'vice-like' grip helps to cushion the plant from damaging wind and secure it in its upwardly mobile form.

The twining stems of *Ipomoea purpurea*

The climbing leaf stems of a clematis

onwards. Many tropical climbers naturally use aerial roots, and 'roots' from stems, as props or supports. A good example is the familiar houseplant Monstera.

Adhesive pads

As if mimicking the little suction pads that frogs and geckos use for scrambling up walls and ceilings, the stems of the Virginia creepers use a splay of adhesive pads at the end of twisting tendrils to climb up walls. These suction pads are an effective adhesive to most surfaces but are thankfully not as damaging to masonry as the adventitious roots of ivy. Blanket coverage of walls is achieved by this simple method of 'suction pad' climbing, giving the plant a secure position to flower and disperse its fruit. This method of clinging onto surfaces is also useful in providing some cushioning and protection for the plant from the ravages of strong winds. You can see the amazing effect of Virginia creepers covering houses, roofs and outhouses in many places, providing seasonal colour changes throughout the year.

Aerial roots

Another effective way of making fast a plant's connection to a support is by encouraging a mass of little 'roots' to grow away from the stem. This is often done with ivy. The 'roots' are more correctly called aerial roots or adventitious roots, since they arise from the stem and not the root. Ivy is popular in the garden, but its tenacious roots will pull out mortar and pieces of masonry rather than break when removed from old walls. These roots act as an anchor point, gripping the surface tightly and allowing the vigorous ivy stems to spread

TIP

Choose a support that will match the size and strength of the climber, and also bear in mind what method the climber uses to cling to the support. A support that is not sufficiently sturdy for a vigorous climber may quickly become overwhelmed by the plant and will eventually collapse.

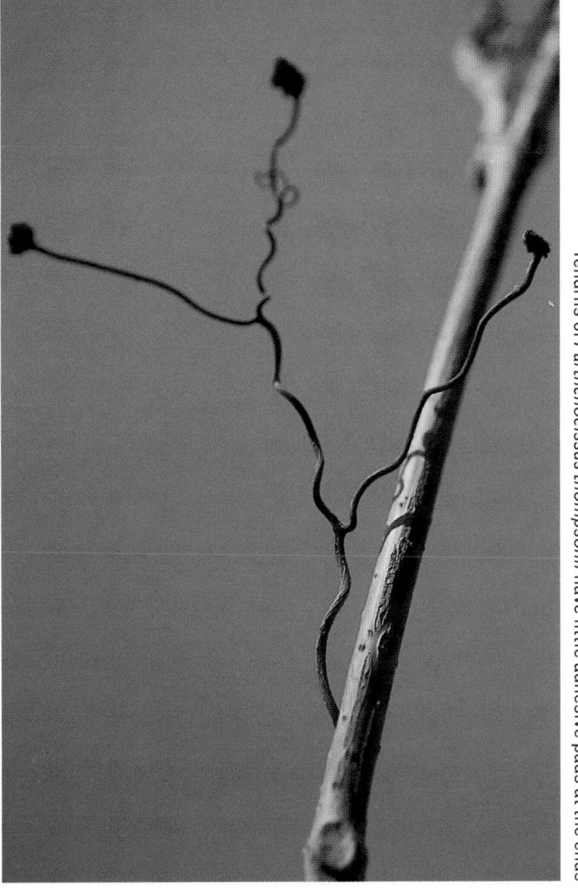
Tendrils of *Parthenocissus thompsonii* have little adhesive pads at the ends

How to Grow Climbers

Walls

Walls provide a uniform surface on which to train climbers, and offer the added advantage of radiating heat to encourage growth or fruit production. If you dislike the appearance of a wall, climbers can be given free rein to cover it up entirely. Equally, with judicious training and pruning, climbers may complement and enhance the appeal of existing fine brick or stonework.

To begin with, choose a wall that is in full sunlight for most of the day, and remember to plant the climber at least 60cm (2ft) away from the base, preferably in water-retaining and well mulched soil, so that the young plant does not become dry. The soil at the bottom of a wall may well contain more bits of cement and crumbling brick or stone than the soil a few steps further away, so this slight gap away is quite important. The next consideration is a means of support for your climber. While allamandas and cobaneas may have to be helped up by tying on to a support system, many ivies and Virginia creepers have no problem in clinging on to the wall itself.

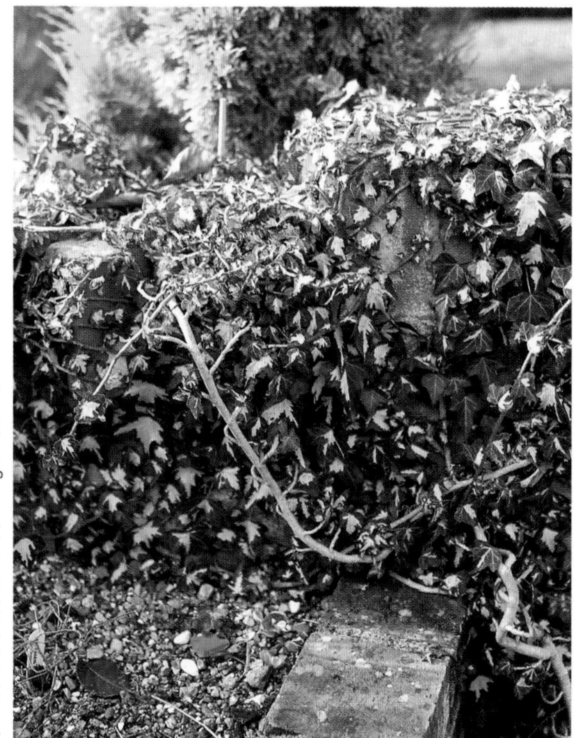

Climbers are useful for covering an old wall

Climbers robustly growing through other plants and trees

Trees and shrubs

In the wild, many climbers naturally grow through shrubs and trees, clinging on to their hosts' branches and stems. This is a marvellous natural phenomenon to emulate in the garden. Trees are for the upwardly mobile climbers such as the Montana clematis, wisterias and honeysuckles. All these are expert climbers and find large trees a great place to venture forth. They will soon conquer even the tallest trees' lofty heights. In the case of montanas, these climbers can overwhelm shrubs and young trees and create a thatch of foliage that blossoms like fallen snow in the spring. Space permitting, letting these climbers have their way is the best course of action, with little or no pruning required. A little visual excitement can be had by incorporating the bright red flame creeper, *Tropaeolum speciosum*, in among the dark foliage of yew or other dark conifers, making a very pleasing summer spectacle.

Herbaceous plants

For those climbers that lack the energy and vigour for long distance growth, such as some of the hybrid and herbaceous clematis varieties, help can be given to enable them to grow through marginal herbaceous border plants. With the addition of some supporting branches of hazel or broom, these plants can be encouraged to twine through asters, lilies and roses. For example, varieties such as *Clematis* 'Victoria' can be grown through the foamy flowers of *Thalictrum aquilegiifolium* 'Purple Cloud'. However, make sure that the climbers are not too vigorous for their hosts.

Many of the New Zealand clematis species and cultivars are very floriferous yet not that vigorous in the garden, and these are best employed trailing from baskets to trickle through adjacent vegetation.

Colour combinations should always be planned carefully before planting. Things to take into consideration include colours of flowers, foliage and fruit. Don't be afraid to be bold with your choice of colours, though. The climber can either complement or contrast with its host plant, or simply extend the season of interest.

Red bougainvillea growing with orange streptosolens against a wall

Hedges

Hedges offer one of the best opportunities to display climbers. Many are in their element twining through a mass of vegetation, and can make an eye-catching feature in the spring. Such species as the *Clematis montana* (many cultivars and species), honeysuckles and wisteria are all good at adding colour to a native hedgerow, or to a tall and dark stand of conifers.

Montana clematis flowers all over a fence, creating a hedgerow

Honeysuckles not only have an incredible smothering effect, practically obscuring any unsightly hedge, but can also produce the most amazing scent. The contrast of conifer foliage and the pure flowers of *C. montana* is well worth promoting and will add colour to dreary conifers. These vigorous climbers may require an annual shearing after flowering has finished to keep them within limits. Neighbours will not always complain about clematis overhanging on their side of the garden fence, but they might not be so keen on intrusive conifers!

TIP

If you are planning to cover an existing, unsightly hedge with a climber, don't plant it in the ground at the bottom of the hedge itself. Instead, plant it to one side and encourage the climber to grow up and around the hedge, just as you would train the plant to clamber up a wooden trellis or wall.

Lending support

Climbers need to secure their tendrils and twirly leaf stems around some support in order to gain height or distance, and subsequently grow. Their lead shoots rotate slowly (obviously not seen with the naked eye) in order to find a suitable support. Without something to cling onto, the climber will make no progress at all and will end up growing itself into a ball that will not produce proper leaves or flowers. Use any of the proprietary sheets of netting, trellis or support systems mentioned earlier (see pages 14–15) to assist the natural growth of climbers and they will quickly scramble up them. The more secure the support you provide for your climber, then the better the results by way of flower production or foliage cover you will receive.

Giving your climber freedom and space, and providing it with adequate water and nutrients, will assure excellent growth and give you endless hours of enjoyment in the garden.

Humulus lupulus aureus (Golden Hop) screening a building

Frames and stakes

The chances are that a nursery-grown climber comes complete with a good rootball, as well as a stake or mini frame. When the de-potted climber is eased into the previously prepared hole, it is essential to leave the stake in the compost and tie the rest of the plant to another support so that it does not immediately flop over. Only when the plant is well established and does not need this initial stake can it be removed, and the plant tied securely to its more permanent frame or support structure. Keeping an eye on the growth of climbers is essential, since a wayward wand of energetic growth can always be tied to the main frame, gaining extra days to flowering that would otherwise be lost if this was left dangling down at the side.

TIP

A wall provides good support for climbers and clematis, but they still need some assistance from a frame or stake. When planting out, do not be tempted to remove the cane stake it came on until the plant has got a good grip on its new support. Best to wait rather than see your new plant blown away in the next strong gust of wind!

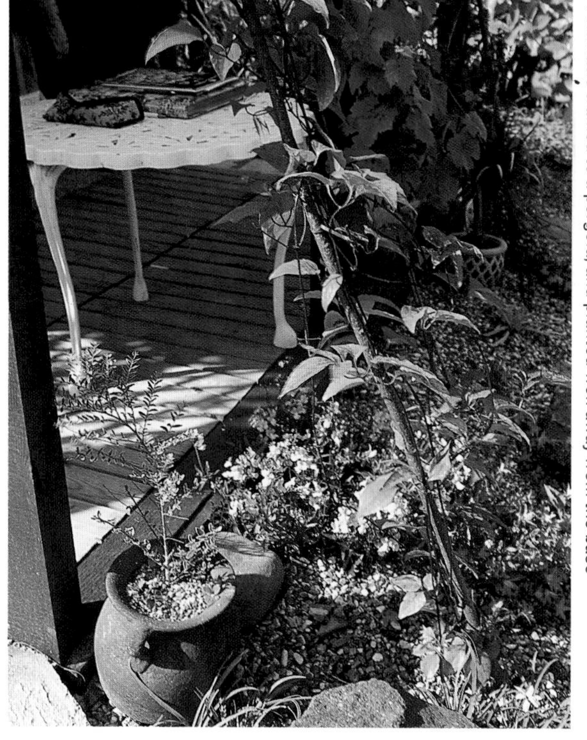

A clematis trained to a pergola, and planted well away from the base

Pergolas and gazebos

Pergolas or arbours and gazebos covered with climbers not only provide a shady seating area in the garden but also a secluded spot. The opportunities for covering a pergola or gazebo with climbers is almost limitless, since a variety of climbers can be planted at the base of each pier (although not too close to the base). Ascendant roses – both ramblers and climbers – are one of the best groups of climbers used to scramble up both wooden and brick piers and to flower along the horizontal beams of a pergola. Honeysuckles and hops are good in temperate climates, bougainvilleas and stephanotis ideal in warmer climates.

Pyramids and pillars

A favourite object for a focal point in a garden is often a pyramid shape that can look equally at home as part of the herbaceous border. On it can be grown a variety of climbing plants, such as roses, which are sometimes better displayed if the trelliswork is painted white or blue for contrast. When orchard and ornament trees have to be cut down, their stumps can be used to make a pillar on which a display of climbers such as scented honeysuckles, as well as ivies, can be trained up together. Jasmines, morning glories and passion flowers all grow well and look good on pyramid-shaped trelliswork, and of course in the kitchen garden, where space is limited, sweet peas and runner beans can be very effectively grown around pillars. A line of pillars constructed along a border or path looks very attractive with rope linking them and climbers trained up the pillars and along the rope chain.

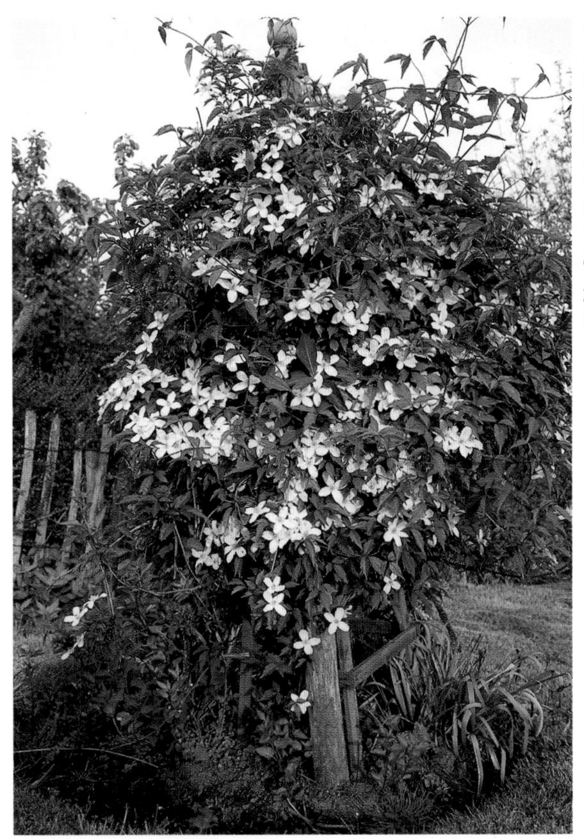

Clematis montana smothering a pyramid

Roses tumbling over a pergola

Planting Combinations

One of the great pleasures of gardening is creating combinations of plants that flower together. In a way, doing this replicates the sequence of events that occurs in the wild, where plants naturally use each other for support in acquiring space and sunshine in order to flower and fruit.

The skill in creating effective planting combinations lies in knowing your plants' habits, growth patterns and flowering times. Experience helps here, too: a knowledge of conditions in your garden is invaluable, in terms of the type and quality of the soil, early and late flowering sites, and the existence of frost-pockets and early sunny sites.

To try out your skills on a small scale, you could grow nasturtiums or thunbergias (Black-eyed Susans) with clematis, or morning glories with clematis on a patio. Both these combinations of plants can be grown in pots, so they are ideal for a small urban garden or a window box. One great advantage of gardening with pots is that combinations can be made up and changed at will.

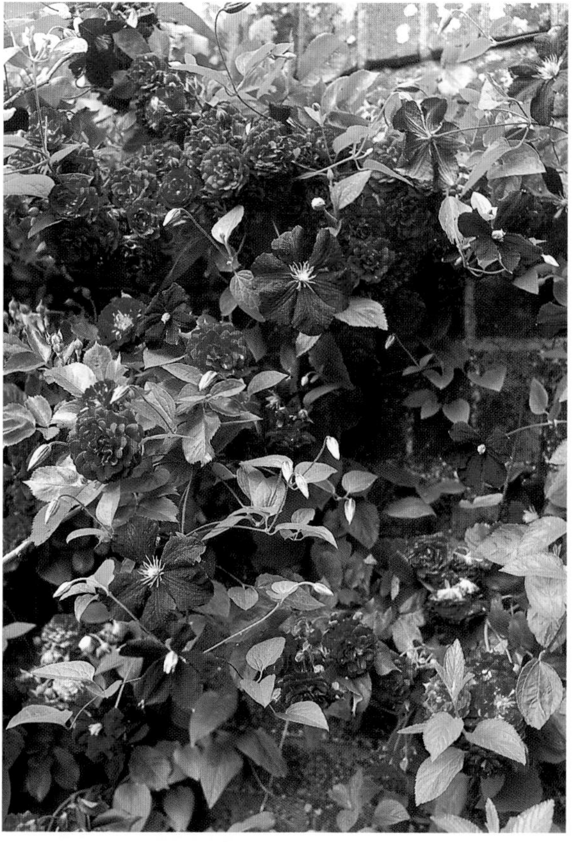

Clematis 'Etoile Violette' and *Rosa* 'William Lobb'

Using climbers effectively

Where you find only one particular kind of flower in bloom, a climber can be quickly and easily introduced to make up just the colour combination you want. The availability of fresh nursery stock at garden centres – often bursting with buds – makes the range of possible combinations almost inexhaustible. If you already have a colour-coded garden, then you have an infinite range from which to choose. A border path can be much improved with the introduction of a vigorous, floriferous climber inserted into a busy flower bed beside it.

Highly effective combinations of climbers can be grown over an arch using, for example, a cucurbit climber twining with honeysuckles, offering scent and visual delight.

Honeysuckles are very useful for smothering old tree stumps, and from

Clematis 'Action Splendour' growing with Ceanothus

within their vigorous growth, snaky herbaceous clematis such as the blue *Clematis* x *durandii* can be encouraged to grow freely.

The rampant growth of wisterias can be used in a multitude of combinations. The sky blue flowers of this plant make a good foil for the many and varied Montana clematis, with their white, cream and delicate pink colours. Montanas and wisterias are both very vigorous plants and make good partners. Both can be used to grow up trees, and a particularly effective combination is blue wisteria with yellow laburnum, as both plants show off their dramatic colours at the same time in spring.

Red nasturtiums growing with *Clematis vitalba*

Combinations for hanging baskets

For hanging baskets, a good combination can be achieved with the trailing stems of Rhodochiton, with its deep purple bells, and variegated leaves of ivy. This can be very easily planted up and makes an interesting display. Many other trailing plants are also effective in hanging baskets and window boxes, because their growing habit helps disguise the sides of the containers and looks dramatic when allowed to cascade around them.

Hanging baskets offer opportunities for quick-change planting combinations with clematis and climbers, no more so than when several baskets containing different combinations are grouped together. If two or three baskets are hung together, it can look like just one enormous arrangement. Alternatively, by hanging several baskets in a line it is possible to create a continuous ribbon of colour.

TIP

Think carefully about which colours work well together when planting combinations. You can create all kinds of effects by combining certain shades or restricting your choice to a single colour scheme. If you are not sure which plants go well together, keep colour schemes simple, ie. just oranges and reds or greens and yellows.

Clematis viticella and *Clematis* 'Abundance'

Rhodochiton growing with variegated ivy

Beautiful bougainvillea

In sub-tropical and tropical climates, and in conservatories around the world, bougainvillea rules supreme, being such a reliable and stalwart climber. In more temperate climates, warm coastal regions or sheltered areas are also suitable for this plant. The vivid bracts of this plant brighten even a dull day in mid-winter. As a vigorous climber grown outdoors, bougainvillea is ideal for mixing with other strident climbers, such as the orange-flowered Pyrostegia. Many a wall in the Mediterranean-type climate of California, the Mediterranean itself, or the western coast of Australia is adorned with this exotic combination. Alternatively, honeysuckles – especially the huge yellow-flowered *Lonicera hildebrandiana* – and bougainvilleas make good companions.

Bougainvillea is also at home with other plants that need the physical support that it can provide, such as the soft blue leadworts, or the uniquely orange streptosolens. These plants make good, colourful and contrasting partners, of which the great garden painter, Impressionist artist Claude Monet, would have approved. Creating colour in the garden is a very personal thing, and open to all sorts of interpretations. Artists often have different insights into colour palettes, as opposed to gardeners who might go for more muted combinations.

Classic combinations

Monet's famous garden at Giverny in northern France is full of climbers, used both in bold contrast with each other and as subtle complementary hues in backdrops. This is particularly the case with the pink roses that are used effectively against the pink stucco of the house, or lost around the lake in the mêlée of foliage provided by willows, lilies, irises and tall grasses. The famous water garden would have no presence without the wisteria and climbing roses which comprise its essential elements.

Creative combinations in herbaceous borders are easy to accomplish, especially if you use clematis and roses. For example, try *Clematis* 'Perle d'Azur' with *Rosa* 'Morning

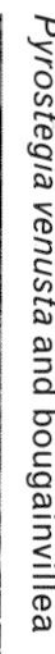

Pyrostegia venusta and bougainvillea

TIP

If you are planning to grow big, heavy climbing plants together in combination, ensure that the structure you grow them upon is strong enough to support their weight. For example, a pergola with brick piers is better suited to the colossal growth of, say, a vigorous wisteria and companion plants than a wooden one ever could be.

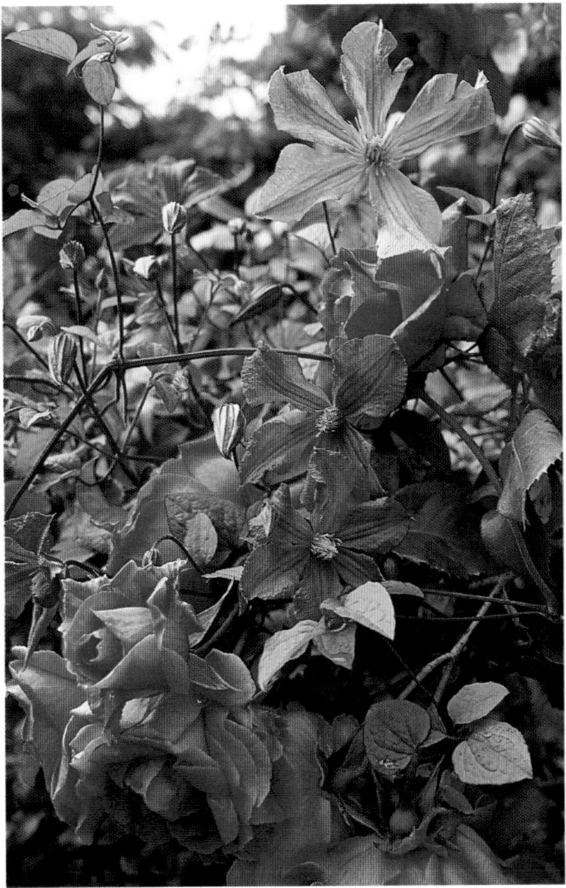

Clematis 'Prince Charles' and *Rosa* 'Pink Favourite'

Jewel', *Clematis viticella* 'Etoile Violette' with *Rosa* 'William Lobb' or *Clematis* 'Stazik' with *Rosa* 'Masquerade'. The choice is yours. Alternatively, if you have an established shrub in the garden, why not decorate it with a clematis? And if you want to see a free-for-all amongst vigorous climbers, plant two Montana clematis together – perhaps a white and a pink one (for example *Clematis wilsonii* and *Clematis montana* 'Marjorie' respectively) – and wait for them to take over an apple tree or hedgerow.

Displaying combinations

Another good place to show off climbing combinations is over pergolas and gazebos. The twentieth century gardeners Gertrude Jekyll and William Robinson, the father of wild flower gardening, both liked to show off Montanas growing rampantly over stout larch posts, their long stems spreading ever onwards and outwards and festooning the bars with their glorious flowers.

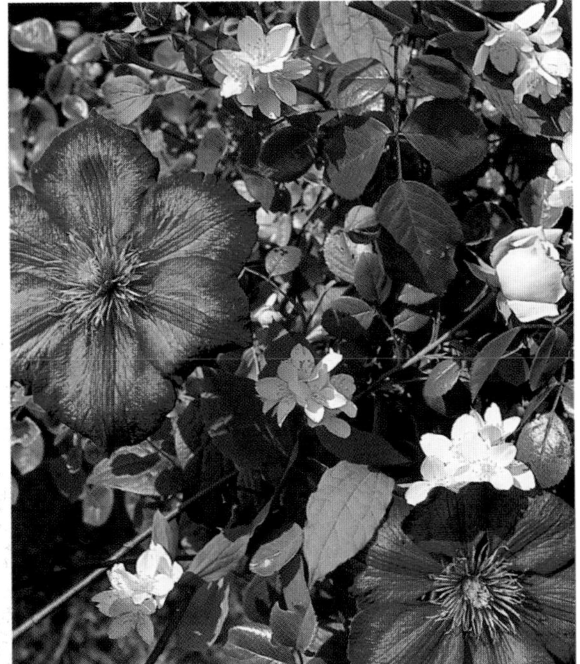

Clematis 'Ville de Lyon', *Rosa* 'Wife of Bath' and *Philadelphus microphyllus*

One of the advantages of pergolas and gazebos is that they can accommodate the rampant nature of climbers and ramblers, allowing you to appreciate just how they would perform in the wild and to admire the beauty of their flowers at eye level. Pergolas in particular provide the perfect showcase for climbing plants, as they are designed for the viewer to pass through and appreciate the plants growing on them close up and at first hand. Flowers grown on gazebos and arches offer a more instant inspirational delight.

Aesthetic considerations

While understanding your garden's particular conditions and the nature of your plants is the key to effective planting combinations, an appreciation of form, texture and above all colour will also help you to succeed. A good basic rule of thumb is that natural combinations work best – that is, plants that would grow together in the wild without the assistance of a gardener, just as nature intended.

Clematis Varieties

With well over 1,500 species, hybrids and cultivars to choose from, clematis can be used to highlight any garden – from brightening up the drab walls of a small, inner city roof garden to enhancing the trellis and archways in the grounds of the grandest country house.

Gardening with clematis is a rewarding experience for any gardener because the variety in colour and form is remarkable – in some years over 100 new varieties have been added. There are red, purple, white, yellow and blue clematis, and flowers that are bell-shaped, tubular, starry, single, double, reflexed or the size of dinner plates. The breathtaking, colourful display of clematis can be simply stunning. Indeed, there are only a few months in the year when there is not a species of clematis flowering in the garden. The different qualities and seasonal displays which characterize the various species shine through from their original roots in the wild – from the mountains of Europe or North America, to areas around the Mediterranean.

Clematis are versatile enough to grow in window boxes, pots, in tubs on patios, on trellises on decks or to take their part in a classic English herbaceous border. Many are hardy, while others – like the hybrids – often need sheltered, sunny aspects. Generally, clematis are fast growers, but there is a tendency for newer cultivars to be less vigorous and more suitable for today's smaller gardens. In fact, 'selective breeding' is targeting the plants that produce the most flowers and which are grown exclusively in small pots. Growth rates may vary across Europe and North America, while gardeners in New Zealand can expect up to 20 per cent extra growth than is recommended elsewhere.

Clematis Alabast

This particular variety is an early, large-flowered clematis and has a very unusual green-cream colour to its sepals, combined with pale yellow anthers in the centre. *C. Alabast* is also known as Poulala and originated from Denmark in the 1980s.

Clematis Alabast

C. Alabast flowers early and the flowers are at their best when they are not in direct sunlight. The plant flowers twice, the first time in the early spring and then again in late summer. Flowers can spread up to 15cm (6in) across and the clematis can reach heights of up to 3m (10ft). To show off this clematis, tie the lead shoots up the trellis or other support so that the flowers will not be restricted. Prune dead or green wood back to two large buds ready for next year's flowering.

Clematis 'Alba Luxurians'

This 'Alba Luxurians' cultivar produces plenty of flowers that appear rather loose and therefore look as if they are nodding in the wind. An attractive and unusual clematis to grow.

This quite unique clematis has camouflaged flowers that give the appearance of green leaves. The colour of the petals varies from white to verdant green. It is a vigorous climber and will do well scrambling nimbly over a wall or up a trellis. The medium sized flowers can spread up to 7.5cm (3in) across and the plant grows to 3m (10ft).

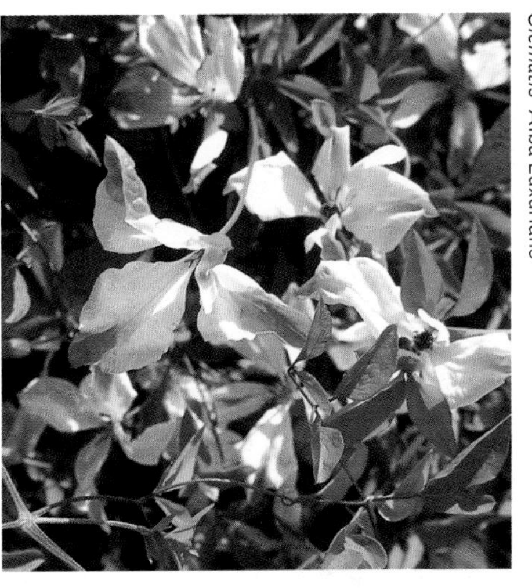
Clematis 'Alba Luxurians'

Clematis 'Arctic Queen'

***C.* 'Arctic Queen' is a prolific flowerer – in fact, one of the best white ones – and is ideal for small gardens or grown in a container on a patio. This cultivar is also known by the name of 'Evitwo', and was raised by Raymond Evison in 1994.**

Clematis 'Arctic Queen'

This is a useful clematis to brighten up either a drab wall or a dull trellis with its abundant blooms. It has large, white flowers that are semi-double to double. The stamens are cream and surround the white female parts of the flower in large numbers. The flowers are produced on both new and old growth, and can spread up to 18cm (7in) across.
C. 'Arctic Queen' itself can grow up to 3m (10ft) in height.

Clematis alpina 'Blue Dancer'

All alpinas have delicate and brittle stems, and, confusingly, living stems that actually look as if they are dead. However, they are experts at zipping up trellis or through shrubs and short bushes.

The attractive feature of *C. alpina* 'Blue Dancer' is the length of the blue sepals, which can grow up to 7.5cm (3in) long. The plant is a vigorous grower, reaching up to 3m (10ft) in height, and producing a mass of beautiful flowers in early spring. It can be grown in a container, or in a trough, and trained to grow up a trellis. This clematis, though, has delicate stems and needs to be kept tied up regularly to avoid distorted growth and damage by strong wind.

It needs to be inspected regularly to keep it confined to the area you want covered or the shrub through which you want it to flower. The flowers are light and dance around in the wind, hence this plant's name. Do not prune in its first year, and after that, only to cut out dead stems and reshape it. It is relatively easy to propagate and the best time to do this is when you prune it.

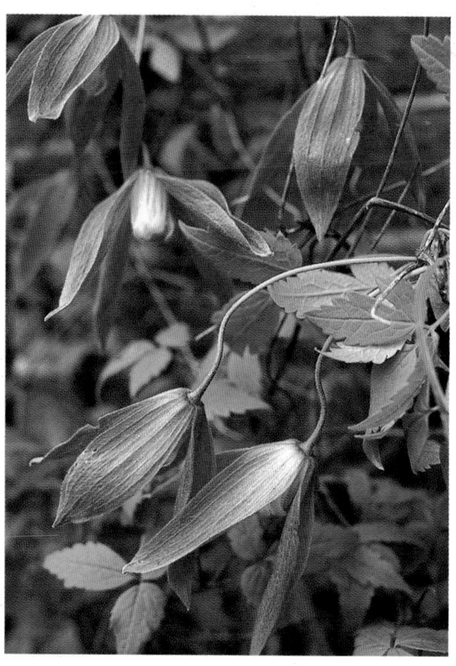

Clematis alpina 'Blue Dancer'

Clematis alpina 'Helsingborg'

This reliable species flowers from mid- to late spring. 'Helsingborg' grows well and its reddish-purple flowers are an attractive addition to any garden or patio. This particular cultivar originates from Sweden.

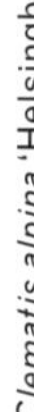

Clematis alpina 'Helsingborg'

With long, curvaceous sepals in a pale reddish-purple colour and light brown-purple petaloid stamens, this alpina hybrid is a vigorous grower like the rest of the species and performs very well competing among other plants such as roses. It can also be grown up against a trellis on its own. Flowers can reach up to 5cm (2in) across and the plant grows to 3m (10ft).

Grown up a support system against a wall or through a low-growing shrub such as a hebe or a pittosporum, *C. alpina* 'Helsingborg' needs to be kept well watered during its spring growth period. The delicate stems of this alpina also need to be tied up so that its flowers are not destroyed by the early spring winds. There is no need to prune 'Helsingborg' in its first or even second year, and only afterwards to reshape it.

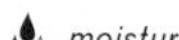

flower | *little moisture* | *moisture* | *wet*

Clematis alpina 'Pink Flamingo'

With its unusual combination of shape and colour *C. alpina* 'Pink Flamingo' can be grown as a garland through shrubs. This is a free-flowering climbing variety, adding a delicate touch of colour to any garden. This attractive cultivar comes originally from Wales.

Clematis alpina 'Pink Flamingo'

This is a favourite clematis among growers. It is a very attractive hybrid because its pinky-white flowers are produced in great abundance over whatever shrub the plant is chosen to grow through. Like all alpinas it needs support and a bit of care and attention to ensure that the lead shoots are not obstructed, and also that they are well tied. Flowers can spread up to 4cm (1in) across, and the plant itself can grow up to 3m (10ft) in height.

Clematis alpina 'Ruby'

This is a very attractive alpina cultivar that is best grown through other vegetation, so that its stunning ruby flowers can pop out the top to be admired. It has thin and delicate stems that need tying back to protect it.

As ruby as they come, the flowers of this dark coloured alpina have contrasting light coloured centres of yellowy-white stamens. This plant is a vigorous hybrid that will reach heights of up to 4m (13ft). The flowers are small and delicate, only growing 5cm (2in) across, and are produced in the spring, just like all the alpina varieties of clematis. There is no need to prune in its first year, and after that only very lightly to shape it. By cutting out a lead shoot this will encourage two other shoots to carry on. The plant needs to be kept well watered during flowering and to be tied up regularly.

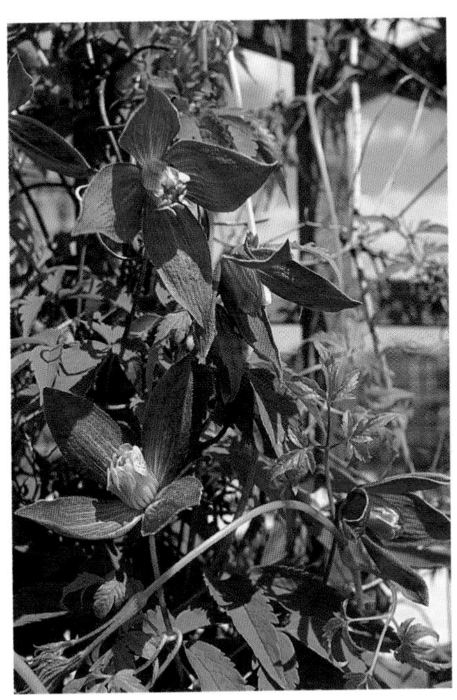

Clematis alpina 'Ruby'

	SPRING	SUMMER	AUTUMN	WINTER	height (cm)	spread (cm)	min temp (°C)	moisture	sun/shade	colours	
Clematis alpina 'Blue Dancer'	● ● ●				300	150	-5°		semi-shady		A keen flowerer if well fed
C. a. 'Helsingborg'	● ● ●				300	150	-5°		semi-shady		Very attractive flowers
C. a. 'Pink Flamingo'	● ● ●				300	150	-5°		semi-shady		Unusual pink and white flowers
C. a. 'Ruby'	● ● ●				400	150	-5°		semi-shady		A strong colour; good for mixing
C. a. 'Rosy Pagoda'	● ● ●				300	150	-5°		semi-shady		Good in containers
C. a. 'White Columbine'	● ● ●				300	150	-5°		sunny		An albino form

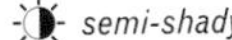

sunny *semi-shady* *shady*

Clematis armandii

The scented armandiis are worth having in any garden, given the right amount of space and dedication. Once established, they are generally fine to maintain and keep healthy, but they can be fickle and some armandiis can be frost sensitive.

Clematis armandii

A species clematis native to China, *C. armandii* is a vigorous, fast-growing climber that is often used in gardens for both its cover and its fragrance. Although it spends most of the year as an evergreen plant with its long shiny leaves, it has an abundance of medium sized and deliciously white scented flowers, which appear in the spring on new growth off a woody plant. Flowers can grow up to 5cm (2in) across and the plant will reach heights of up to 6m (20ft). Unfortunately, this good looking clematis is relatively difficult to propagate from, compared with most others.

Clematis armandii 'Apple Blossom'

One of the many attractive armandii cultivars, 'Apple Blossom' has subtle colours, with a hint of apple blossom. It climbs very well and produces attractive bunches of flowers in early spring. The foliage, like that of all armandiis, is shiny and attractive.

The apple blossom connection is through the undersides of the medium sized flowers, that have an attractive hue of pale rose. Just as fast-growing as the true species, this is a worthwhile variety to grow. It is more difficult to propagate than other varieties and often costs more than other clematis to buy, but it repays the gardener with masses of foliage and flowers. Flowers are up to 5cm (2in) across and the plant can grow up to 6m (20ft).

Clematis armandii 'Apple Blossom'

	SPRING	SUMMER	AUTUMN	WINTER	height (cm)	spread (cm)	min temp (°C)	moisture	sun/shade	colours	
Clematis armandii	flower, flower			flower, flower	600	300	-5°	little moisture	sun		The native species – full of hardiness
C. armandii 'Apple Blossom'	flower, flower			flower, flower	600	300	-5°	little moisture	sun		Subtle hues of colour under petals

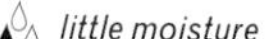 *flower*  *little moisture* *moisture* *wet*

Clematis 'Bees' Jubilee'

C. 'Bees' Jubilee' is a very attractive clematis which will brighten up any garden or patio area. It is a compact plant, which makes it ideal for small gardens and for growing in pots or containers on a patio.

Clematis 'Bees' Jubilee'

This attractive hybrid has large, stunning two-tone flowers with a central star of deep purple and the outer petals a pale white-rose. Its flowers can grow up to 15cm (6in) across, and they bloom from mid- to late summer. Because this plant grows in a compact manner, *C.* 'Bees' Jubilee' is suitable for growing in containers on patios or trained up and across low walls, preferring to be situated in partial shade rather than bright, direct sunlight. The plant will reach up to 3m (10ft) in height, and spreading as far as 1m (3ft) across.

Clematis 'Beauty of Worcester'

Although not a vigorous grower, this clematis is well worth the trouble of cultivating because its large flowers look particularly attractive and the multitude of different shaped sepals are fascinating.

This clematis can produce both single and double deep-blue flowers – although not at the same time! The double flowers start in late spring or early summer, and the single ones in late summer, continuing right into the autumn. *Clematis* 'Beauty of Worcester' sports an attractive rich tapestry of deep blue-purple flowers. The flowers are able to grow up to 15cm (6in) across and the plant will climb up to 1.5m (8ft) in height if allowed to grow freely.

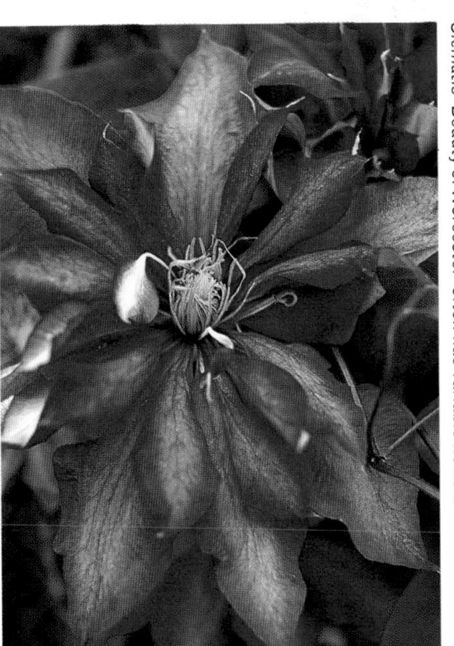

Clematis 'Beauty of Worcester' often has variable flowers

Clematis 'Beauty of Worcester'

Keep this plant well watered and regularly tied up to ensure that it reaches its full potential and is not stunted. Prune back to a good pair of buds in late winter or early spring.

Clematis 'Belle of Woking'

This attractive clematis is very rewarding once it is established. The flowers fade quickly and become almost white in strong sunlight. It may be grown in a container and shown in a small courtyard garden.

This clematis has large, double flowers that are a silver-mauve colour when new and fresh. This variety thrives well in full sunlight. The flowers can grow up to 10cm (4in) across and the plant itself can reach up to 1.5m (8ft), with a spread of 1m (3ft). It grows to a medium height and needs to be kept well watered. The large flowers look superb grown intermingled with a rose up against a wall or up a trellis. It can also be grown in a container and the flowers make good cuttings – however, there may not be sufficient flowers if the plant is not well established. Prune back to a good pair of buds in late winter or early spring.

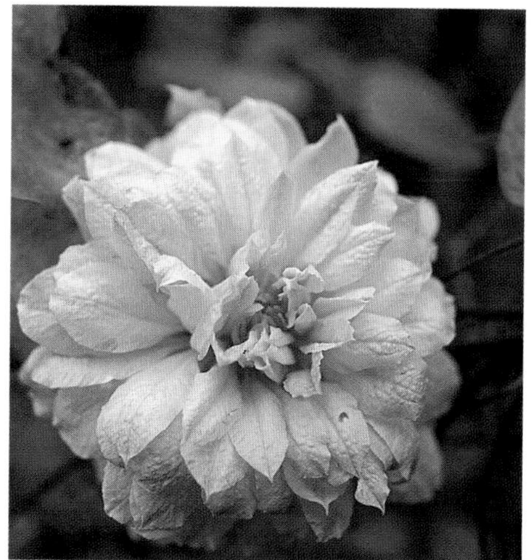
Clematis 'Belle of Woking'

Clematis 'Blekitny Aniol'

The interesting colour of this clematis is best made use of as a combination in an herbaceous border. It should be grown through other border plants, as these will give it support for climbing and enable it to flower from its secure position.

Otherwise known as 'Blue Angel', the medium sized flowers on this clematis are very delicate, with a crushed silk appearance and grooves along the centre line of the petals. This hybrid grows to about 1.5m (5ft) and its thin stems need to be tied up if grown up a trellis or support system. The delicate, silky flowers can reach up to 7.5cm (3in) across.

C. 'Blekitny Aniol' is expert at growing through other shrubs, which it uses for support. The flowers are popped out between the host shrub at convenient places, making an attractive focal point of colour in the border. Any dead stems on the plant need to be cut back to two buds in the late winter or early spring.

Clematis 'Blekitny Aniol'

Clematis 'Blekitny Aniol'

 *flower*  *little moisture*  *moisture*  *wet*

Clematis 'Charissima'

Flowers of this clematis always look eye-catching because of the two tones of alternating pink on the sepals. *C.* 'Charissima' begins to flower in the early summer and continues until early autumn, flourishing both in sun and shade.

This clematis has beautiful medium sized flowers that produce different degrees of pink, ranging from pale pink towards the centre of the flowers to a stronger pink towards the outside. Flowers can grow up to an impressive 18cm (7in) across, and the plant can reach heights of about 3m (10ft).

The great advantage of growing *C.* 'Charissima' is that when it is established it produces lots of large flowers, often overlapping. It needs to be kept well trained and well watered to perform at its best. At the end of winter or the beginning of spring, it needs to be pruned back to a pair of fat buds, which will allow it to grow strongly and flower in early spring.

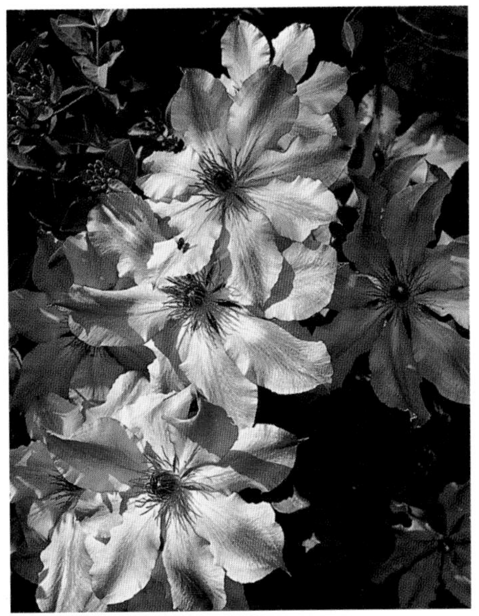

Clematis 'Charissima'

Clematis cirrhosa 'Wisley Cream'

This is a persistent, evergreen climber that flowers during some of winter's most inclement weather. However, *C. cirrhosa* is not a terribly vigorous variety, and it will fail if it is neglected – which does not apply to many other clematis – so ensure that it is planted in a sheltered spot.

Clematis cirrhosa 'Wisley Cream'

The green, yellow bells of this cultivar are distinctive, and the small, delicate flowers are produced from late autumn through to early in the new year on last year's stems. The evergreen *cirrhosa* species, from which it is derived, is native to the Mediterranean region and is fairly hardy. On a warm winter's day, the flowers have a delicate scent. The appearance of this clematis can be improved by pruning it hard back occasionally, which causes the plant to shoot from the base. Flowers grow up to 2.5cm (¾in) long and the plant will, exceptionally, reach up to 4m (13ft).

	SPRING			SUMMER			AUTUMN			WINTER			height (cm)	spread (cm)	min temp (°C)	moisture	sun/shade	colours	
Clematis cirrhosa 'Wisley Cream'	●	●									●	●	400	150	-5°		sunny		An unusual green for the garden
C. c. 'Freckles'	●	●									●	●	400	150	-5°		sunny		Creamy pink flowers

sunny  semi-shady 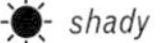 shady

Clematis 'Comtesse de Bouchaud'

A classic old variety originating in France, this is a reliable clematis for any garden. It grows to 3m (10ft) and can be mixed with other plants as it climbs up a wall or through shrubs. Characteristically, it has petals that are bent back or reflexed.

This widely appreciated clematis is a late, large-flowering variety that has wonderful, soft pink flowers set off by yellow stamens. Flowers can grow up to 12.5cm (5in) across. A good mixer in the herbaceous border.

As a late-flowering clematis, it needs to be pruned well back at the end of the year, cutting out at least two-thirds of the plant back to a pair of fat buds. These will be the lead shoots for next year. The new growth then needs to be tied up as it begins to shoot forward in the spring. *C.* 'Comtesse de Bouchaud' is a versatile plant, thriving equally whether grown up walls, mingling in between shrubs, entwining itself up a tree or clambering up a tripod structure in a pot. A very attractive clematis, it always needs to be kept well watered.

Clematis 'Comtesse de Bouchaud'

Clematis 'Countess of Lovelace'

This plant's large pink flowers are very appealing for any gardener and it can be used to great effect in borders. This clematis is also ideal for a container, but as it has weak stems, it will always need to be tied up.

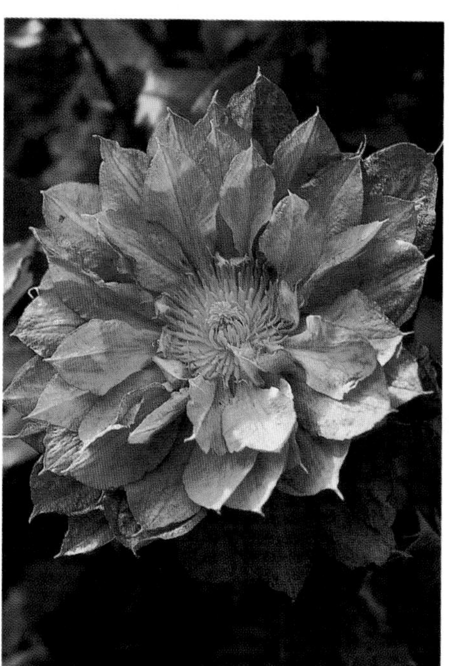

Clematis 'Countess of Lovelace'

Growing to about 2.5m (8ft), *C.* 'Countess of Lovelace' is a versatile plant, producing double flowers in early summer and single flowers in late summer. The pink flowers typically have pointed petals and yellow anthers. Flowers can grow up to 15cm (6in) across and the plant can reach heights of up to 2.4m (8ft).

Its variety of different shaped flowers makes this clematis a particularly interesting variety. As for pruning, it needs to be trimmed in late winter or early spring by being cut back to a pair of well-developed buds.

This plant will grow well in a container and can therefore be used as a display plant on the patio. It can be grown equally well up a trellis or trained up a wall. Because its flowers are particularly attractive and conspicuous, it is an extremely popular plant for any garden.

Clematis 'Crimson King'

The bright red colour of this clematis' flowers is appealing and can be used to great effect in the garden wherever striking colour combinations are required. Plant it beside a clematis with light flowers or among evergreen shrubs for great contrast.

Clematis 'Crimson King'

Sometimes known as 'Crimson Star', the large, stunning flowers are strikingly red and star-like, with a contrasting pale centre area. It flowers in mid-season – usually as singles, but occasionally as semi-double flowers. Flowers can be up to 18cm (7in) across and the plant will climb to 3m (10ft).

Prune this clematis at the end of winter or the beginning of spring back to a pair of large buds ready for spring growth. Tie up the new shoots as they grow on, and then just sit back and wait for the extravagant flowering.

Clematis x durandii

***C.* x *durandii* scrambles rather than clings to get around and this plant will readily find ways of spreading through neighbouring plants in the border, usually given a little help with training from the gardener.**

One of the most popular of herbaceous perennial clematis, this plant dies off to ground level in winter, only to reappear in the spring and shoot up among other low growing plants. The soft indigo-blue colours of its small flowers are extremely attractive, with distinctive, golden yellow anthers, and are borne on long stems that always need support. Flowers grow to about 10cm (4in) across and the plant barely reaches 1.8m (6ft) in height.

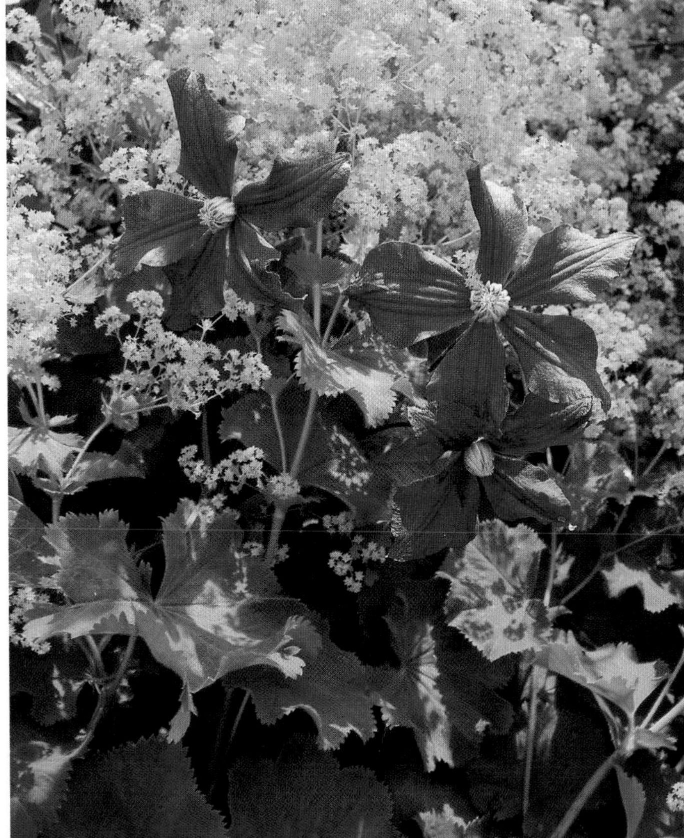

Clematis x durandii

Clematis 'Duchess of Edinburgh'

The huge, double flowers of this cultivar are magnificent, making quite an impressive feature on a trellis or growing up against a wall. The transformation of the flowers from a green colour to white is well worth the wait.

Clematis 'Duchess of Edinburgh'

The double flowers take a while to develop, during which time they are a glorious green and then mature to white. The size of a fist, the flowers come out in two phases from the early summer until the autumn, the latter ones being smaller. The flowers do not seem to look like most other clematis, being almost paeony-like in form. They are in flower for a long period and change colour as they mature; it is worth trying to collect seed once this stage is passed. Prune in late winter or early spring by cutting back to a pair of buds. This will produce new growth in spring. Keep well watered. The plant grows to about 3m (10ft).

Clematis 'Early Sensation'

Like some of the newer cultivars, this particular clematis can be smothered in massed ranks of flowers that make an eye-catching display in any garden in the spring. It is compact and low, but produces a vast array of flowers.

True to its name, this hybrid clematis produces a shower of early flowers that is quite simply sensational! The flowers have a pale, greenish-yellow tint (which is typical of a few clematis species), but this particular one lightens as the flowers mature in the warmer conditions of late spring to early summer. Older specimens actually grow fewer and smaller flowers. A clematis to grow for its abundant display of flowers, not for its height, as it barely reaches 1m (2–3ft). It can look attractive scrambling out of a trough on a patio or over a scrubby area of the garden that needs covering up.

Keep 'Early Sensation' well fertilized and watered to ensure a good crop of flowers for as long as possible into early- to mid-summer.

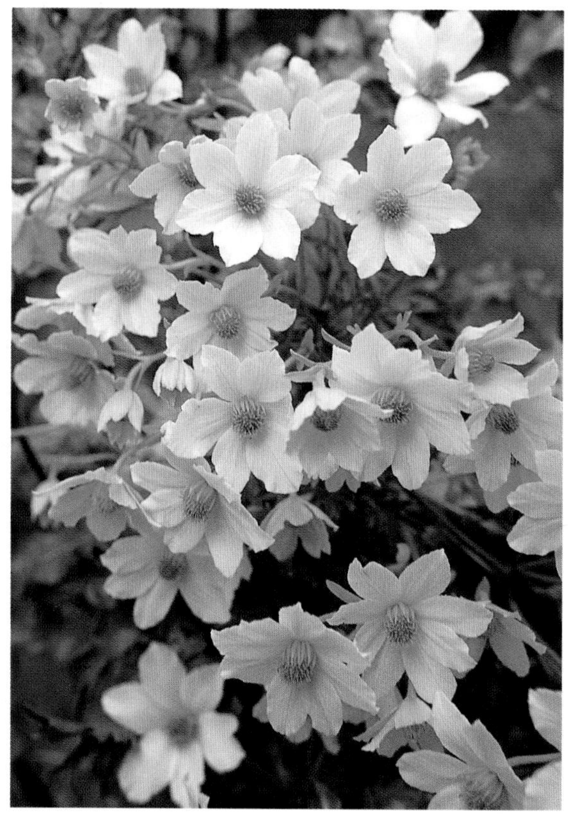
Clematis 'Early Sensation'

Clematis 'Edward Pritchard'

This cultivar has its place in the herbaceous border, with its mass of stems and their attendant flowers. As it grows neither at ground level, nor reaching very high, its place is in the middle level of the classic herbaceous border, where it mixes well.

Large numbers of small flowers are produced on this plant, rather like a blizzard, each having a delicate cross of white with pink tips. The effect can be extremely attractive in an herbaceous border where the surrounding shrubs help to support this hybrid, which originates from Australia. Not a particularly high-growing clematis, 'Edward Pritchard' reaches only about 1m (3ft) in height.

For best results grow this clematis in the sunniest position in the garden. Not only will this help its flowering, it will improve the delicious scent that the tiny flowers give off. Remove all dead material at the end of the season.

Clematis 'Edward Pritchard'

Clematis 'Elsa Spath'

Once known as *Clematis* 'Xerxes', this is a fine cultivar that can be well employed as a display plant on a patio. It grows to over a metre (3ft) high in a container and will smother the canes with foliage and flowers.

A large-flowered cultivar from Germany at the end of the 19th century, 'Elsa Spath' is considered a fine plant for growing in the garden or patio due to its reliable flowering over a long period, lasting from early on in the summer until the autumn. It has single flowers, reaching an impressive 16cm (6in) across, with overlapping, rich mauve-blue sepals and red anthers. This clematis can grow up to 3m (10ft) and is an ideal climber to train up against a wall.

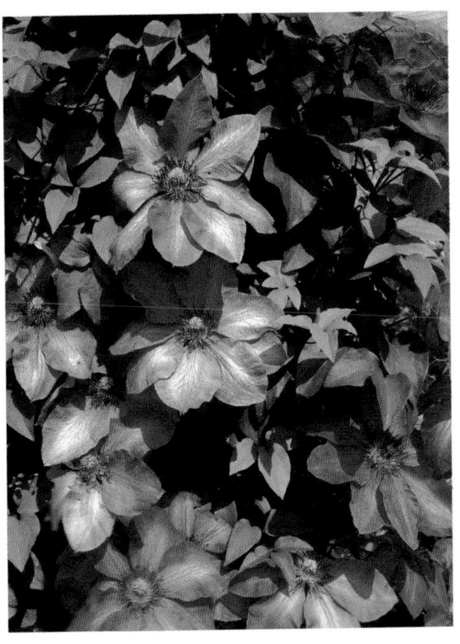

Clematis 'Elsa Spath'

Clematis 'Ernest Markham'

A reliable performer, *Clematis* 'Ernest Markham' is ideal when trained to grow up against a wall, or intermingling among shrubs in the herbaceous border. This climber can make a vivid colour contrast in any garden or patio.

This late, vigorous, large-flowered cultivar is a favourite for locations in full sun. The rich, magenta flowers have a central boss of yellow, making them very distinctive and attractive flowers. It can grow to about 4m (13ft) in height.

To get the best results from this plant, and the flowers in particular, position 'Ernest Markham' in the sunniest spot in the garden or up against a sun-drenched wall where heat from the sun will be reflected. At the end of the winter or in early spring, cut the plant right back to the ground ready for strong spring growth.

Clematis 'Ernest Markham'

Clematis 'Evening Star'

This stunning clematis is quite spectacular in any border or patio display. The large flowers of this dinner-plate clematis are equally at home in an herbaceous border or potted up in a large container.

Also known as 'Evista', this hybrid clematis was raised at the end of the 20th century and grows well in an herbaceous border, since it grows to a medium height and can be seen at about 1m (3ft) from the ground.

The flowers of this variety are large – almost dinner-plate in size – and are produced in moderation from early to late summer. However, due to their large size the flowers are susceptible to wilt, so cut back any affected stems to healthy growth, to prevent this from spreading.

Clematis 'Evening Star'

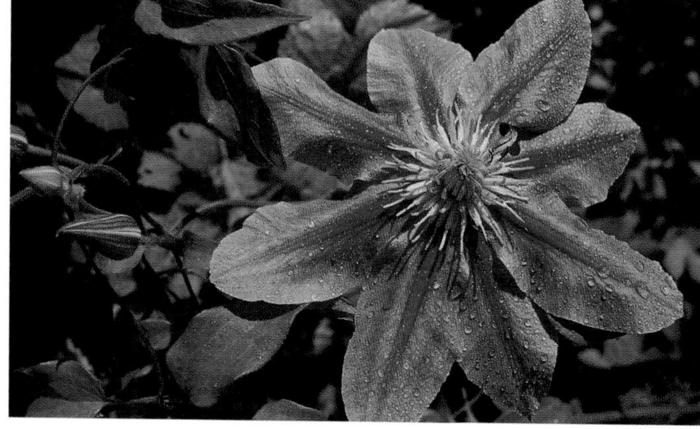

Clematis 'Evening Star'

'Evening Star' can also be grown effectively up against an old tree stump or up a piece of trelliswork. It does not get overloaded with flowers, and two or three might be a good, annual display. The large, attractive flowers more than compensate for its lack of extravagance with blooms. Towards the end of the winter or in early spring, prune back the plant to the ground and wait for new shoots in the spring. Mark its spot, as there are many other early herbaceous plants that will soon smother its position before this clematis appears again.

Clematis 'Fairy Queen'

Well worth waiting for, the flowers on this clematis are as large as dinner-plates. They tease gardeners by displaying plump buds for weeks before magically unfurling on a nice warm late spring or early summer's day.

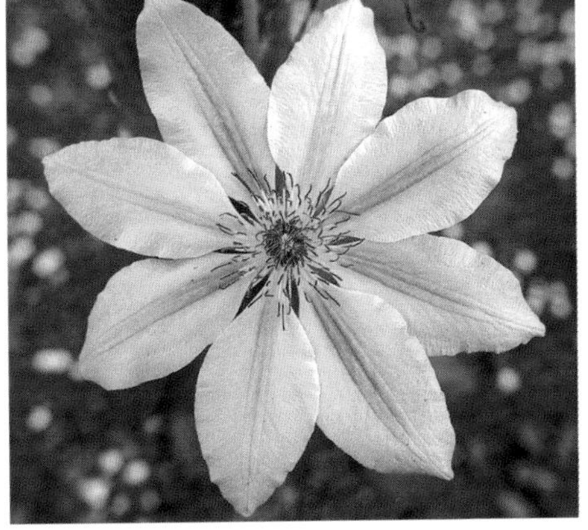
Clematis 'Fairy Queen'

It takes two months to produce the large buds that precede the impressive fairy-like flowers of this early summer hybrid. Reaching about 2m (7ft) in height, it can easily be grown up a tree or small bush.

Not noted as being vigorous, this climber needs to be pruned back to a pair of fat buds at the end of winter or the beginning of spring. Old, dead shoots should be cut off. The plant tends not to overproduce lots of stems, so those that do appear need to be tied up securely, ready to bear the big flowers.

Clematis 'Fireworks'

Resplendent and magical with its stunning bold colours, this is another of the dinner-plate-sized clematis that makes a valuable container plant. Its large, attractive flowers last a long time and attract a variety of pollinators.

The large summer flowers are stridently coloured in red and magenta, displaying darker colours along the length of its broad sepals. The central boss is creamy purple, dispensing heaps of pollen onto the sepals when ripe. It reaches up to about 1.2m (4ft) in height.

Prune back both old and green stems at the end of the winter or early spring to a pair of large buds. The plant will sprout upwards from these buds in the spring.

Clematis 'Fireworks'

Clematis 'Fireworks'

This clematis will do fine for a time kept in a pot or container on the patio, but after a couple of years it needs to be replanted in the soil where it will perform much better. It needs to be kept well watered and tied up securely at all times, so that it can produce its large, early flowers without the risk of wind damaging the plant. Watch out for wilt and at the first sign, cut back any affected stems to healthy growth, to prevent this spreading through the plant.

Clematis flammula

A native species that can be relied upon to give lots of colour at the end of the summer, this clematis produces plenty of white, star-shaped flowers that enliven any dull autumnal day or lend colour to any shady corner.

Also known as the Pure White Clematis, this species of clematis is native to the Mediterranean. It produces masses of scented flowers in late summer to early autumn, and is rampant, reaching heights of up to 4.6m (15ft). The plant prefers a well-drained, sheltered and sunny site. It is hardy and resistant to disease, and can be relied upon to cover up any dull surface as it spreads to about 1m (3ft) in width.

Grow this clematis in full sun. It can even thrive in coastal gardens within splashing distance of the sea, in the sand and fully exposed to the elements. It is a fairly drought-resistant plant and will equally grow around a scree bed or edge of an herbaceous border. At the end of the season it can be cut right back, allowing the old stems to produce new shoots. Flowering at the end of the season is a great advantage, where many other plants have succumbed in the hot weather.

Clematis flammula

Clematis florida 'Sieboldii'

An eye-catcher for detail if ever there was one, the extraordinarily large flowers of this particular cultivar are excellent if grown in pots or containers where they can be shown off to their full advantage.

Unique among the varieties of clematis for the shape of the flowers, *C. florida* 'Sieboldii' has an extremely large, purplish boss ringed by six white sepals. The incredible uniformity and simplicity of the flowers are very appealing. It flowers from early summer on stems to about 3m (10ft).

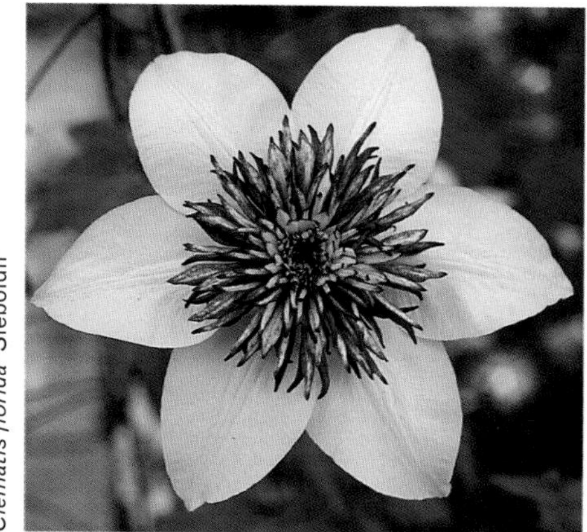

Clematis florida 'Sieboldii'

Flowers are produced on the current season's growth, so for pruning purposes, cut away last year's old growth at the end of the winter. This will allow for new shoots to grow out in the spring, thereby producing a good crop of the white and purple flowers. Keep well watered and grow the clematis in a sunny position in the garden, preferably up against a sun-drenched wall in a pot or container. Propagate from cut stems, each with a pair of leaves and buds.

Clematis 'Fuji-musume'

One of the biggest of the 'dinner-plate' varieties, this oriental cultivar makes a bold statement both in shape and its deep purple colour. It is excellent for growing in a container, brightening up any patio or placed against a drab wall or dull fence.

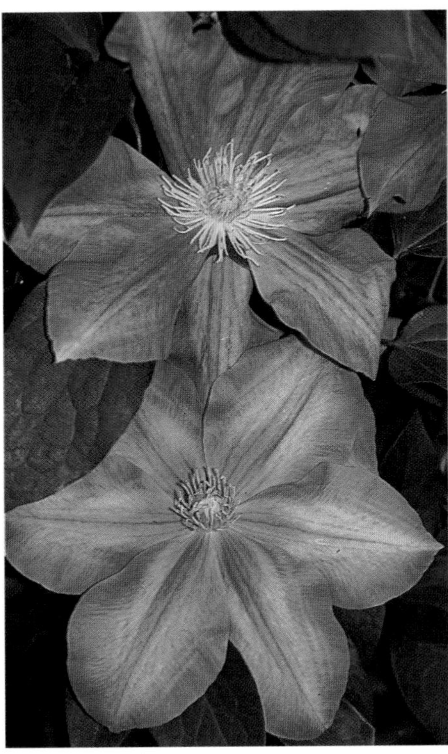

Clematis 'Fuji-musume'

The attractive flowers are stunning, reaching to 13cm (about 5in) across, and of a deep rich, purple colour. This Japanese hybrid was raised in 1952 and grows to about 1m (3ft) in height. It is ideal grown in a container for display. It flowers from the early summer to the autumn.

The fact that the plant does not grow very high means it can be put to a useful role in decorating an herbaceous border around the middle height level, or for providing vivid colour in a container trained up a trellis or other support system. Try growing next to another clematis with contrasting flowers. Towards the end of the season or in the new year, prune back the plant's dead stems to a pair of fat buds. These will be the new shoots in the spring. Once these shoots start coming up, they need to be firmly tied up the supporting cane or trelliswork, as they need to be secure when its vast flowers come into bloom.

Clematis 'Gillian Blades'

One of a number of white clematis, this particular variety is grown for the purity of its white flowers and its reliability. The colour contrast of the white and the yellow boss of the flowers also adds interesting appeal.

This hybrid has medium-sized white flowers of around 16cm (6in) across, which are borne on growth up to about 1.8m (6ft) in height. Typically, the edges of the sepals are wavy, and the central boss area has a touch of pale yellow. It flowers from mid-summer until the autumn and produces an abundance of flowers if kept well watered. The best spot in the garden is in a sunny site with well-drained, fertile, humus-rich soil.

Propagation of this clematis can be achieved either from taking cuttings of the stems with buds in the spring or growing on from the seeds. Prune back to a good pair of buds at the end of the winter or beginning of spring.

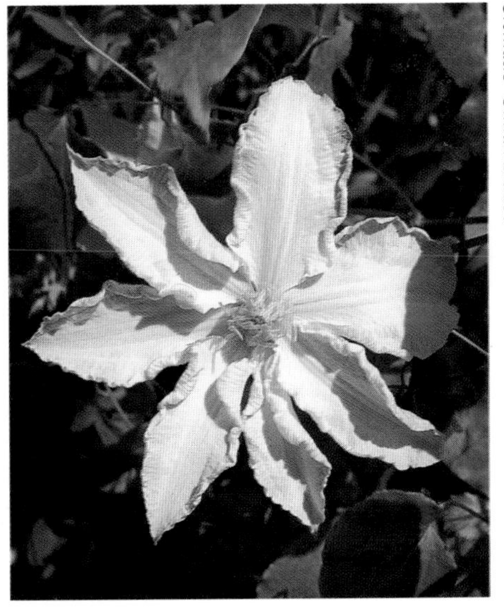

Clematis 'Gillian Blades'

Clematis 'Gipsy Queen'

The dark and sombre colours of the flowers are very appealing and are characteristic to this cultivar. The plant grows well through shrubs and trees, and shoots out flowers intermittently from its stems.

With its reliable growth and flowering, this is a popular variety that bears lots of rich, dark-purple flowers on stems up to 3m (10ft) tall. It is easily grown through trees or in a hedgerow, and flowers during the early summer onwards.

At the end of the winter or early spring, cut most of the plant back to a pair of healthy looking buds. These will be the lead shoots for the following year's growth. *C.* 'Gipsy Queen' is a very popular and widely available vigorous climber, and is a classic clematis originally raised in England as long ago as 1877. The rich colour of its flowers makes it an ideal choice for gardeners who enjoy colour combinations, as this plant provides a vivid contrast to other clematis species, as well as many trees, shrubs and flowers.

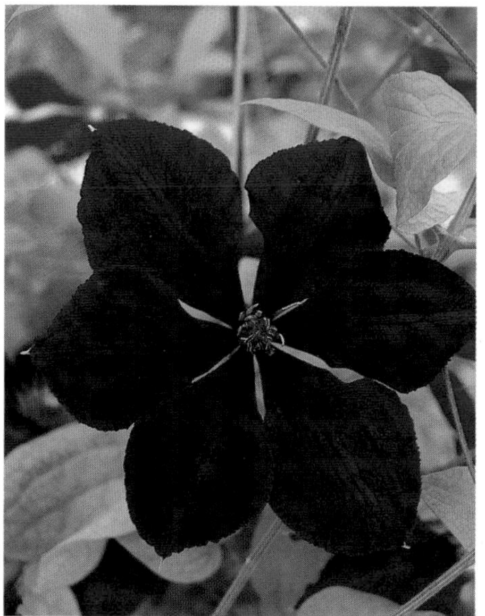

Clematis 'Gipsy Queen'

Clematis 'Golden Tiara'

A vigorous clematis that can be grown up canes, this wonderfully bright variety will reward the gardener with beautiful sprays of deep yellow, pointed flowers, contrasting with their chocolate boss centres.

Clematis 'Golden Tiara'

Bold and bright yellow flowers festoon this vigorous hybrid that can be easily trained to grow up tripod structures, through shrubs or up a trellis on a wall, reaching about 2.4m (8ft) in height. The chocolate centred boss makes an equally bold statement, particularly contrasting with the vibrant yellow.

Keep newly planted specimens well watered until established and mulch in the spring with well rotted manure or garden compost. Watch out for slug attack, especially on fresh young growth, and aphids later on in the season. *Clematis* 'Golden Tiara' likes a sunny position in the garden. Towards the end of the year, the dead and dying vegetation can be cut right back to allow new growth to appear in the following spring. This clematis can make all the difference to a colourful display up a pergola in the garden or trellis on the patio.

Clematis 'Grandiflora sanguinea'

This is an excellent climber that performs well in the garden, especially if trained up a feature structure. It has large numbers of colourful flowers borne from its stems and it can be mixed with other climbers and shrubs.

Exuberant in growth to 3m (10ft), this clematis, with its modest medium sized flowers, is excellent for training up pergolas and over arches. It has a clear, open growth with long stems and the flowers are a soft, velvety rose-red colour, with slightly crimped edges.

For best results, plant in a sunny position in the garden. After flowering, at the end of the year or at the beginning of spring, prune back the plant to a pair of fat buds. Be sure to tie up the new shoots when they come through, so that the plant performs and flowers well the next season.

Clematis 'Grandiflora sanguinea'

Clematis 'Guernsey Cream'

There are not many cream clematis that are more aptly named than this particular cultivar, with its creamy yellow sepals and anthers. The large, single flowers can reach up to 12cm (5in) across, providing a lovely display for the garden.

Quite symmetrically complete, the purity of this variety, named after one of the Channel Islands, makes this variety of clematis a particular favourite among many gardeners. The suffusion of cream over the whitish sepals is quite a characteristic feature. The plant grows to a height of about 2.4m (8ft) and is best grown with dappled shade since the flowers fade in direct sunlight.

As an early, large flowering clematis, it needs to be pruned back to a pair of plump buds in late winter or early spring. The resultant new shoots need to be tied up to ensure continued expansive growth.

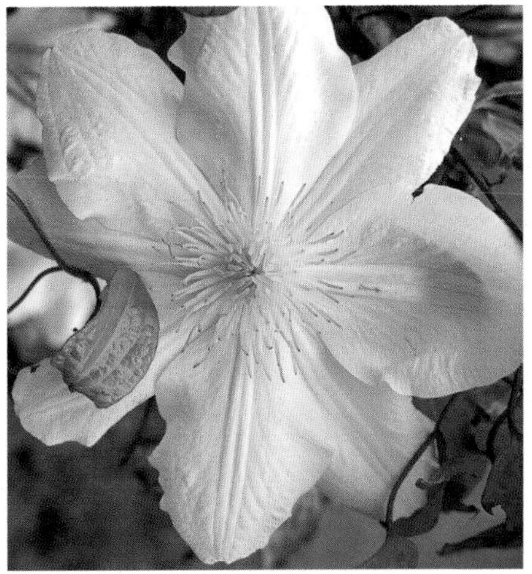

Clematis 'Guernsey Cream'

Clematis 'Hagley Hybrid'

When planted in a pot, this hybrid grows well on many stems and can be mixed with other climbers in the same container. What it lacks in vigour it certainly makes up for in a reliable spread of delicate, soft pink flowers.

Clematis 'Hagley Hybrid'

A faithful and reliable clematis for a pot or container, this produces chintzy pink flowers, about 10cm (4in) across, from early summer up until the autumn. Its stems run to about 1.5m (5ft) and it is easy to grow, preferring as much sunlight as possible to grow through trellis or shrubs, where it needs to be supported or tied up.

The precise colour shade of Hagley Hybrid's flowers is unique, and this hybrid has great appeal. To carry on having a great crop of flowers year after year, prune the clematis back to a pair of large buds in late winter or early spring. Tie up the new shoots securely, as otherwise they can ramble away and produce imperfect flowers.

Clematis 'Hagley Hybrid'

Clematis 'Henryi'

This is a stunning, all-white clematis that has beautiful pure white petals and a chocolatey central boss area. The flowers are among the largest of all clematis, growing up to 20cm (8in) in diameter – a magnificent sight in the garden.

Clematis 'Henryi'

This mid season, large-flowered clematis hybrid is popular throughout the whole of Europe and also the USA. It grows to about 3m (10ft) and produces pure white flowers that are extremely attractive. The central boss has chocolate, purple-tipped white stamens that look like matchsticks.

Being one of only a few white clematis, this hybrid is a popular choice for a container or trained up a trellis or tripod. It needs to be pruned back to a pair of big buds in late winter or early spring. The delicate new shoots should be tied up securely to hold the plant up when the large flowers bloom.

 *flower*  *little moisture* 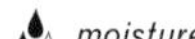 *moisture* 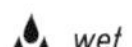 *wet*

Clematis heracleifolia 'Côte d'Azur'

One of a number of heracleifolias, this has a hint of the blue of the Mediterranean in its petals that gives it its cultivar name. The flowers on heracleifolias are gathered together in little garlands of colour in a tubular shape, characteristic of this species.

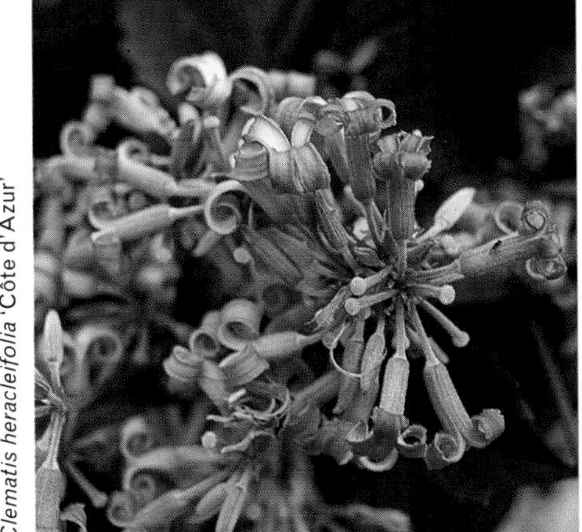

Clematis heracleifolia 'Côte d'Azur'

This is one of a number of cultivars of the popular herbaceous clematis. Not being a climber like most other clematis, this variety dies right down to the ground in winter. It then shoots back up again from ground level in spring, reaching about 1.2m (4ft) in height, producing bright blue clusters of flowers between its large leaves. This clematis is a good grower for the lower levels of the herbaceous border, scrambling along and covering the ground. Given a sunny situation in good garden soil, this variety will give great pleasure during the summer.

	SPRING			SUMMER			AUTUMN			WINTER			height (cm)	spread (cm)	min temp (°C)	moisture	sun/shade	colours	
Clematis heracleifolia 'Côte d'Azur'			●	●	●								120	100	-5°	💧💧💧	sunny	■	A fine blue colour. Needs support
C. heracleifolia var. *davidiana*			●	●	●								120	100	-5°	💧💧💧	sunny	■	Needs support
C. heracleifolia var. *davidiana* 'Wyvale'				●	●	●							75	100	-5°	💧💧💧	sunny	■	Light- to mid-blue flowers

Clematis 'Huldine'

The dainty flowers are particularly attractive and are best grown in such a position where the sunlight falls through the petals. Grow it so that the flowers are at least at eye level or along the top of a wall to catch the light.

Unique among clematis in having bands of purple on the underside of its sepals, the top side of the attractive flower is pure white. This hybrid has an open sort of growth and will vigorously scramble over hedges, walls and up trellis to about 3m (10ft) in height and 2m (7ft) wide. It flowers from the early summer onwards, reaching 6–7cm (about 3in) across.

The plant can be quite vigorous, producing lots of flowers along fences and wall tops. Prune back at least three-quarters of its old growth in the winter or early spring, thus allowing the plant to flower on its new extensive growth. It is a popular and reliable hybrid that makes a good visual display clambering up trellises in the garden or on a patio.

Clematis 'Huldine'

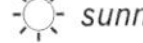 *sunny*  *semi-shady*  *shady*

Clematis integrifolia 'Rosea'

Integrifolias **are a large group within the clematis family. They are derived from the native species** ***C. integrifolia*** **and share the characteristic of having an abundance of small, bell-shaped flowers, sometimes with the tips of the petals turned up.**

Clematis integrifolia 'Rosea'

There are more than a dozen cultivars of *integrifolias* and this is one of the most attractive pink forms. The plant is a low growing clematis, only reaching about 60cm (2ft), and therefore is ideal for an herbaceous border. It is a late flowering cultivar, bearing extremely large numbers of charming, bell-shaped pink flowers, and because it flowers from mid-summer until the autumn, brings a touch of colour to the garden even when summer is over.

	SPRING			SUMMER			AUTUMN			WINTER			height (cm)	spread (cm)	min temp (°C)	moisture	sun/shade	colours	
C. i. 'Hendersonii' *hort*			●	●	●								60	60	-10°	wet	☼		Needs some support; pert, pink flowers
C. i. 'Olgae'			●	●	●								60	60	-10°	wet	☼		Needs some support; pert, pink flowers
C. i. 'Pangbourne Pink'			●	●	●								60	60	-10°	wet	☼		Needs some support; pert flowers
Clematis integrifolia 'Rosea'			●	●	●								60	60	-10°	wet	☼		Needs some support; pert, pink flowers

Clematis 'Jackmanii'

The species ***C.*** **'Jackmanii' offers a number of useful cultivars for the garden. They are all excellent for growing against walls of houses, over porches or around windows since they are particularly vigorous and have an abundance of flowers.**

This is a species of clematis that has especially attractive, medium sized flowers that boast a deep, rich purple colour. There are other cultivars that are larger or white, and they are all good at growing up brickwork, reaching about 3.6m (12ft) with a little support to help it on its way. They flower abundantly during the hot summer months in the warmest spot in the garden, and are highly reliable climbers.

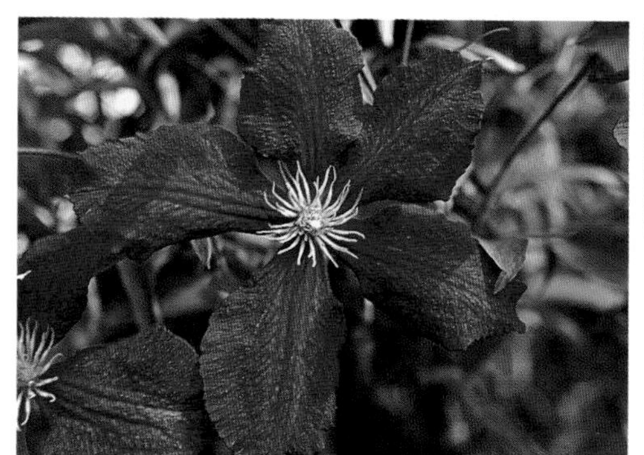

Clematis 'Jackmanii'

	SPRING			SUMMER			AUTUMN			WINTER			height (cm)	spread (cm)	min temp (°C)	moisture	sun/shade	colours	
Clematis 'Jackmanii'				●	●	●	●						360	120	-10°	wet	☼		A hardy native species
C. 'Jackmanii' 'Alba'				●	●	●	●						360	120	-10°	wet	☼		Good against a wall
C. 'Jackmanii' 'Superba'				●	●	●	●						360	120	-10°	wet	☼		Good against a wall

● *flower*  *little moisture* *moisture* *wet*

C. 'John Huxtable'

This chance seedling with strident, white flowers was taken from its pink parent *C.* 'Comtesse de Bouchaud' (see page 42). Another of the rather scarce all-white varieties, this clematis looks stunning grown next to a darker, contrasting one.

This all-white clematis has great presence not only in the form of the flower, but in the lines of the buds and the verdant green of the foliage. It grows to about 1.2m (4ft) and flowers, sometimes prolifically, from mid-summer onwards, lasting well into the autumn.

Clematis 'John Huxtable' is good at producing contrasting colour combinations, such as a striking white against a dark yew hedge. Only reaching a relatively short height, it is ideally suited for growing within an herbaceous border. As a late, large-flowering cultivar it needs to be pruned back to the ground at the end of the season or at the beginning of the spring. To reduce disease from the above-ground material and to reduce untidiness, it is probably better to remove the material in late winter. This is also true for many other varieties of late-flowering clematis.

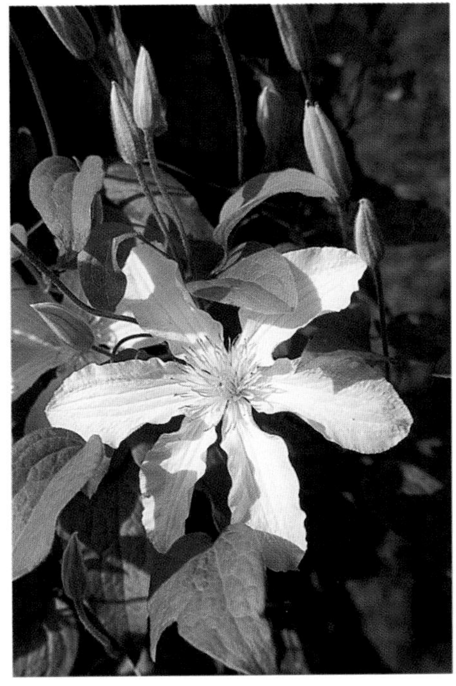

Clematis 'John Huxtable'

Clematis 'Kardinal Wyszynski'

Originally raised by Brother Stefan in Warsaw, Poland, it is also known as 'Cardinal Wyszynski', named after a Polish Cardinal who was killed in the Second World War. It comes from the Jackmanii species of clematis.

This reliable clematis has striking blood-red flowers that are borne on strong growth reaching up to 2.4m (8ft). It is one of the large-flowered clematis and is in bloom from mid-summer to autumn. The flowers can grow up to nearly 13cm (5in) across.

Clematis 'Kardinal Wyszynski'

The brilliance of the red flowers are very useful in contributing to colour combinations in gardens. For example, try planting 'Kardinal Wyszynski' next to the yellow leaf form of Choisya. The petals of the clematis flower are held very stiffly and are usually quite pointed. Train this one up a trellis, tripod or among other plants within an herbaceous border. It also looks good grown in a container. Being a large, late-flowering hybrid, 'Kardinal Wyszynski' needs to be cut down to ground level at the end of the winter or beginning of the spring. It also appreciates being securely tied to a support if not used in the border among other plants.

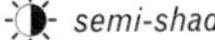

Clematis 'Lasurstern'

A highly reliable clematis, 'Lasurstern' performs well in the garden, and a plant in full flower can have over 150 blooms fully open at the same time. The sight can be staggering, and being as floriferous as that, it does not need mixing with others.

Growing to about 1m (3ft), this is an early flowering, large-flowered clematis that is much favoured in gardens. It makes a spectacular display up against a wall as it bears masses of stunning, large blue-purple flowers, each able to grow up to 15cm (6in) across, with wavy-margined, overlapping sepals and cream anthers. Petal colours can fade in the sun and severe winters may damage early top growth.

For best results, prune back to two large buds at the end of the winter or the beginning of the new year, removing perhaps half to three-quarters of the dead and green wood. Two new shoots will arise from here in the spring and these shoots need to be tied up to make the plant secure for the new flowers.

Clematis 'Lasurstern'

Clematis 'Lincoln Star'

Planted in a container, this cultivar is a little timorous at growing and flowering but it does produce some interesting and bright flowers. Grown in a bed – like many other cultivars – with more free access to nutrients, it grows more vigorously.

True to its name, the stunning flowers are indeed star-like, with the tips of the petals pointed and unfurled. It flowers from late spring through to early autumn and its beautifully artistic flowers can reach up to 12cm (5in) across. Growing to 2.4m (about 8ft), the plant's pink petals and deep maroon boss stamens are particularly attractive.

This cultivar grows to medium height, so it can be grown within an herbaceous border. Prune it back to a pair of fat buds during winter or new year, cutting out any dead stems.

Clematis 'Lincoln Star'

wet

Clematis macropetala

There is a huge number of *macropetala* from which to choose, of different colours and flower shapes. The *macropetalas'* characteristics are vigorous growth and small flowers with interesting ends to their petals, often pointed or long and reflexed.

Clematis macropetala

This is a species clematis native to China and Siberia. It is one of the earliest flowerers of the clematis family, beginning in early spring (although occasionally certain varieties wait until the summer). This clematis sports small violet-blue flowers that at first look as though they are double, having four long sepals with short petaloid stamens within – the outer coloured violet-blue and the inner cream. This plant is a vigorous deciduous climber, preferring a sheltered but sunny position, and is easy to propagate by layering. *C. macropetala* will grow to 2.7m (9ft). It sometimes repeat flowers in the summer.

Clematis macropetala 'Markham's Pink'

Growing vigorously up trellises or over arches, this cultivar is one of the most popular of all clematis, with its very attractive flowers. *En masse* the flowers put on a worthwhile show and *macropetala* is generally a reliable variety.

Clematis macropetala 'Markham's Pink'

At least 25 *macropetala* cultivars such as this pink one are known to the horticultural world and they are all good value in the garden. Typically, this variety has a very open habit, and it scrambles readily through shrubs and up trellises, always needing support, and producing vast quantities of double pink flowers. It grows up to 3.4m (10ft).

Light pruning is recommended. This should be restricted to removing any dead or damaged stems after flowering. The plant should be encouraged to grow by tying or cutting back to restrict growth. It is best grown through other vegetation.

	SPRING			SUMMER			AUTUMN			WINTER			height (cm)	width (cm)	min temp (°C)	moisture	sun/shade	colours	
Clematis macropetala	●	●	●	●									270	150	-10°				A hardy species clematis
C. m. 'Lagoon'		●	●	●									270	150	-10°				Was called 'Blue Lagoon'
C. m. 'Markham's Pink'		●	●	●									340	150	-10°				Strong pinks make this a favourite
C. m. 'White Lady'		●	●	●									270	150	-10°				Delightful white flowers

 sunny 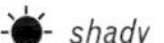 semi-shady shady

Clematis 'Madame Baron Meillard'

The best place to grow this particular plant is up against a wall where it can get maximum sunshine and warmth. It needs as much sunshine as possible and then it will reward the gardener with a good flush of flowers late in the year.

A late flowering autumn clematis, this has pretty, lilac pink flowers with green anthers, reaching up to 12.7cm (5in) in diameter. The plant is vigorous and needs to be situated in a very sunny position to get the most out of it. It grows to 4m (13ft).

Since 'Madame Baron Meillard' flowers late in the summer it can be pruned down to ground level after it has flowered, over the winter or early in the new year. This will allow it to grow on substantially during the summer to produce its crop of flowers. The shoots from the new buds should be securely tied up and the plant allowed to grow up to its required position. In milder areas it could be pruned back to a pair of healthy buds, removing half to three-quarters of its growth above ground.

Clematis 'Madame Baron Meillard'

Clematis 'Marie Boisselot'

A highly recommended and extremely reliable cultivar, this can have over a hundred blooms in flower at the same time. It was once called *C.* 'Madame Le Coultre', but is currently named after the Frenchwoman Marie Boisselot, who raised it in 1885.

With a regular tendency to produce masses of pure white flowers, this vigorous hybrid is a must to decorate a garden gate, an arbour or areas of trellis. The flowers are up to 17cm (7in) across with cream anthers, and are produced from mid-summer onwards. The plant can grow up to 3–4m (10–13ft).

Clematis 'Marie Boisselot'

Clematis 'Marie Boisselot'

The flowers are particularly attractive, with large uniformly-shaped petals, each with a couple of ridges running along the centre line, and a fine display of stamens in the centre of the flower. Prune back to a pair of fat buds in the winter or early spring, or cut to ground level, particularly if you wish for late summer and autumn flowers.

Clematis 'Miss Bateman'

As a very reliable clematis, this is best grown in a container on a patio or in an herbaceous border where its white flowers can be appreciated. The flowers produce a lovely faint-scented bouquet of violets.

The white flowers of the 'Miss Bateman' variety typically have red anthers that distinguish it from other white clematis. The flowers grow up to 10cm (4in) across and the plant can reach up to nearly 1m (3ft) high. The plant flowers twice, first in early summer and then again in late summer.

There are many places this cultivar can be grown – either in a container, in a border or up a trellis, tripod or against a wall. Being an early large-flowered hybrid, *Clematis* 'Miss Bateman' can be pruned back to a pair of fat buds during the winter or early in the new year. The new shoots that arise from the buds should be tied up to stop damage and to direct the plant towards the areas in which you want it to flower.

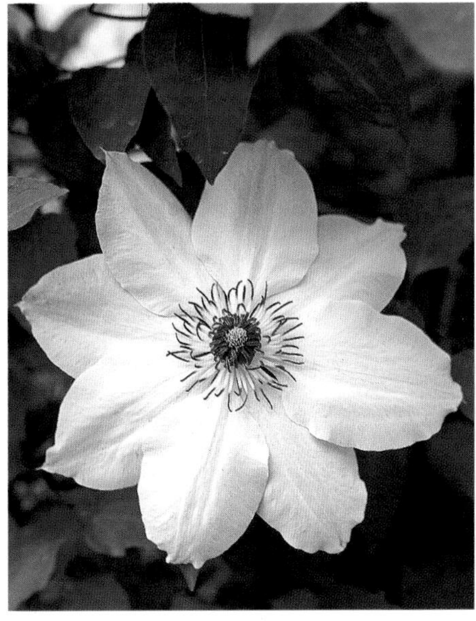

Clematis 'Miss Bateman'

Clematis 'Madame Grangé'

This old French cultivar is free flowering and is of particular use in the garden, since it comes out late in the season. It can be grown in an herbaceous border mixed with other plants or otherwise grown up a trellis.

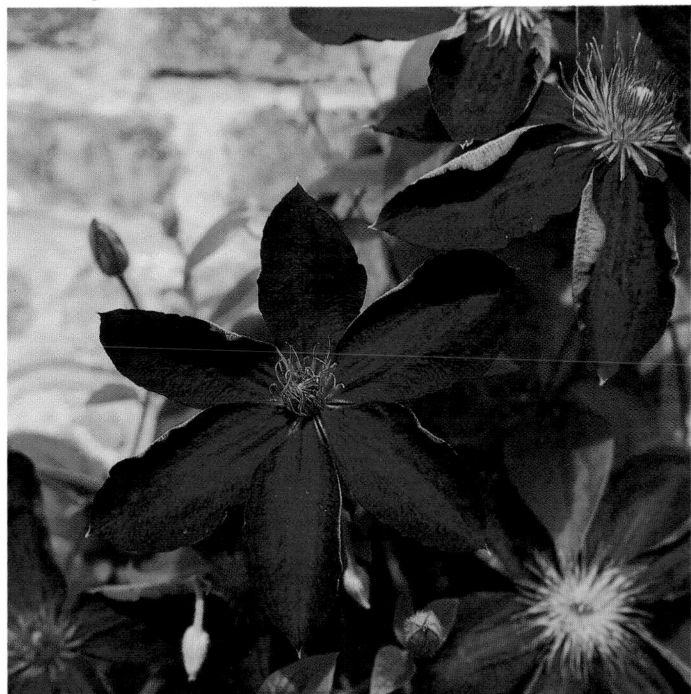

Clematis 'Madame Grangé'

Fading with age and sunshine, this late flowering clematis has particularly attractive dusky purple flowers with a yellow-purple boss. The impressive flowers can grow up to 13cm (5in) across and the plant is able to reach up to 3m (10ft). It flowers from mid-summer until the autumn. In the garden it is ideal as a dark contrast to light backdrops.

After it has finished flowering, prune this clematis back to the ground during the winter months, taking off all the dead and any remaining green wood. Clear up the cut material, and either burn or compost. New shoots will arise in the spring. These should be tied up to stop any wind damage and to direct the plant into the areas you want it to expand to or to cover. Grow it up trellises, walls and especially among herbaceous plants. This clematis looks best set against a light background for contrast.

Clematis montana

The Montana species is the mainstay of spring clematis. There are many cultivars and they are mostly characterized by having small pink or white flowers that are produced in extraordinary numbers. A mature plant can have over a thousand flowers. The climber itself is exceedingly vigorous and can swamp small trees.

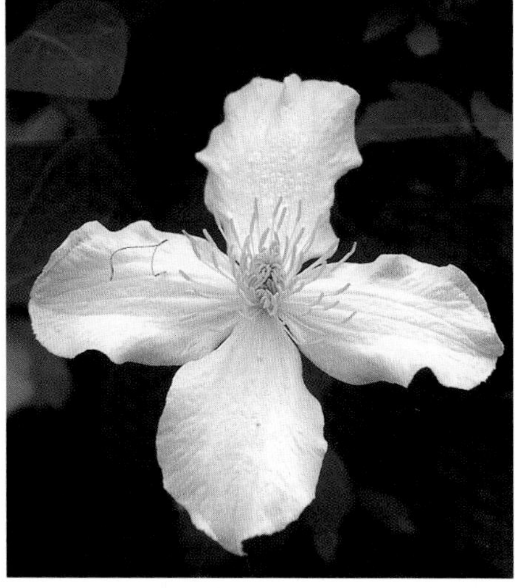

Clematis montana

This is a species clematis, native to China, that is a very vigorous grower indeed. It is widespread in Europe, where it can reach just over 9m (30ft) in height. The flowers are white, fading to pink, but it is in the soft pinks that the large number of cultivars have been developed. Montanas flower in late spring.

Pruning is restricted to cutting out any dead wood and shaping the plant. After a few years montanas produce lots of 'thatch' (masses of inter-twining stems). This needs to be thinned carefully, since the thatch contains living material (mostly on the outside) and dead material on the inside (usually, but not always).

Clematis montana 'Broughton Star'

Like a number of montana cultivars, this one's dark foliage is seen for most of the year and makes an important contribution to foliage effects in the garden. The springtime flowers, in deep pink fading quickly to pretty pale pink, complement the faint ruddiness in the young foliage.

A vigorous growing vine, this 'Broughton Star' will grow to just over 6m (20ft) along a trellis. In the spring it produces a large amount of stunning rich pink double flowers that fade eventually to pale pink.

The sepals are reflexed. A most attractive feature of this particular variety is the dark foliage, which contrasts well against the stunning pink of the flowers.

If you have space there is no need to prune this clematis back for a number of years. It can be allowed to grow along a trellis or up a tree. Eventually you may wish to restrict its growth, in which case prune off the stem. There will always be wayward stems to prune off, whenever they do not add to the aesthetics of the plant, as well as any dead stems.

Clematis montana 'Broughton Star'

Clematis montana 'Continuity'

Mounds of pink flowers cover this cultivar that, once established, gives a fine display of typical rampant montana behaviour. But unlike the other montanas, it goes on flowering for much longer than the four week period the petals normally last for.

Characteristically vigorous, *C. montana* 'Continuity' will smother a garden shed with a large amount of foliage and a capping of quite attractive pale pink flowers. It is difficult to propagate, due to its hollow stems, and grows to just over 6m (20ft).

Unless it is intruding into areas you would prefer it not to, every other year or so cut back wayward stems, any dead material and thin out any thatch that has developed. The fact that this clematis is a relatively continuous flowerer during the spring and summer is a great advantage.

Clematis montana 'Continuity'

Clematis montana 'Elizabeth'

A firm favourite for those gardeners who want a reliable pink montana, this particular variety produces a mass of beautiful soft pink blooms in its one time flush of flowers, which takes place in the spring. Like most other montanas, it grows rapidly immediately after petal loss.

Clematis montana 'Elizabeth'

This plant has perfectly formed small, pink flowers contrasting against a background of dark foliage, making this strongly scented montana a good mixer. Smelling variously of chocolate and vanilla, it will grow to just over 6m (20ft) and can be grown alongside lighter coloured plants to show off the foliage, or alternatively with colour-matching subjects.

For the best results, prune out any dead material and thatch whenever necessary, and cut off wayward stems as they appear. However, there is generally no real need to interfere with the development and growth of these plants unless space in the garden is at a premium.

Clematis montana 'Freda'

This variety is particularly useful for smaller gardens, since it has a more compact growth pattern than the other montanas. Despite this, however, it is still able to grow up to 8m (26ft) if given sufficient time and space.

'Freda' has very uniform pink flowers measuring about 2.5cm (¾in) across with dark foliage, making this a useful addition for the back of the herbaceous border, perhaps growing up a red brick wall. It grows well in most soils and aspects, and the punctuations of pink against the dark foliage are well worth having and make an attractive feature in the garden.

There is very little pruning required in young specimens. During the winter, prune out any dead or wind-damaged stems. In older specimens, thin out any developed thatch. Encourage the plant to reach different areas by tying up lead stems and training them where you want them to go.

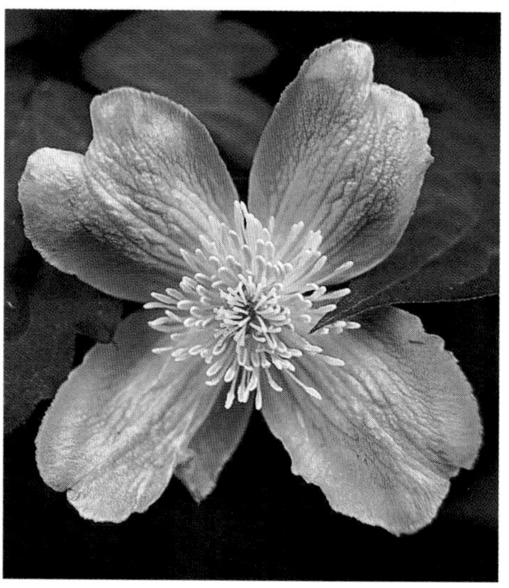

Clematis montana 'Freda'

Clematis montana 'Mayleen'

This particular montana cultivar has pink flowers that produce a strong scent of vanilla. Attractive and rampant at the same time, 'Mayleen' can be employed to grow over fences and trellises with relative ease.

Small pink flowers, with slightly reflexed sepals, are produced in masses over a mature specimen of 'Mayleen'. Like so many other montanas, their best display occurs from about the third year after planting, when they have massed ranks of stems.

The plant will grow to about 6m (20ft).

Check the plant for any dead and damaged stems, and prune these off. In older plants, thin out any thatch accordingly, being careful to remove only dead stems, and shape the plant to your requirements.

Clematis montana 'Mayleen'

 *flower*  *little moisture*  *moisture*  *wet*

Clematis montana 'Odorata'

Although it is named 'Odorata', the scent of this clematis is subtle and not overpowering. In common with other montana cultivars, this is just as vigorous and an excellent scrambler. The flowers are produced as a sheet of colour in the spring.

A vigorous climber, this montana will smother a small tree or grow rampantly along a hedgerow, producing a sheet of small, pale pink flowers from early to late spring. Although not especially over-powering in scent, the flowers do produce a sweet perfume on warm days. It will grow to just over 6m (20ft) and the flowers can reach around 6cm (2in) in diameter.

After a few years this clematis may need to be kept in check, as it could easily take up too much space in the garden if it is left to its own devices. Judicious cutting back to shape the plant should be carried out, alongside thoroughly pruning out any dead and damaged stems. Removing stems growing in the 'wrong' direction will also help keep the plant's growth in check and improve its general shape.

Clematis montana 'Odorata'

Clematis montana 'Tetrarose'

This particular montana variety is characterized by its four petals and green bronzy foliage and serrated leaflet margins. Its relatively large flowers grow up to 7.5cm (3in) in diameter.

The uniformity of the pretty pink flowers is typical of this cultivar, and it contrasts well with the mass of yellow stamens at the centre of the flowers. Growing vigorously up to 10m (33ft), it can be grown in any aspect but may not be advisable to grow in a small garden or patio.

Clematis montana 'Tetrarose'

	SPRING			SUMMER			AUTUMN			WINTER			height (cm)	spread (cm)	min temp (°C)	moisture	sun/shade	colours	
Clematis montana		●	●	●									900	250	-10°				A vigorous species montana
C. m. 'Broughton Star'		●	●	●									600	250	-10°				Star-like flowers
C. m. 'Continuity'		●	●	●	●	●							600	250	-10°				Continuous flowering
C. m. 'Elizabeth'		●	●	●									600	250	-10°				Softest-pink flowers
C. m. 'Freda'		●	●	●									800	250	-10°				Looks great against red bricks
C. m. 'Mayleen'		●	●	●									600	250	-10°				A soothing pink colour
C. m. 'Odorata'		●	●	●			●						600	250	-10°				Not wildly scented, but subtle
C. m. 'Tetrarose'		●	●	●									1,000	250	-10°				Geometrically pink

 *sunny*  *semi-shady* *shady*

Clematis 'Mrs Cholmondeley'

A classic clematis originating from 1873, this old but reliable variety is an excellent choice for the garden since its large flowers are particularly attractive up against a wall or trellis, and its spiky seed heads are of great interest.

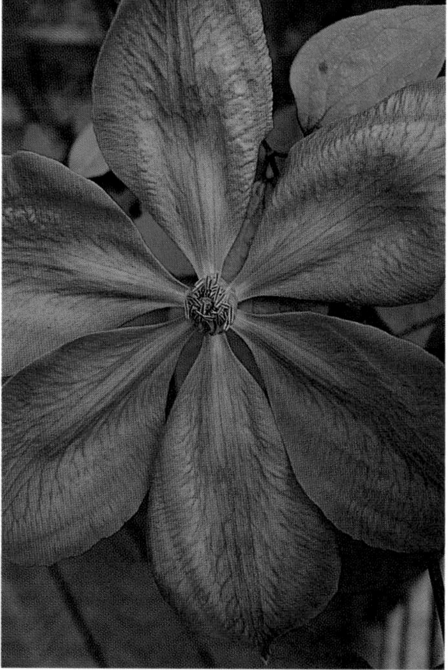

Clematis 'Mrs Cholmondeley'

An ideal candidate for a container, this clematis will scramble to about 1.5m (5ft) along trellises, and having been well watered will produce quite a number of large blue-purple flowers, each up to 20cm (8in) across. It is in flower by the early summer and continues flowering sporadically until late summer.

If taken out of the container after a few years, it will double its size and do very nicely trained up a tripod within an herbaceous border. After flowering, perhaps after an early autumn flush of flowers, prune it well back to a pair of fat buds, so that in the following spring these will become the lead shoots that will start the plant off for the new season. Ensure that lead shoots are tied up, otherwise the plant will look bedraggled and unsightly and will be unable to support its large-sized flowers.

Clematis 'Mrs George Jackman'

A good plant from this variety trained up against a wall is likely to produce over 30 flowers at the same time. This is what you should achieve with good ground conditions and plenty of water. The large flowers will make a distinguished display.

Dating from 1877, this is a large-flowered cultivar that produces masses of semi-double flowers, up to 15cm (6in) in diameter, from early summer onwards. It also flowers later in the year, this time with single blooms. It does well in a container, and will grow to an impressive 2.5m (8–9ft) in height.

During the winter or early spring, prune most of its dead and green vegetation back to a couple of plum buds. These will be the starter buds in spring. Be sure to tie up the new shoots that will arise from these buds securely, so that they are not damaged by spring winds. This clematis makes a useful colour contrast against a bare brick wall.

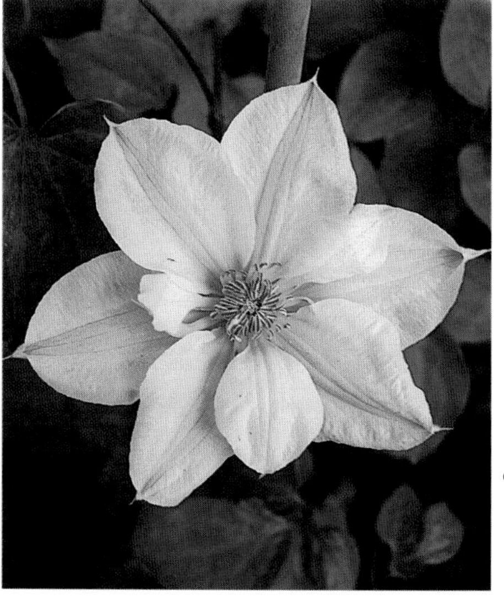

Clematis 'Mrs George Jackman'

Clematis 'Multi Blue'

Raised in 1983, this unusual flower has its merits grown in a smart pot or container and supported on canes where it can be inspected and appreciated in all its glory at head height. This spectacular clematis is more of a reproductive confusion, with a mass of central petaloids and a total lack of anthers, yet at the same time its flowers appear quite stunning.

Originally found in Holland, this clematis has a stunning central boss of petaloids in a blueish-purple hue. The flowers are attractive in both late spring and late summer, and may be either single or double. It grows to around 2.4m (8ft) in height.

During the winter or early spring, cut out any dead and green stems and prune back to a pair of potentially good buds lower down on the plant. When these sprouts shoot in the spring, tie these up to minimize damage from wind or heavy rain, and direct them to spread out over the area you want it to cover.

Clematis 'Multi Blue'

Clematis 'Nelly Moser'

Widely grown around the world, this is a very popular clematis for its large, colourful and attractive flowers. Good healthy plants produce masses of flowers at the same time, but they do have a tendency to fade in full sun.

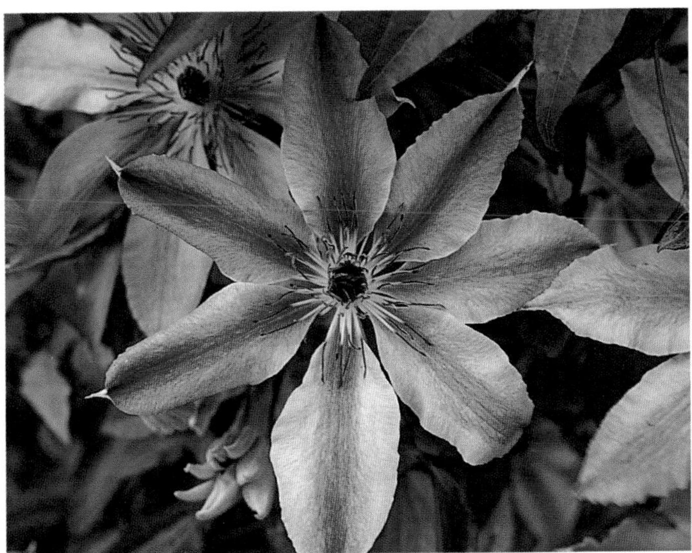

Clematis 'Nelly Moser'

A very popular cultivar, this plant is vigorous to 3m (10ft) and produces vast quantities of impressive, large flowers measuring up to 17cm (7in) across. The colour of the sepals is typical, being white with a suffusion of the palest pink and a single purple band down the middle.

Well after flowering, in winter or early in the new year, prune off at least half to three-quarters of the dead and living stems back to a pair of promising buds. These will be the lead shoots in the following spring. Be sure to tie these shoots up to encourage the plant to grow in the direction you wish, and to minimize any damage to the shoots while growing from spring winds. A position in dappled light is best.

Clematis 'Niobe'

This clematis' most distinguishing feature is its very long flowering period. This free-flowering variety is particularly recommended for growing in containers. It also thrives and looks good mixed with other plants in the herbaceous border.

Clematis 'Niobe'

The typical feature of this Polish hybrid is the combination of dark red sepals with a bold boss of yellow stamens. This clematis flowers from late spring until autumn, producing flowers up to 15cm (6in) across and can grow up to 4.6m (10ft) in height. 'Niobe' is a very attractive plant for a patio pot or grown in a window box trailing up some trellis on a veranda wall or over a porch way.

As this is an early large-flowering clematis, it needs to be pruned during the winter or during the early part of the year, back to a pair of plump buds. Cuttings for propagation can also be taken at this time. New growth needs to be tied up as it develops. Keep 'Niobe' well watered both before and during flowering.

Clematis 'Patricia Ann Fretwell'

A reliable producer of big handfuls of flowers, the 'Patricia Ann Fretwell' variety produces a limited number of flowers year after year. It should be grown just for the stunning flowers, which are best shown off growing through other vegetation.

Also known as 'Parfar', this clematis produces magnificent blooms that are as big as a fist in all dimensions. The large, double-pink flowers are produced in late spring, always after the montanas, and grow with thin stems among taller herbaceous border plants. The plant will scramble around and grow to about 1.5m (5ft) in height.

A regular flowerer and popular cultivar, this clematis is best pruned back to a pair of fat buds during the winter or early in the new year. Pruning should include old stems and leaves that can be either composted or burnt. The remaining stems should be tied up to the supporting plant or trellis, and the new growth can be tied up as it develops.

Clematis 'Patricia Ann Fretwell'

Clematis 'Perle d'Azur'

With Jackmanii parentage, this is a classic clematis that is highly recommended for gardens. As 'Perle d'Azur' flowers so prolifically, it can be used as a backdrop to alcoves and seating areas, creating a superb spread of colour across a large area.

A great performer against a wall, this clematis will run riot over many square metres (yards), producing a mass of blue-purple flowers from late spring onwards. The medium-sized flowers of this plant make a great cover for dull surface areas. This variety is widely available but is unfortunately difficult to propagate.

As a late large-flowered cultivar 'Perle d'Azur' needs to be pruned back to a good pair of buds, close to about 30cm (1ft) from the ground.

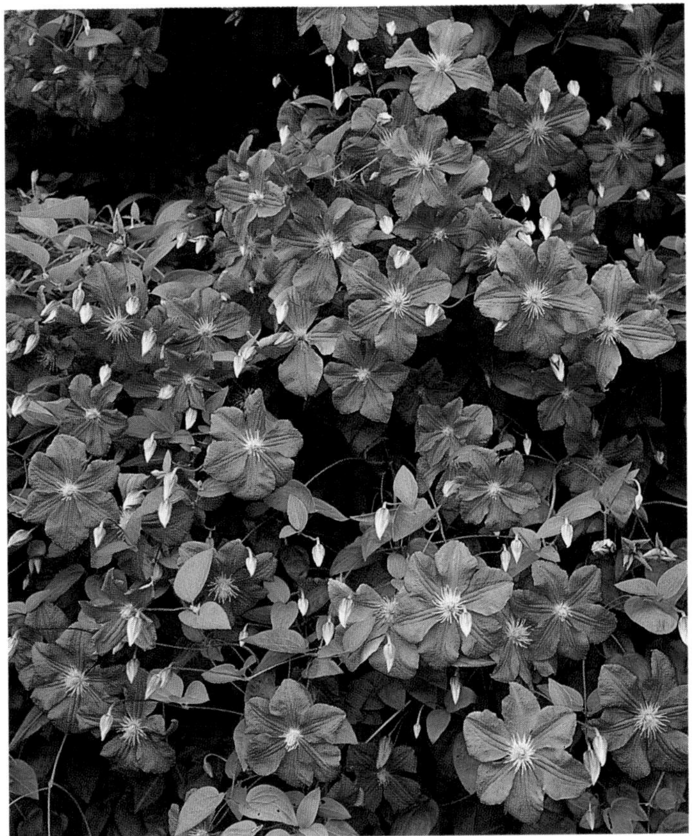

Clematis 'Perle d'Azur'

Clematis 'Perrin's Pride'

This variety is a useful dark-purple, large-flowered clematis which looks impressive planted in the herbaceous border growing through plants, particularly against a background of evergreen shrubs.

'Perrin's Pride' is a reliable climber that will grow to 3m (10ft) in height. It has large purple flowers, up to 15cm (6in) across, which first appear in the early summer, followed by a second flush later in the same season. A characteristic feature of this clematis is its dull yellow anthers in the flower centre.

Keep this clematis well watered before and during flowering. As a late large-flowered cultivar it needs to be pruned back to a good pair of buds close to about 30cm (1ft) from the ground. Take stem cuttings at the same time.

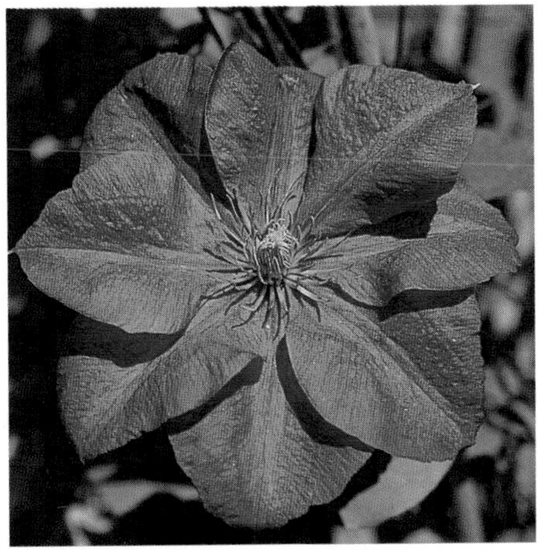

Clematis 'Perrin's Pride'

Clematis 'Petit Faucon'

Grown for its unusual twisted flowers, this clematis is an interesting compact variety that can be grown in patio gardens, in containers or overhanging low walls. The steely blue colour of this variety is particularly appealing.

Also known as 'Evisix', this variety arose as a seedling from a nursery on the island of Guernsey. Its twisted sepals on its small flowers are characteristic, and will flower for up to three months. Good for draping over a wall, or through herbaceous plants, as it only grows to about 1m (3ft).

Clematis 'Petit Faucon'

Clematis 'Pink Fantasy'

This shade of pale pink in a large-flowered clematis is not that common, and the plant can be most usefully grown in the herbaceous border of a garden, entwined around other plants such as low growing shrubs.

Originating in Canada, this variety is a very suitable hybrid for containers and has pale pink flowers which are a little more firmer and pert than the 'Hagley Hybrid' variety (see page 52). Its flowers, which bloom in the summer, are about 10cm (4in) in diameter and the plant will run to about 2.4m (8ft).

Keep this clematis well watered before and during flowering. As a late large-flowered cultivar it needs to be pruned back to a good pair of buds close to about 30cm (1ft) from the ground during winter or early spring. Compost or burn all dead stems and leaves. Stem cuttings that include a pair of buds can be used at this time for propagation. During the spring make sure that the new shoots are tied up in the direction you want them to grow.

Clematis 'Pink Fantasy'

Clematis 'Polish Spirit'

Both garden designers and those interested in colour co-ordination in the garden may find this plant a useful mixer, as its dark colours will contrast or colour match beautifully with many other border plants.

Clematis 'Polish Spirit'

This stunning clematis, which was named in honour of the Polish people during the Second World War, produces rich velvet-maroon flowers roughly 7cm (2in) across, with the plant itself growing to about 4m (13ft). It flowers freely from mid-summer until the early autumn, and is vigorous enough to grow into a small tree or hedgerow.

Since this is a viticella type of clematis, it is best to prune this cultivar during the spring by cutting back all last year's growth of stems and leaves. This should be removed back to pairs of new buds that will start the new year's growth. New shoots can be tied up to begin with, allowing the plant to develop healthily. Keep this clematis well watered before and during flowering. During the autumn make cuttings from stems, keeping a pair of buds for each cutting before putting them into compost.

Clematis 'Prince Charles'

This clematis is ideal for containers or grown specifically for cut flowers. The flowers may be borne in very large numbers. This variety performs well when trained along a trellis or through pergolas from where its flowers can tumble freely.

Originally raised in New Zealand, this variety has a bluish-purple flower that is somewhat variable in colour, depending on how much sunlight the plant receives. It has characteristic yellow anthers, and the flowers are borne freely, giving the impression they are nodding. The flowers are up to 10cm (4in) across and the plant grows energetically up to 2.5m (8ft).

Keep well watered before and during flowering. As a late large-flowered cultivar it needs to be pruned back to a good pair of buds about 30cm (1ft) from the ground during winter or early spring.

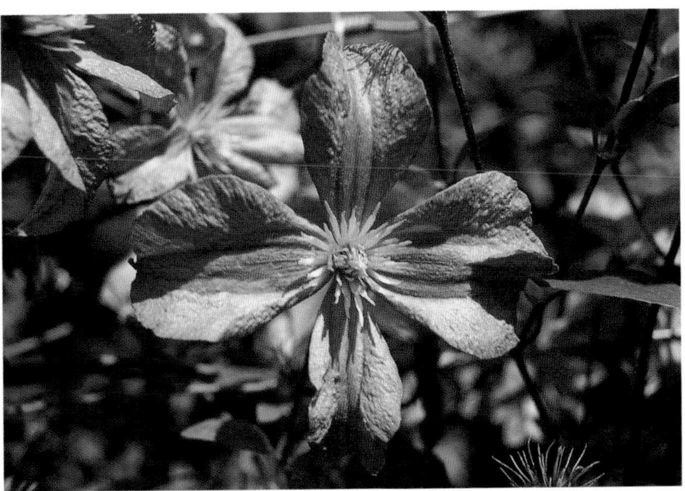
Clematis 'Prince Charles'

Clematis 'Princess of Wales'

The bright colours of this clematis are most effective when it is planted up a pillar or trellis where the small but beautiful flowers can be best appreciated. It is fairly vigorous and the flowers are very shapely. This variety can also be grown through other plants, producing a dazzling display of delicate colour.

Clematis 'Princess of Wales'

With clear, bell-shaped flowers, *Clematis* 'Princess of Wales' is an attractive variety that can grow up to 3m (10ft) in height. Originally raised in the late 19th century, it has other invalid, but still popular, names such as 'The Princess of Wales' and 'Princess Diana', after the most famous owner of the plant's title.

This clematis should be cut right back to a good pair of buds close to about 30cm (1ft) from the ground during winter or early spring. Tie up the new shoots as they emerge in the spring to prevent wind damage and to assist the plant's growth.

Clematis recta

A species clematis which produces lots of foliage and flower – as well as producing a heavy, sweet scent – this plant makes a useful addition to borders and can be grown next to red gladioli to make a contrasting combination.

This clematis, native to southern Europe, has several known cultivars and subspecies, including some with dark foliage. It is perfect for planting in the herbaceous border and, with the help of adjacent plants or support, can grow to around 1.5m (5ft). Late flowering, the scent of *C. recta* attracts colourful butterflies and useful hoverflies, whose larvae feed on those troublesome aphids which will try and attack the plant. As an herbaceous clematis, this species dies back to ground level during the winter.

During the winter or early in the new year, prune the plant back to ground level and compost or burn debris. When new shoots are produced in the spring, tie them up to supports to prevent damage.

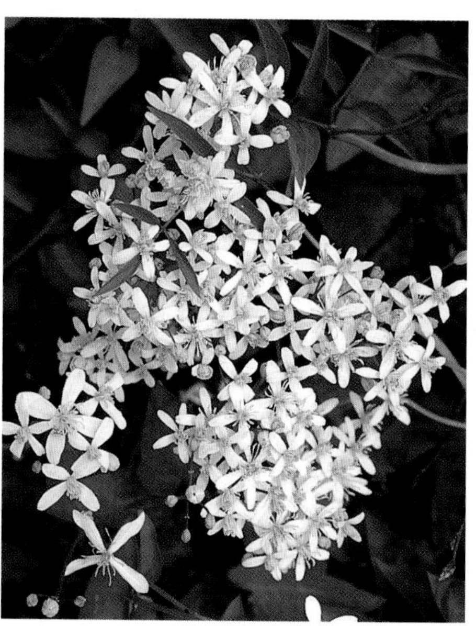

Clematis recta

	SPRING			SUMMER			AUTUMN			WINTER			height (cm)	spread (cm)	min temp (°C)	moisture	sun/shade	colours	
C. recta			flower	flower	flower	flower	flower						150	75	-10°	little moisture	sun/partial shade		An herbaceous perennial
C. r. 'Velvet Night'			flower	flower	flower	flower	flower						150	100	-10°	little moisture	sun/partial shade		Dies down in winter

flower · little moisture · moisture · wet

Clematis rehderiana

Growing abundantly in gardens, this species clematis does well against walls or through trees, and produces masses of foliage and flowers. The pale yellow bell-shaped flowers are produced in little clusters that are particularly attractive.

This very vigorous clematis can climb to 7m (23ft) and is therefore able to cope with clambering up and through reasonably large trees. Its flowers are a very unusual shape for a member of the clematis family. These cowslip-scented, bell-shaped flowers are a creamy yellow colour that are produced from mid-summer to late autumn. *Clematis rehderiana* originates from China.

Prune this species during the winter by removing all of the years' growth that has died down. This should be either composted or burnt. In the spring new shoots can be tied up to begin with and to allow the plant to develop healthily. This plant needs plenty of space to grow happily, so allow for this. Keep well watered before and during flowering. During the summer make cuttings from stems, keeping a pair of buds for each cutting before putting them into compost.

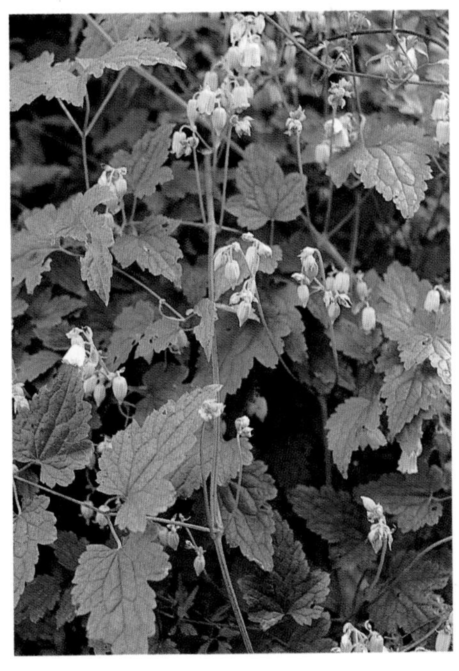

Clematis rehderiana

Clematis 'Rhapsody'

The blue colour of the sepals on this clematis is truly remarkable and for this reason it is often best grown in a container to show off its floriferous display in all its glory. This particular variety is quite compact in its growth.

Clematis 'Rhapsody' has six pointed blue-purple sepals, with magnificent flowers up to 12.5cm (5in) in diameter.

Clematis 'Rhapsody'

This plant can grow up to 2.5m (8ft) in height and is suitable for growing up a wall or, for visual impact, planted in a container to brighten up a dull patio or paved area. It also works well climbing up a trellis or fence and can also be encouraged to grow amongst roses and other shrubs. It comes into flower from early summer and lasts up until the autumn.

Whilst this plant is in bud it needs to be kept well watered right up to, and during, flowering. During the late winter or early spring the dead stems and leaves should be cut back to a pair of fat buds close to about 30cm (1ft) from the ground. Cuttings for propagation may be made at this time, which involves taking short pieces of stem, each with a pair of buds, dipping the cut surface in hormone powder to assist with growth and then placing them into compost.

Clematis 'Rouge Cardinal'

This clematis has a rather grand and sophisticated deep red colour, like the 'Polish Spirit' variety, and is well disposed to grow up red brick walls where it colour matches the bricks. It is a hybrid from the Jackmanii variety (see page 54).

A popular clematis, this rewarding variety produces a good quantity of deep red-maroon flowers, each about 10cm (4in) across. The plant is excellent growing up a wall, as it will show off its flowers up to 3m (10ft). It does need support, however, since it has feeble stems.

Being a trouble-free variety, 'Rouge Cardinal' can also look stunning grown through low shrubs such as heathers, with the deep red, late-summer flowering blooms providing an extra colour contrast. It prefers to be planted in the full sun for best results.

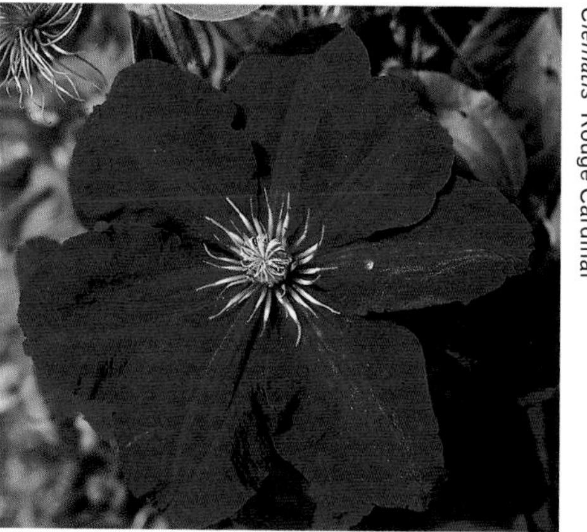

Clematis 'Rouge Cardinal'

Clematis 'Royal Velours'

This particular cultivar is ideal for growing up a wall or even covering up an ugly drainpipe by training it up strategically placed trellis. Due to its stunning colour, 'Royal Velours' is also excellent for making cut flowers.

This clematis hybrid typically features small flowers growing in clusters. The rounded sepals of this plant are a rich maroon with a satin, velvety finish, and the sepals are a drab yellow colour. The flowers are about 5cm (2in) in diameter and the plant will grow to about 2.5m (8ft) in height. It bears its flowers from early summer through to the autumn.

After flowering, in the autumn and during the winter period, cut back any dead stems and leaves to a series of paired buds that look large enough to start off the following year's growth.

Clematis 'Royal Velours'

Clematis 'Royal Velvet'

Also marketed under the name 'Evifour', this clematis can be grown in a container to make a feature in a small garden. It has dark foliage and can be mixed with other species to make an attractive focal point in a border.

Clematis 'Royal Velvet'

This cultivar is a large-flowered clematis with flowers up to 15cm (6in) in diameter from late spring to autumn. The sepals are a rich purple and the anthers have a reddish tinge, making them an attractive feature. Growing to about 1.8m (6ft) in height, this plant looks splendid if it is grown in containers.

This clematis is best pruned back to a pair of fat buds during the winter or early in the new year. Pruning should include old stems and leaves that can be either composted or burnt. The remaining stems can be tied up to the supporting plant or trellis, and the new growth should be tied up as it develops.

Clematis 'Ruby Glow'

Delightfully coloured with pink blooms, this is an early, large flowering clematis. Grown in a small garden this plant excels in pots and containers and can equally be grown successfully either up a trellis or a wall.

This cultivar is aptly named with its pink sepals suffused in ruby, alongside its dull-red anthers. The impressive, large flowers are up to 17cm (7in) in diameter. It has two flushes of flowers, one in the spring and the second crop produced in the summer. It is ideal for containers, growing up to around 2.5m (8ft) in height. Use it to brighten up a dull corner or to enliven a plain terrace.

Prune this clematis back to a pair of fat buds during the winter or early in the new year. Pruning should include old stems and leaves that can be either composted or burnt. Tie up remaining stems to the supporting plant or trellis, and the new growth should be tied up as it develops.

Clematis 'Ruby Glow'

Clematis 'Snow Queen'

An early large flowering clematis with pointed sepals, this plant has compact growth combined with a propensity to flower enthusiastically, which makes it an excellent subject to grow in a small garden.

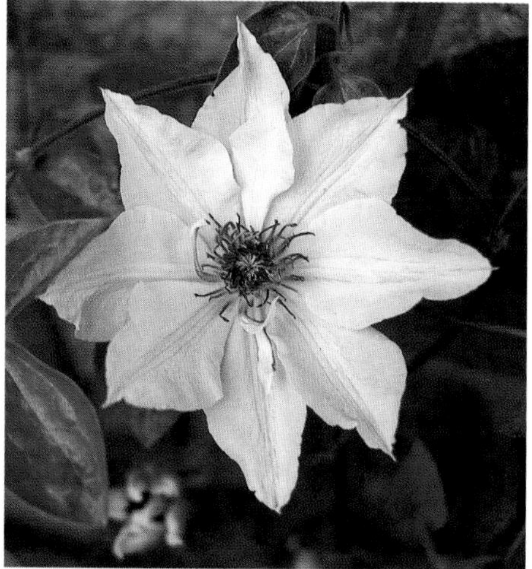
Clematis 'Snow Queen'

Originating from New Zealand, this clematis has pointed white sepals each with palest yellow along the centre line. The flowers are up to 10cm (4in) across and the plant can grow up to 2.4m (8ft). Coming into flower both in early and late summer, the cultivar is good to grow in containers and to use for cutting. Late-summer flowers have hints of pink.

During the winter or early in the new year, prune the plant back thoroughly to a pair of fat buds. When new shoots are produced in the spring, tie them up to supports to prevent damage and to encourage healthy growth.

Clematis 'Star of India'

Accentuating a tendency to be star-like, the tips of the sepals of this clematis are often pointed. An old English clematis, this vigorous, large-flowered variety is well worth growing in the border, or up a trellis or pergola.

Almost squarish in shape, the pink flowers have just four to six rounded sepals in the form of a star. The flowers are up to 10cm (4in) in diameter and the plant grows to about 3m (10ft). This clematis is free-flowering, making it ideal to mix with other plants.

Keep this clematis well watered before and during flowering. As a late large-flowered cultivar it needs to be pruned back to a good pair of buds close to about 30cm (1ft) from the ground during winter or early spring. Compost or burn all dead stems and leaves.

Stem cuttings that include a pair of buds can be used at this time for propagation. During the spring make sure that the new shoots are tied up in the direction that you want them to grow. This will reduce the chances of damage from storms. The pink flowers of this clematis can be combined in the herbaceous border with roses and many other shrubs. The plant can also be grown up trellis or a tripod and through shrubs, its squarish flowers being a little different from those of most other cultivars.

Clematis 'Star of India'

Clematis 'Stazik'

A slow but reliable flowerer and mixer, this cultivar puts on a good display of velvet-burgundy blooms each year and quietly gets on with its flowering among other species without gaining much extra height.

Clematis 'Stazik'

Growing among open shrubs such as roses, 'Stazik' is a good herbaceous mixer that will run to about 1.2m (4ft) in height. The flowers are up to 7.6cm (3in) across and are a rich burgundy velvet with a suspicion of red along the centre line of the sepals. The filaments are white with burgundy anthers.

When planning your herbaceous border with this clematis as a mixer, choose shrubs whose colours will contrast strongly with the sumptuous reds of 'Stazik'; blue and pink hues work particularly well.

This plant needs to be cut right back to a good pair of buds close to about 30cm (1ft) from the ground during winter or early spring. Tie up the new shoots as they emerge in the spring to prevent wind damage and to encourage healthy growth.

Clematis 'Sugar Candy'

Dinner-plate sized flowers are produced in abundance on this large-flowered clematis cultivar. To get the most out of this magnificent plant, grow it in full sunlight where it will perform best of all, really showing off its splendid blooms.

Also known by the name 'Evione', this clematis produces spectacular large flowers, the sepals being pink with a contrasting purple-red down the centre line. It is good value, particularly for its abundance of large, colourful flowers from early to late summer.

When buds are produced, water the whole plant thoroughly, and continue to do so once the flowers have opened.

Clematis 'Sugar Candy'

Clematis terniflora

This is the kind of useful clematis that you can almost forget about, since it is fairly hardy and will flower prolifically in the autumn without fail. Typical of a species clematis, it is a strong grower with tough, woody stems. It was previously known as *Clematis maximowicziana*.

Clematis terniflora

Commonly known as the Sweet Autumn Clematis, this plant is true to its name as it produces a show of sweet-scented flowers in the autumn. Native to the east coast of North America, it is a rampant grower, typically reaching 4.6m (15ft). The star-shaped flowers themselves are small, up to 2.5cm (1in) across, but produced in very large numbers. This climber is an ideal choice for a trellis.

Once established, this clematis tends to produce a lot of knotted vegetation – a mass of new and old growth – and this 'thatch' should be selectively thinned out to make room for the new growth and accompanying flowers. The plant will tolerate quite a hard prune during the winter period or early in the new year and will produce long stems that can then be tied up to save them from wind damage.

Cuttings for propagation may be made at the same time as pruning. This involves taking short pieces of stem, each with a pair of buds, dipping the cut surfaces in hormone powder to encourage vigorous growth and then placing the cuttings into compost.

Clematis 'The Bride'

The simplicity and uncomplicated manner of the flower and foliage are the most appealing features of this lovely white clematis. It does not have complex features, such as double flowers, twisty shapes or colour variations like so many other clematis.

The very attractive flowers are a pure white with a tinge of greenish yellow through the centre, growing to around 7cm (3in) in diameter. The stamens are a wonderfully contrasting yellow. The plant itself grows to about 2m (7ft) in height. The cultivar belongs to the Jackmanii group of clematis. Its flowering season is from the early summer onwards.

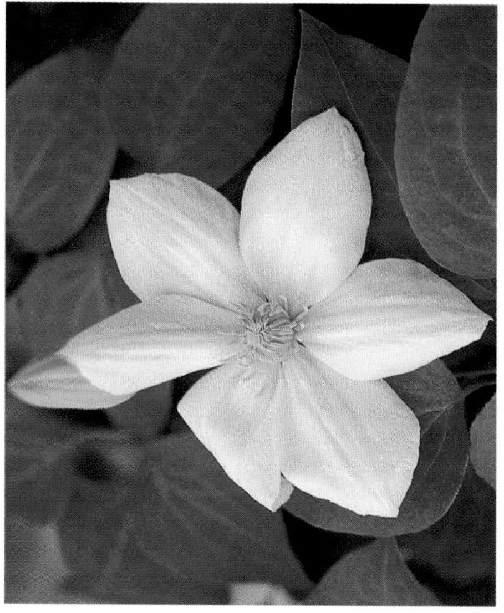

Clematis 'The Bride'

Clematis 'The President'

A large-flowered clematis, this is a classic old variety that has been grown for more than 100 years. It has a compact form and does well in containers. It can also be grown up trellis and pergolas, and will reward you with plenty of flowers.

Hugely popular, because of its depth of colour and long flowering time, this cultivar is used a great deal against house walls, on trelliswork and in containers. The large flowers are of a stunning rich purple-blue hue, reaching up to 15cm (6in) across. *Clematis* 'The President' flowers vigorously throughout the summer, stopping only at the onset of autumn. The plant will grow up to 3m (10ft) in height if it is given adequate support.

Clematis 'The President' is best pruned back to a pair of fat buds during the winter or early in the new year. This includes old stems and leaves that can be either composted or burnt. The remaining stems should be tied up to the supporting plant or trellis, and the new growth can be tied up as it develops.

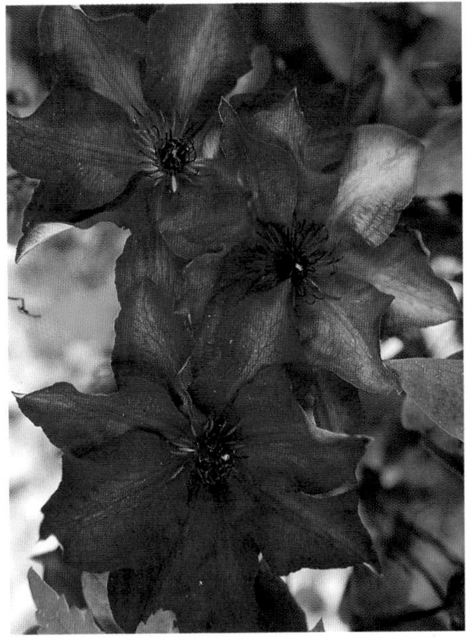

Clematis 'The President'

Clematis 'Twilight'

Grown through other climbers or plants in the herbaceous border, this large-flowered pink clematis is a particularly good mixer of medium height. Its compact form lends itself to cultivation in containers and it is ideal for small gardens.

With a rounded symmetry, *Clematis* 'Twilight' has very attractive lavender-mauve sepals and a large boss of cream and pale yellow. Flowers can grow up to 15cm (6in) in diameter and the plant can reach as much as 2.5m (8ft) in height.

This plant is a real garden brightener, especially in a small space. It is best pruned back to a pair of fat buds during the winter or early in the new year. Pruning should include old stems and leaves that can be either composted or burnt. The remaining stems should be tied up to the supporting plant or trellis. This will encourage active new growth in the spring.

Clematis 'Twilight'

Clematis 'Victoria'

A classic English clematis which is nearly 150 years old and dates back to the Victorian era. It is a large, late-flowering cultivar that combines superbly among roses and contrasts well against a light background, such as a white wall.

This old clematis, named in honour of Queen Victoria, is much favoured among gardeners today for its propensity to climb over walls and trellises. It is a prolific flowerer and its mauve-purple flowers are about 10cm (4in) in diameter. The plant will scramble to about 3m (10ft) and it flowers from around mid-summer onwards.

After its summer exhuberance this clematis needs to be cut right back to a good pair of buds close to about 30cm (1ft) from the ground during winter or early spring. This will allow new shoots to spring forth in the growing season, and these should be tied to supports.

Clematis 'Victoria'

Clematis 'Ville de Lyon'

Originating from viticella parentage, this is a reliable clematis for training up a pillar or growing through other vegetation in the border. It has a fairly leafless base, which can be covered by a host plant, allowing 'Ville de Lyon' to burst through the top.

An old clematis variety, this makes a good plant to train up a pillar, spilling over with its maroon flowers up to 12cm (5in) in diameter. The sepals are dusted like moths wings, with light coloured scales. This variety will grow up to 3m (10ft) and comes into flower from early summer.

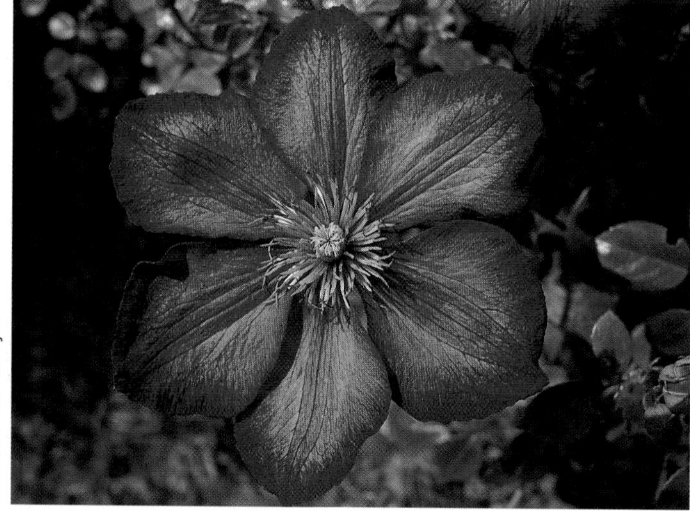

Clematis 'Ville de Lyon'

This is a very popular cultivar which is easily mixed with other clematis or grown through roses or other herbaceous plants. Its reddish colour combines well with rose pink and white flowers. Keep well watered from the spring onwards so that the full compliment of buds develops into a mass of flowers.

During the late winter or early spring the dead stems and leaves of this plant should be cut back to a pair of fat buds close to about 30cm (1ft) from the ground. Cuttings for propagation may be made at this time. This involves taking short pieces of stem, each with a pair of buds, and placing these into compost after dipping the cut surfaces in hormone powder.

Clematis vitalba

This extremely hardy plant is a rampant growing clematis, also known as Traveller's Joy. It is accustomed to romping through yew trees in its natural habitat on chalky soils. In the garden, it is tamed only by the secateurs to keep it within bounds.

Clematis vitalba

Native to Western Europe, this is a vigorous climber which, if left to its own devices, will scramble on several stems to as much as 15m (50ft). Harnessed in the garden it will make 2.5m (8ft) easily in opposite directions. It is an ideal plant for growing in trees, along trellises or used for screening. As well as looking good, it has scented flowers and attractive seed heads, from which the nickname of Old Man's Beard is derived.

Unless you want a sea of seeds wafting over the garden during the autumn, cut this plant hard back to its principal stems. These may be large and fibrous, depending on the age of the plant. All the vegetation can be cut off, allowing you then to prune the plant to where you want the show of foliage and flowers next year. There is no doubt that this plant will always benefit from a very hard prune, with a huge amount of new growth following.

Clematis 'Venosa Violacea'

A viticella cultivar, this clematis is a very attractive addition to any trelliswork or wall where its bright flowers can be appreciated. The intensity of its attractive markings varies from country to country, depending on stock.

This is a very appealing cultivar with its wonderful contrasting bands of colour on its sepals. This banding is variable. The purple-white flowers are about 5cm (2in) in diameter and the plant will scramble up pillars or over trellis to about 3m (10ft). Its magnificent flowers are produced from mid-summer through to late autumn, providing the garden with some welcome late colour.

As a viticella cultivar this clematis needs to be pruned back to a good pair of buds close to about 30cm (1ft) from the ground during the winter. Take stem cuttings at the same time.

Clematis 'Venosa Violacea'

Clematis 'W.E. Gladstone'

With large, blue floppy dinner-plates as flowers, this is a classic clematis that flowers over a long period from mid-summer onwards. It can add a dash of perfect colour grown in a courtyard garden and is suitable for taking cuttings.

This old English clematis has large, single, flowers growing to around 20cm (8in). The sepals are pale blue with a boss of maroon anthers. This variety grows to about 3.7m (12ft) given adequate support to bear the weight of its blooms, and flowers from early summer through to the autumn.

Clematis 'W.E. Gladstone'

Clematis 'Wada's Primrose'

This particular clematis, originating from Japan, is a very suitable plant to grow in a small garden in a container, or in a border trained up some trellis to give it added support. Its fat, soft grey-green buds open to delectable primrose colours in early summer, fading to white as the season progresses.

Pale primrose in colour, this large-flowered cartwheel-like clematis is worth growing in a container, along a trellis or even up a pillar. Its flowers, which can grow as much as 18cm (7in) in diameter, bloom from early summer onwards and last until the autumn, but fade both with age and if positioned in full sunlight. On a pyramid-shaped support or trellis it will exceed 2.5m (8ft) in height, but in a container it will grow to just over 1m (3ft).

Clematis 'Wada's Primrose'

Whilst this clematis is in bud it needs to be kept well watered right up to, and during, flowering. During the late winter or early spring the dead stems and leaves should be cut back to a pair of fat buds close to about 30cm (1ft) from the ground. Cuttings for propagation may be made at this time. This involves taking short pieces of stem, each with a pair of buds, dipping the cut surfaces into hormone powder to encourage healthy growth and then placing the stems into compost. This is one of the more popular clematis varieties which will always reward you with lots of large flowers.

Clematis 'Warszawska Nike'

A good mixer and excellent flowerer, this Polish cultivar has spectacular blooms that vary somewhat from a deep ruby colour through pink-maroon to a dark chocolate-velvety hue. This variety of colour is due to different root stock and age.

Also known as 'Warsaw Nike', this is another stunning variety which will make an impact in the garden. The flowers have highly contrasting bright maroon sepals with a large cream boss, and can grow up to 15cm (6in) across. The plant comes into flower, often prolifically, from early summer onwards and can reach up to 3m (10ft) in height.

During the spring make sure that the new shoots of this clematis are tied up in the direction you want them to grow. Once established, the plant can produce lots of flowers that will look very attractive on a medium sized-plant.

Keep this clematis well watered before and after the onset of flowering. During winter and spring, prune the plant back to a good pair of buds close to about 30cm (1ft) from the ground. Compost or burn all dead stems and leaves. Stem cuttings that include a pair of buds can be used at this time for propagation.

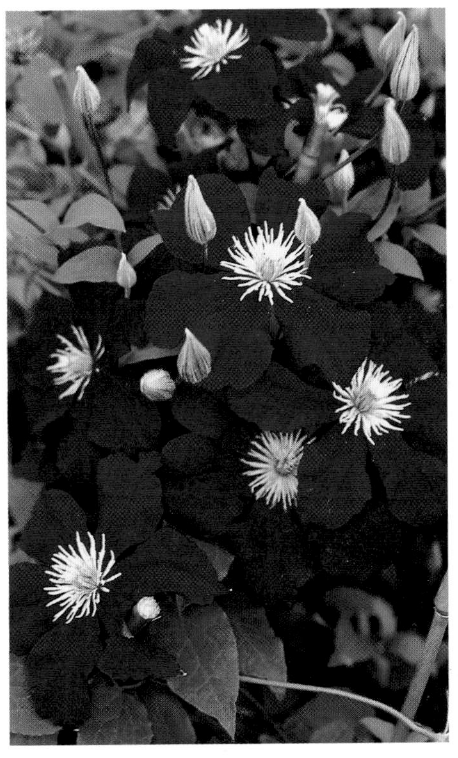

Clematis 'Warszawska Nike'

Clematis 'William Kennett'

This attractive variety can be grown in an herbaceous border where it will happily grow through plants, mixing and contrasting well with its host plants. It looks equally good either planted by itself in a container or trained to clamber up trelliswork, where it can show off its beautiful flowers.

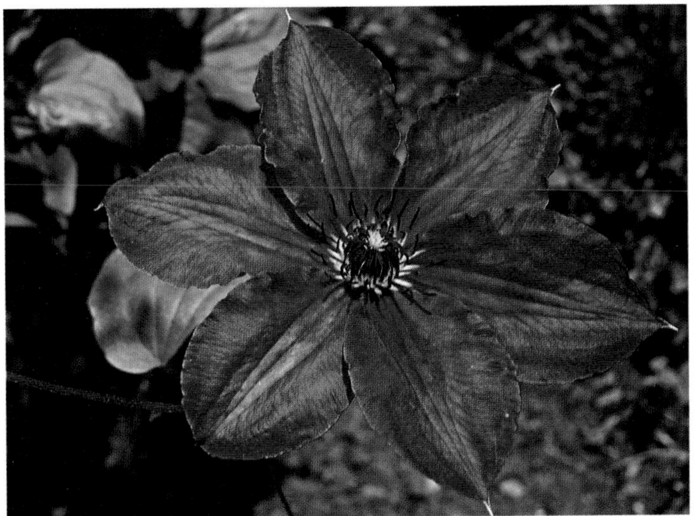

Clematis 'William Kennett'

An English cultivar which is over 100 years' old, this is a large-flowered clematis that has overlapping sepals. The dark purple-blue flowers are up to 15cm (6in) in diameter, with lovely maroon stamens in the centre. The plant can grow up to 2.5m (8ft). It comes into flower in early summer, lasting until the autumn.

This clematis is best pruned back to a pair of fat buds during the winter or early in the new year. Pruning should include old stems and leaves that can be either composted or burnt. The remaining stems should be tied up to the supporting plant or trellis, and the new growth can be tied up as it develops.

Climbers

The world of climbers is unbelievably diverse with the majority of our common climbers coming from the tropics. Their role in the garden is to use other plants or features, such as walls or trellises, to clamber skywards, shrouding unsightly objects and delighting us with their flowers and foliage.

Many of these climbers can be found cavorting among the canopy of rainforests and in clearings, scrambling about in the sunshine, producing flowers and then dispersing fruits. We have come to use these climbers for the house and garden, and our efforts to accommodate them have inevitably to include ensuring that they receive lots of heat and sunshine. Many of the tropical climbers described in this book can be grown as houseplants or conservatory plants, and in warmer areas grown outdoors.

How these plants climb is also variable, from those with climbing stems and tendrils, to suckers and aerial roots. There are those that sprawl over other vegetation, and there are trailing and pendant climbers – reaching downwards and outwards, rather than being upwardly mobile. There are some species, such as Aeschynanthus, Allamanda and Euonymus, which are sprawlers that need support. Some are climbers that are best used as ground cover plants. There are climbers that are treated as annuals, but which may be perennial in the wild. The climbing world is full of contrasts, with toxic climbers, including the beautiful gloriosas, dregeas and epipremums, contrasting with those with edible parts such as ipomoeas, passifloras and bomareas. Some climbers give off a beautiful perfume, such as jasmines, honeysuckles and sweet peas, while others are grown for their attractive foliage and are useful in small courtyard and town gardens, such as Ampelopsis and Parthenocissus.

Abutilon

Trailing abutilon

A native species from Brazil, this tropical climber does well in temperate climates and is a firm favourite on patio trellis, where its bright flowers can be much appreciated. The tri-coloured flowers (red and yellow with purple stamens) on the *A. megapotamicum* variety hang from the stem and are about 12cm (5in) long.

Most members of the Abutilon family are not climbers but are shrubs or small trees, so *A. megapotamicum* is unusual within its genus. Grown in the garden it performs as an evergreen or partial evergreen, and with its unusual flowers it makes an attractive feature worth mixing with another similar sized climber such as a clematis for its colour effects. Care should be taken to keep the plant well supported and ensure it is in a sunny position but with occasional shade. Cut out any tangled patches to allow the long arching stems to grow more freely. *A. megapotamicum* is frost hardy.

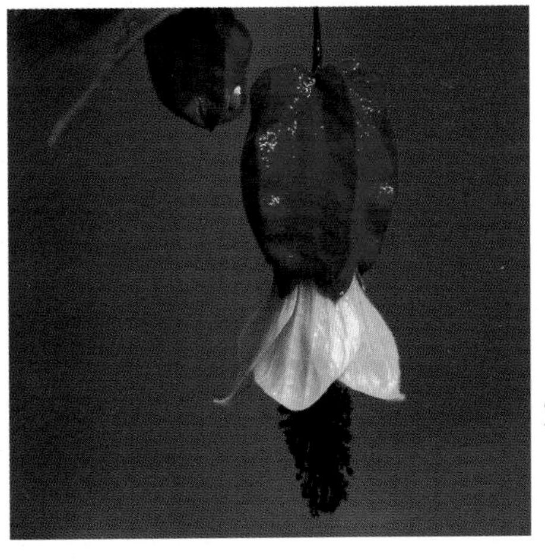

Abutilon megapotamicum

	SPRING	SUMMER	AUTUMN	WINTER	height (cm)	spread (cm)	min temp (°C)	moisture	sun/shade	colours	
Abutilon megapotamicum		flower flower flower	flower		200	200	-5°	wet	sunny		Attractive on trellis
A. megapotamicum 'Variegatum'		flower flower flower	flower		200	200	-5°	wet	sunny		Suitable for a yellow garden theme
A. megapotamicum 'Wisley Red'		flower flower flower	flower		200	200	-5°	wet	sunny		Fiery red
A. x milleri (A. m. x A. pictum)		flower flower flower	flower		250	250	-5°	wet	sunny		Lobed leaves

Actinidia

The Actinidia genus, of which there are about 40 species, are mostly climbers originating from Asia.

Actinidias are generally vigorous climbers, especially the kiwi fruit (*A. deliciosa*), and with its huge wands reaching 8m (26ft) they need to be cut back in smaller gardens. *A. kolomikia* is more restricted in its growth and needs all encouragement to get over a garden wall or trellis. Virtually no pruning is needed.

Actinidia kolomikia

	SPRING	SUMMER	AUTUMN	WINTER	height (cm)	spread (cm)	min temp (°C)	moisture	sun/shade	colours	
Actinidia arguta		flower flower flower	flower		700	150	-15°	moisture	semi-shady		'Tara vine'
A. deliciosa		flower flower flower	flower		1,000	610	-5°	moisture	semi-shady		Single sexed plants
A. kolomikia		flower flower flower	flower		550	180	-15°	moisture	semi-shady		Scented
A. polygama		flower flower flower	flower		460	240	-15°	moisture	semi-shady		'Silver Vine', scented

 *flower*

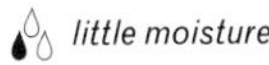 *little moisture*

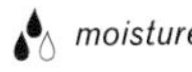 *moisture*

 *wet*

 *sunny*

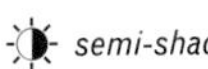 *semi-shady*

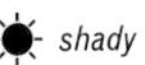 *shady*

A

Climbers

Aeschynanthus

Variation among these colourful trailing plants centres on the colour of the tubular flowers and the leaves, some of which are bronze to black. Grown in a conservatory or greenhouse, or outside in warmer climates, these are from the hot rainforest and their high humidity requirements should be respected.

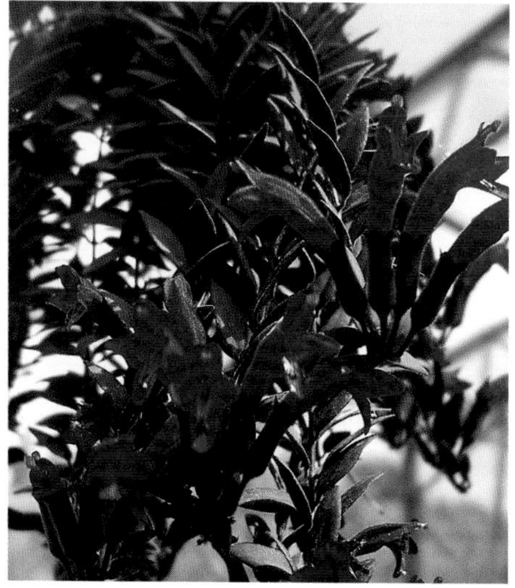

Aeschynanthus lobbianus

Native to the sub-tropical forests of the Himalayas through to China, this is a group of some 100 species that are related to Columneas (see page 98) and, like them, are frequently grown in hanging baskets. In the wild they are trailing plants that make use of other plants to get around. *A. lobbianus* make excellent subjects in hanging baskets, as they overflow with flowers along the trailing stems. Each flower is a long curved tube. Grow them outside in the hottest place in the garden or on the patio. Water regularly before flowering and then sparingly afterwards. Take care, as these trailers are frost tender. *A. lobbianus* is also known as the Lipstick vine.

	SPRING			SUMMER			AUTUMN			WINTER			height (cm)	spread (cm)	min temp (°C)	moisture	sun/shade	colours	
Aeschynanthus lobbianus			flower	flower	flower	flower	flower			flower			90	30	5°	little moisture	sun		Also *A. radicans* var. *lobbianus*
A. longicaulus			flower	flower	flower	flower	flower			flower			90	30	5°	little moisture	sun		Named after its long leaves
A. speciosus			flower	flower	flower	flower	flower			flower			90	30	5°	little moisture	sun		Trailing perennial

Akebia

Chocolate Vine *or* Fiveleaf Akebia

Best grown in an acid or loam soil, this is a good plant for screening a wall or trellis and it has the advantage of attractive foliage and scented flowers. It grows well up to fence height and needs plenty of room in a good, sunny position. Not for small courtyards.

A native of Asia, this semi-vigorous climber produces lots of chocolate coloured flowers from spring onwards that are scented. The flowers tend to be produced within the attractive foliage and are therefore not always evident. Named after its five leaflets on each leaf, *A. quinata* also has a three-leaflet leafed relative, *A. trifoliata*. The Chocolate Vine is a hardy plant and a semi-evergreen climber that

Akebia quinata

 *flower*  *little moisture*  *moisture* 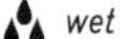 *wet*

needs space. It only rarely produces sausage-shaped fruits and is more of a foliage plant than a flowering plant. In due course Akebia will smother a wall or trellis, so do not plant it close to other plants. General garden soils that are well drained are best for this climber. Plant it in full sun for best results and keep the plant well watered. Prune the plant after flowering by cutting back and thinning out any thickets. *A. quinata* is generally not troubled by pests and diseases.

	SPRING			SUMMER			AUTUMN			WINTER			height (cm)	spread (cm)	min temp (°C)	moisture	sun/shade	colours	
Akebia quinata	●	●	●	●	●	●							1,000	120	-15°		sunny		'Fiveleaf Akebia', scented
A. quinata (Cream form)	●	●	●	●	●	●							1,000	120	-15°		sunny		A light coloured variety
A. trifoliata		●	●	●	●	●							1,000	120	-15°		sunny		Three leaves, also called *A. lobata*

Allamanda

Golden Trumpet or Common Allamanda

Ideal for hot spots and for growing in pots and conservatories, *A. cathartica* is a tropical plant with beautiful yellow flowers. The sap is poisonous and contact with the skin should be avoided, so do not plant in areas where children are likely to be around. This is a classic climber for warm climates.

Originating from South and Central Americas, this is a genus that has gone global in all tropical and semi-tropical parts of the world as a reliable climber and flowerer. It is more of a scrambler than a full-blown climber. In temperate climates it does well in full sun, and is a good performer in conservatories. The large flowers are pure yellow. There are a dozen species of Allamanda, not all with yellow flowers, but *A. cathartica* is the one that lends itself to gardens, there being several cultivars.

A. cathartica does even better when it is fed continually in the spring. Plant in fertile soil in borders or rich compost in hanging baskets, preferably up against a wall in full sun. Take care to keep well watered and ensure it is well drained. After flowering it can be kept fairly dry. Cuttings can be made from old or new wood, but watch out for fungal attacks on the leaves and flowers.

Allamanda cathartica

	SPRING			SUMMER			AUTUMN			WINTER			height (cm)	spread (cm)	min temp (°C)	moisture	sun/shade	colours	
Allamanda blanchettii					●	●	●	●	●				300	210	5°		sunny		Trumpet-shaped flowers
A. cathartica					●	●	●	●	●				580	240	5°		sunny		Large yellow flowers
A. cathartica 'Hendersonii'					●	●	●	●	●				200	120	5°		sunny		Buds are bronze in colour

sunny 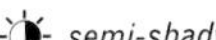 *semi-shady* 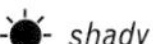 *shady*

Ampelopsis

Blueberry Climber

A general purpose climber ideal for town or country, the Ampelopsis berries provide food for birds and the plants display an attractive autumn foliage. The Blueberry Climber uses tendrils and is vigorous, needing plenty of space and support.

A. glandulosa var. *brevipedunculata* 'Elegans' with *Clematis* 'Mme Baron Veillard'

Named after its blue fruits, this deciduous genus is native to the woodlands of north-east Asia. It is ideal in urban gardens since it thrives in either sun or shade, climbing up concrete walls. It should be kept well watered, but not overwatered, and needs plenty of support. Its leaves are three- or five-lobed and turn red in autumn, dropping and producing more throughout the winter. It is from the same family as the grape and its small grape-like fruits change from ivory to a bright metallic blue in the autumn. *A. g.* var. *brevipedunculata* 'Elegans' is an appealing variety that has mottled white and green leaves with pink stems, ideal as a mixer with varieties of clematis.

	SPRING			SUMMER			AUTUMN			WINTER			height (cm)	spread (cm)	min temp (°C)	moisture	sun/shade	colours	
A. glandulosa var. *brevipedunculata*					●	●	●	●	●	●			460	120	-15°	moisture	◐		Highly versatile
A. g. var. *brevipedunculata* 'Elegans'					●	●	●	●	●	●			300	120	-15°	moisture	◐		Ideal as a houseplant
A. megalophylla					●	●	●	●	●	●			1,000	120	-15°	moisture	◐		Native to China

Antigonon

Confederate Vine

Perfect for smothering pergolas, gazebos, walls and fences, this tropical climber is best outside only in the hottest locations, especially in all areas with Mediterranean or sub-tropical climates. It produces lots of sprays of pale pink buds that break into exciting pink flowers. It is a vigorous climber that can produce dense vegetation.

Native to Mexico, this deciduous vine has a host of names such as Rosa de Montana, Queen's Wreath, Corallita, Mexican Creeper and Coral Vine. *A. leptopus* has delicate pink flowers (there is also a white form), borne as long trailing sprays, each bloom being about

Antigonon leptopus

 *flower*  *little moisture*  *moisture* 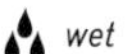 *wet*

3cm (1in) long. Its dark green leaves are either heart shaped, arrow or triangular. The plant is excellent for providing plenty of interesting foliage, in this case dressed with intermittent sprays of pink flowers. It is a good mixer with other vigorous climbers, such as Aristolochia. The roots should be covered with mulch to prevent frost damage during the winter months and watered regularly during the summer.

	SPRING			SUMMER			AUTUMN			WINTER			height (cm)	spread (cm)	min temp (°C)	moisture	sun/shade	colours	
Antigonon leptopus					●	●	●	●	●				1,220	360	0°		sunny		Edible roots
A. leptopus 'Alba'					●	●	●	●	●				1,220	360	0°		sunny		A white form

Aristolochia

Dutchman's Pipe *or* Pelican Flower *or* Birthwort

The biodiverse world of Aristolochias is always worth dabbling in, whether it is in the garden or house. Their flowers are peculiarly attractive, if sometimes disagreeably scented. Their sap is poisonous, so avoid planting where children play. Despite these caveats, their beauty and contribution to foliage are over-riding features.

With over 300 species native mostly to Latin America, Aristolochias are an unusual group of climbers. This is because of their bizarre shaped flowers that are like wavy ear-trumpets, sometimes accompanied by a musky smell. Their dark, mottled colours and shape are unique and endearing.

Aristolochia littoralis

Aristolochias can be grown in gardens or conservatories and are fairly hardy. Even though they are drought-tolerant in the wild, these climbers should be watered regularly in the garden or conservatory.

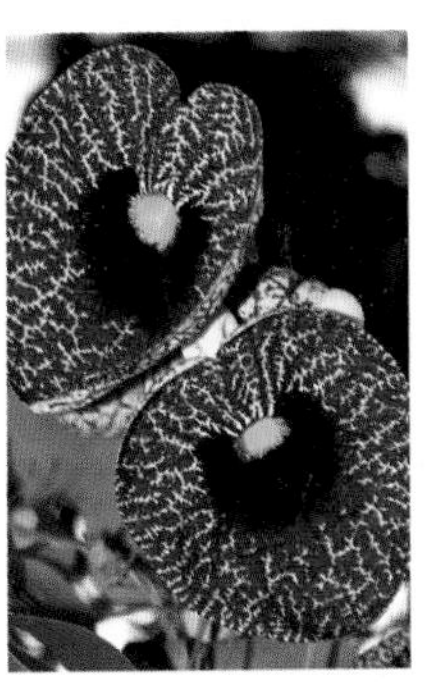

Aristolochia littoralis

The larger-flowered Aristolochias are more suitable for conservatories where they will reach the roof. The scrambler *A. clematitis* is a pest of vineyards in southern France, but is not so vigorous in temperate climates. Grown outside in warm locations, they can be vigorous if in a hot and sunny location and are excellent for foliage. It is fairly disease resistant, as its poisonous foliage has few defoliators.

	SPRING			SUMMER			AUTUMN			WINTER			height (cm)	spread (cm)	min temp (°C)	moisture	sun/shade	colours	
Aristolochia clematitis			●	●	●								90	30	-15°		semi-shady		Spreads by roots; native to Europe
A. gigantea				●	●	●							1,000	500	5°		sunny		Evergreen twiner
A. grandiflora				●	●	●							1,000	500	5°		sunny		Flowers up to 18cm (7in) across
A. littoralis				●	●	●							760	360	5°		sunny		'Caligo Flower'
A. macrophylla				●	●	●							1,000	500	-5°		semi-shady		'Dutchman's Pipe'

sunny 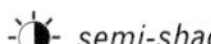 *semi-shady* 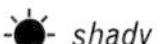 *shady*

Beaumontia

Nepal Trumpet Flower *or* Herald's Trumpet *or* Easter Lily Vine

This is one of just a few semi-tropical evergreen climbers that are vigorous enough to reach to an upstairs window and pervade the room with scent. Its arching stems can be used to make attractive bowers and arches, really showing off and making the most of its fragrant flowers.

Originating from the foothills of the Himalayas, *B. grandiflora* is a fairly vigorous climber with a dramatic spreading habit. As you can see from this specimen below, photographed on the French Riviera, this rampant climber will easily reach the roof of the first floor of most buildings. Climbing by means of semi-twining branches, it bears trumpet-shaped white flowers that grow nearly up to 13cm (5in) long. The shape of the flowers gives it its Easter Lily Vine name. The dark green leaves are oval, being downy below.

This plant grows best outside on a warm wall facing the sun, and is ideal for all areas that have a warm or Mediterranean-type climate. For those gardens in a temperate climate it can be grown in a conservatory, especially for its scent. Keep *B. grandiflora* well watered, taking care, however, not to overwater; water sparingly in winter. Generally, once the plant has become established, it does not require too much attention.

If you want to keep the spread of this vigorous plant in check, prune back after flowering. It is also fairly trouble-free from pests and diseases, although red spider mite may be a problem if this climber is grown inside in a conservatory.

Beaumontia grandiflora

 *flower*

 *little moisture*

 *moisture*

 *wet*

Billardiera

Climbing Blueberry *or* Purple Apple

Ideal for a drought garden, this genus has both yellow-green flowers and purple fruits, though not at the same time, creating a dramatic change in a garden. It is more a decorative species for a rockery or wall in full sun since it is rather sedentary, conserving plant growth in exchange for producing more flowers and fruits.

Belonging to the Pittosporum family, Billardiera is a genus of nine species native to Australia. The plant is named after the French botanist de la Billardière, who collected examples in Australia in the late eighteenth century. It is one of those fascinating desert plants that develops a large underground tuber, enabling it to grow back after fire or drought, making this climber ideal to grow in a hot garden, preferably with light, sandy soil. The elongated bell-shaped flowers of *B. longiflora* are borne in rather large numbers over the plant and are pendulous. They change into fleshy purple fruits that are both unusual and extremely attractive. The stems are very wiry and twist around each other.

Billardiera longiflora

Billardiera longiflora. The fruits may be red, white, purple or pink

This is not a particularly rapid- or vigorous-growing climber and can be successfully grown in a conservatory or cool greenhouse. It is a trouble-free plant, which requires the bare minimum in care. It generally looks after itself as it does not need too much water, and very little pruning is required as it is a fairly slow grower. However, removing thatch will help its appearance and growth, as well as preventing a possible build up of spiders, which love nesting in its wiry enclaves.

	SPRING			SUMMER			AUTUMN			WINTER			height (cm)	spread (cm)	min temp (°C)	moisture	sun/shade	colours	
Billardiera longiflora				●	●	●							150	30	-5°				Drought specialist
B. scandens			●	●	●								360	30	0°				Known as 'Common Apple Berry'

 *sunny* 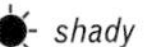 *semi-shady* *shady*

Bomarea

Climbing Alstroemeria

One of the many tropical climbers for the garden, this Latin American species is ideal for hot walls and trellises. It grows fast and tall, and produces lots of clusters of orange-yellow flowers. *B. caldasii* is the most popular species of this genus.

Originating from the rainforests of Central and South America, this is a vigorous plant that climbs using long twining stems. *B. caldasii* is herbaceous, dying down during the winter to its tuberous roots. Its flowers are produced as pendulous umbels and are attractively coloured with orange on the outside and yellow on the inside. It has lance-shaped leaves that arise from succulent stems. There are 50 species of Bomareas and their flowers range from yellow and green through to red and pink. Keep the plant moist, watering well and giving the plant a good dose of fertilizer in the spring. Try growing from seed, which is surprisingly easy.

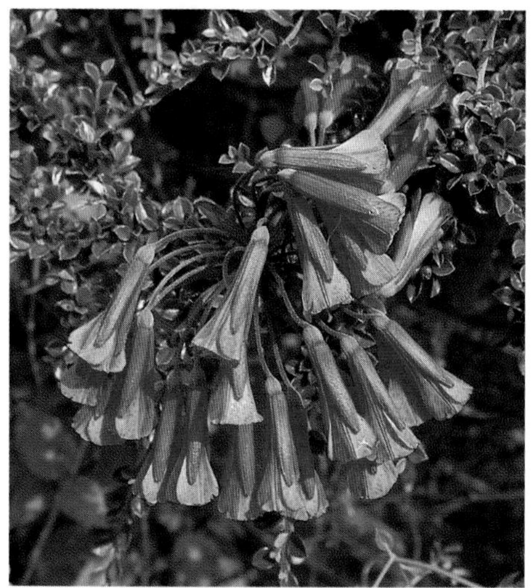
Bomarea caldasii

	SPRING			SUMMER			AUTUMN			WINTER			height (cm)	spread (cm)	min temp (°C)	moisture	sun/shade	colours	
Bomarea andimarcana	flower	flower	flower	flower	flower	flower	flower	flower	flower				300	120	-5°	moisture	sun		Also called *B. pubigera*
B. caldasii			flower	flower	flower	flower	flower	flower	flower				240	120	0°	moisture	sun		The most popular species
B. edulis				flower	flower	flower	flower	flower	flower				300	120	-5°	moisture	sun		Edible roots
B. patacocensis				flower	flower	flower							460	120	0°	moisture	sun		Deciduous, with spotted flowers

Bougainvillea

Bougainvillea

A species to suit many spaces in the garden, from a potted plant in the house, a sprawler in a conservatory, grown as a standard in a pot, allowed to flourish in a hanging basket or garlanded around a pergola in more sub-tropical climes. The stems of a bougainvillea are tough and spined, but its flowers are always magnificent.

Bougainvillea 'Miss Manila'

Bougainvilleas have contributed greatly to the colour and sparkle of many a garden around the world, especially in the tropics and in conservatories. One of the great advantages of bougainvilleas is that in cultivation they can sometimes be kept in flower all year round.

Bougainvillea takes its origins as a wild plant from the rainforests of Brazil; in milder, temperate climates it can perform very successfully under glass in a conservatory or growing up a warm, sheltered, preferably sun-drenched, wall. The lively coloured bracts, usually in pink

 *flower*  *little moisture* 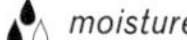 *moisture* 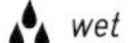 *wet*

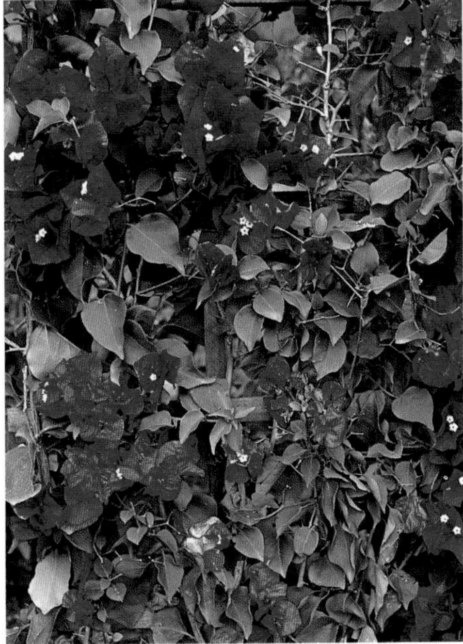

Bougainvillea x buttiana 'Multicolor'

and red, but sometimes in orange and white, are borne off the tough woody stems of this highly reliable climber. The spectacular flowers ensure that this plant will be at home in any small garden, as well as clambering spectacularly over archways, pergolas or high walls in a slightly larger garden.

As a small plant, bougainvilleas can be grown in a pot on the patio, taking them indoors during the winter months as a houseplant. Mature specimens, trained over walls or archways, can effectively cover quite large surfaces. However, whether your Bougainvillea is mature or young, all need tying to a support for climbing. As for looking after, once the plant is established you should only need to water occasionally, particularly during the winter months. If growing in a conservatory, make regular checks for spider mite, but apart from that this plant is generally trouble-free from pests and diseases.

Named after the French navigator De Bougainville, there are about 14 species and well over 160 cultivars that are on the market resulting from hybridization. All take some beating from other climbers for the sheer brilliance of their colours.

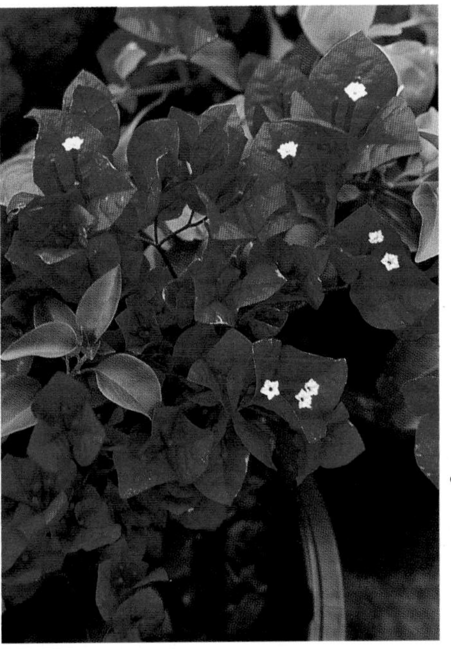

Bougainvillea 'Oo-la-la'

	SPRING	SUMMER	AUTUMN	WINTER	height (cm)	spread (cm)	min temp (°C)	moisture	sun/shade	colours	
Bougainvillea x *buttiana*					1,200	120	0°				Hybrid of *B. glabra* and *B. peruviana*
B. x *buttiana* 'Multicolor'					610	120	0°				Two coloured flowers on same plant
B. x *buttiana* 'Raspberry Ice'					1,200	360	0°				Unusual variegated leaves
B. glabra 'Snow White'					610	120	0°				An unusual white form
B. 'Miss Manila'					610	120	0°				An interesting shade of marbled red
B. 'Oo-la-la'					610	120	0°				After the effect it has on observers
B. 'Scarlet O'Hara'					1,200	120	0°				Also 'Hawaiian Scarlet', 'San Diego Red'
B. spectabilis					1,200	360	0°				The regular form

 *sunny* 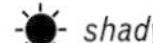 *semi-shady* *shady*

Campsis

Trumpet Creeper *or* Trumpet Vine

Grown in the conservatory or outside in a sunny position, this is a vigorous vine that has attractive flowers. The climber needs to be supported before it is established. It mixes well with climbing roses and is excellent to grow up against brick walls.

Campsis x tagliabuana 'Madame Galen'

There are just two species of Campsis, one native to North America (*C. radicans*), the other to China (*C. chinensis* or *grandiflora*) as its latin name acknowledges. Both inhabit woodlands in warm climates, so in temperate climates one might expect to grow these in warm hot spots, perhaps with dappled shade. Ideal places include up against walls that radiate lots of heat or entwining up and around other plants. The vines and their varieties are very vigorous and the foliage comprises large leaves with pinnate leaflets. The more fertile the soil, the more vigorous the growth. The orange to yellow flowers, according to variety, are borne on big trusses. They are deciduous and frost hardy. Keep well watered, but not in marsh-like conditions.

	SPRING			SUMMER			AUTUMN			WINTER			height (cm)	spread (cm)	min temp (°C)	moisture	sun/shade	colours	
Campsis grandiflora						flower	flower	flower	flower				1,000	360	-5°	moisture	☼		Excellent against a hot sunny wall
C. radicans						flower	flower	flower	flower				1,000	360	-5°	moisture	☼		Vigorous climber
C. radicans f. *flava*						flower	flower	flower	flower				1,000	360	-5°	moisture	☼		A yellow flowered variety
C. x tagliabuana 'Mme Galen'						flower	flower	flower	flower				1,000	360	-5°	moisture	☼		Hybrid of *C. grandiflora* and *C. radicans*

Cardiospermum

Balloon Vine *or* Heart Pea *or* Heart Seed

With 14 species to choose from, there is great potential from these exuberant tropical climbers for producing large, balloon-like fruits adorning some fascinating foliage. Cardiospermums are perennials but are often grown as annuals or biennials since they are readily propagated by seed.

Native to various tropical climates around the world, including India, Africa, North and South America, Cardiospermums are really grown for their inflated fruit capsules and their interesting evergreen foliage. In the wild they grow in forest margins scrambling up trees. In the garden they keep their

Cardiospermum halicacabum

 *flower*

 *little moisture*

 *moisture*

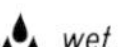 *wet*

scrambling characteristics and will readily climb through other vegetation or up canes using their tendrils. In frost-prone areas, grow outdoors as a half-hardy annual or in a temperate greenhouse. Keep these climbers well watered, but take care not to over soak the soil, and thin back at the end of the year in early to mid-winter.

The green-white flowers are very small. Leaves have divided leaflets, slightly reminiscent of Anthriscus or Cannabis, or of a fern, and make an ideal foliage effect in the garden. The fruits change from green to brown. The *C. halicacabum* species shown here is also called Love in a Puff or Winter Cherry.

	SPRING	SUMMER	AUTUMN	WINTER	height (cm)	spread (cm)	min temp (°C)	moisture	sun/shade	colours	
Cardiospermum grandiflorum		● ● ●	● ● ●		360	90	5°		☼		An herbaceous vine
C. halicacabum		● ● ●	● ● ●		360	90	5°		☼		Evergreen tendril climber

Celastrus

Bittersweet *or* Staff Vine

A valuable plant for autumn colour in a garden, this is a group of deciduous climbers that grow strongly, providing cover up walls and trellises. They grow in ordinary garden soil and provide attractive oval foliage with berries. Male and female flowers in green, yellow or white may be produced on different plants.

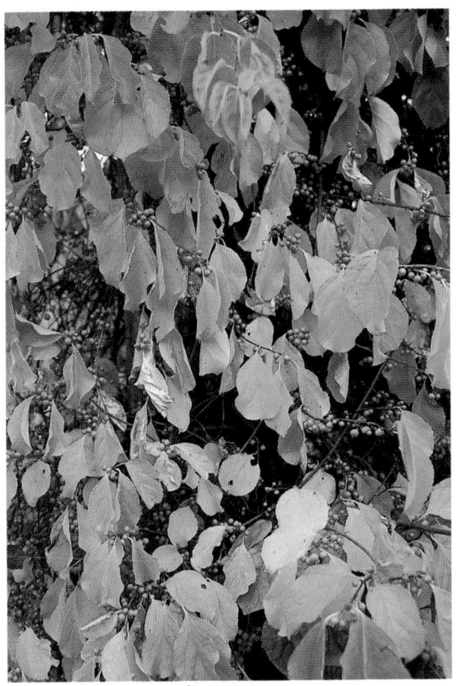
Celastrus orbiculatus

This genus represents 30 species from two areas in the world, for instance the Oriental Bittersweet, *C. orbiculatus,* and the American Bittersweet, *C. scandens.* As its 'scandens' name suggests it is a climber, and a vigorous one to 9m (30ft). A veritable 'staff vine', it needs a sturdy tree through which to climb. What is most spectacular about this species is the rich yellow-orange colours of the leaves in the autumn. It also sports clusters of orange and red berries that are not particularly attractive to birds. However, as a vigorous vine, it fills a colourful slot against a wall or up other vegetation at a time of year when there is sometimes a lack of colour in the garden. Keep well watered in a good, fertile soil. It can be grown from seed and cuttings can be taken from young or old wood and from the roots. As for general care, cut out old stems to open up the plant.

	SPRING	SUMMER	AUTUMN	WINTER	height (cm)	spread (cm)	min temp (°C)	moisture	sun/shade	colours	
Celastrus orbiculatus		● ● ●			1,370	120	-15°		☼		Oriental bittersweet, hardy
C. scandens		● ● ●			1,000	120	-15°		☼		American bittersweet, hardy

 *sunny* 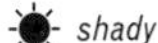 *semi-shady* *shady*

Cissus

Cissus

A very versatile group of vigorous climbers, Cissus can be grown outdoors in warm climates or as houseplants all round the world. Favourite species include the Kangaroo vine (*C. antarctica*), the Water vine (*C. hypoglauca*), the Grape ivy (*C. rhombifolia*) and the Ivy of Uruguay (*C. striata*).

There are 350 known species of Cissus, and the genus is the largest of the grape family (Vitaceae). Other species to which cissus are related are the Boston Ivy and Virginia Creepers. All cissus are vigorous climbers. They are among the largest vines growing in the rainforests of South America and north eastern Australia, where they form huge lianas (climbers of the tropical forest), rambling through the trees. They have therefore adapted to living in partial shade, which is why they are so good as houseplants. Grown outside in warm climates, their foliage makes a useful contribution for covering up walls, but the flowers they produce are negligible.

Cissus sp.

Cissus rhombifolia

These plants are best grown in fertile soil, which should be changed every year if the cissus is grown as an indoor plant. Their favourite site is in a shady position, kept well watered but not saturated. As this plant tends to look after itself, very little care is required. Even though it prefers fertile soil, it is tolerant of impoverished soil and can survive as a neglected houseplant. Cissus is generally trouble-free from pests and diseases.

	SPRING			SUMMER			AUTUMN			WINTER			height (cm)	spread (cm)	min temp (°C)	moisture	sun/shade	colours	
Cissus antarctica	●	●	●	●	●	●							1,520	120	5°	little moisture			Kangaroo vine
C. discolor				●	●	●							2,400	120	5°	little moisture			Dark red berries
C. hypoglauca				●	●	●							2,400	120	5°	little moisture			Water vine
C. quadrangularis				●	●	●	●						300	120	5°	little moisture			Native to Africa and India
C. rhombifolia				●	●	●							300	120	5°	little moisture			Grape ivy
C. striata				●	●	●							1,000	120	5°	little moisture			Ivy of Uruguay

● *flower*  *little moisture*  *moisture* 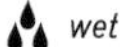 *wet*

Clerodendrum

Glory Bower *or* Glorybower

Most of the genus of Clerodendrums include trees or shrubs and herbaceous plants, but the climbers among the 400 species are well worth growing for the garden. Hailing from the tropical forests they can grow vigorously even when planted in poor soils or restricted in small pots on a patio.

Probably the most widespread Clerodendrum climber grown is the 'Bleeding Heart Glorybower', *C. thomsoniae*, which is a very reliable climber. It grows around the world as an evergreen shrubby vine in warm gardens, as a stunning container plant or trained over trellises and pergolas, or even indoors as a houseplant. Clerodendrums prefer a sunny position with dappled shade and they should be kept well watered in drought conditions in well drained soil. Although it will survive in poor soils, a rich, fertile soil is what this plant prefers. It produces an abundance of attractive, delicate creamy-white flowers in the summer, particularly in hot, sunny conditions, which are in fact bracts around red flower tubes. Like many of the Clerodendrum genus, the female part, or stigma, protrudes out of the flower.

If pruning is necessary, wait until the plant has flowered. Generally, clerodendrums are fairly trouble-free from pests and diseases.

Clerodendrum thomsoniae

Clerodendrum thomsoniae

	SPRING			SUMMER			AUTUMN			WINTER			height (cm)	spread (cm)	min temp (°C)	moisture	sun/shade	colours	
C. myriacoides 'Ugandense'					✿	✿	✿	✿	✿				360	90	5°	💧	semi-shady		Vivid blue to violet flowers
C. splendens				✿	✿	✿							300	90	5°	💧	semi-shady		Salverform, bright scarlet flowers
C. thomsoniae				✿	✿	✿							180	90	5°	💧	semi-shady		Bell-shaped, white and crimson flowers

 *sunny* 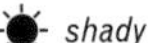 *semi-shady* *shady*

Clianthus
Parrot's Bill

The reds of Clianthus always add a hot element to any warm border, and the suggestion of a Mediterranean style garden. These evergreen members of the pea family have attractive pinnate foliage, like those of Acacia.

Clianthus puniceus

Clianthus is a species native to the warm scrublands of Australia and New Zealand. In the wild they compete for space and light by scrambling over plants; in the garden they are scandent, thus needing support to carry them aloft. There are just two species employed in the garden – *C. formosus*, an ideal trailer for hanging baskets or conservatories, and *C. puniceus* that grows well in warm borders and conservatories. Occasional thinning is required but mostly it does not need pruning. Keep well watered but not saturated.

	SPRING			SUMMER			AUTUMN			WINTER			height (cm)	spread (cm)	min temp (°C)	moisture	sun/shade	colours	
Clianthus formosus				✿	✿	✿							20	100	5°	moisture	☼		Sturt's desert pea; hanging baskets only
C. puniceus		✿	✿	✿									400	300	-5°	moisture	☼		A New Zealand native
C. p. 'Albus'		✿	✿	✿									400	300	-5°	moisture	☼		Has white claws
C. p. 'Red Cardinal'		✿	✿	✿									400	300	-5°	moisture	☼		Brighter colours than the norm

Cobaea
Cup and Saucer Vine

'Mexican ivy' or 'Monastery Bells', to give it its other names, can be grown in light or shade and responds well in gardens. The unusual shape of the large fragrant flowers are a welcome addition to any garden's vertical surfaces.

C. scandens is an extremely vigorous climber that in the wild scrambles and clambers over scrub and forest. In the garden its energy can be harnessed up a wall, where it will reward with plenty of cup-shaped flowers after which it is named. The flowers are normally violet to bright green. Grown as an annual in colder climates, it is a tender plant, except in sub-tropical climates where it becomes woody. Be sure to cover its roots during winter. Prune in the spring.

Cobaea scandens

	SPRING			SUMMER			AUTUMN			WINTER			height (cm)	spread (cm)	min temp (°C)	moisture	sun/shade	colours	
Cobaea scandens					✿	✿	✿	✿	✿				1,060	90	5°	moisture	◐		Very vigorous climber
C. scandens f. 'Alba'					✿	✿	✿	✿	✿				760	60	5°	moisture	◐		Flowers fading to white

✿ *flower* | *little moisture* | *moisture* | *wet*

Cocculus

Carolina Snailseed

A subject for the wild garden, this is a great smotherer and will grow to 3.5m (12ft) over a wall or fence. Its clusters of red berries are an attractive feature and a lure for birds. An unusual plant in gardens, it is best treated as an annual.

Known by a variety of names such as Carolina Moonseed, Red Moonseed, Red-berried Moonseed, Coral-beads and Snailseeds, *Cocculus carolinus* is a native climber from the eastern coast of the USA. The fruits are always produced in dense clusters. The berries are either red or black. The flowers are small and inconspicuous. Cocculus leaves are heart-shaped and are borne on twining stems.

The nature of this plant's growth is rather like Convolvulus (see page 98), being vigorous and prolific in leaf production. The plant should be kept moist in partial shade, and is best cut back in the autumn. The bark and seeds are poisonous, so do not grow if children are likely to be around. This is an ideal plant for a wildflower garden.

Cocculus carolinus

Codonopsis

Bonnet Bellflower

Always needing winter protection in temperate climates, the flowers are attractive in a variety of blue hues. They can be grown in borders or rockeries and are scandent rather than climbing, so they always need some support.

Codonopsis convolulacea

Mostly native to China, Japan and the Himalayas there are over 30 species of Codonopsis. In the wild they occur on scree-slopes, scrambling over rocks or over low vegetation. Some are therefore best suited for rock gardens, others contribute to vertical space in the herbaceous border. The bell-shaped nature of the flowers is obvious across the species, and many species have the typical soft pale blue colours seen among bellflowers. Plant in acid, sandy soil and keep well watered. Grow in a greenhouse in cold climates.

	SPRING			SUMMER			AUTUMN			WINTER			height (cm)	spread (cm)	min temp (°C)	moisture	sun/shade	colours	
Codonopsis clematidea					●	●	●						150	90	-15°	💧💧💧	☼		A sprawling plant
C. convolulacea				●	●	●							180	60	-15°	💧💧💧	☼		Slender, twining plant
C. lanceolata							●	●	●				90	30	-15°	💧💧💧	☼		Long leaves; winged seeds
C. meleagris				●	●	●							30	15	-15°	💧💧💧	☼		Inside of the flowers spotted
C. tangshen				●	●	●							180	60	-15°	💧💧💧	☼		From China; spotted flowers
C. vinciflora				●	●	●							90	30	-15°	💧💧💧	☼		Ideal for rockeries

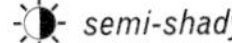 *sunny* 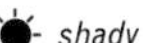 *semi-shady* *shady*

Columnea

Goldfish Plant

Goldfish plants get their name from the bright orange colour of the flowers. There are many cultivars available from nurseries including variegated leaf and those with red and brown flowers. They belong to the African violet and Gloxinia families.

Columnea x banksii

Often grown in hanging baskets in temperate areas, goldfish plants are native to the rainforests of South and Central America. They typically live on other plants high in the canopy, where they root in the leaf litter that collects on branches and are drizzled upon by mist. This can be emulated by spraying if the plants are kept in a conservatory or greenhouse. Keep well watered to start and then ease off when more mature. In sub-tropical areas, grow them on limbs of garden trees with epiphytic ferns for an attractive display.

	SPRING			SUMMER			AUTUMN			WINTER			height (cm)	spread (cm)	min temp (°C)	moisture	sun/shade	colours	
Columnea x banksii	✿	✿	✿	✿	✿	✿							120	30	5°	little moisture	☼		Hybrid of *C. schiedeana* & *C. oerstediana*
C. microphylla	✿	✿	✿	✿	✿	✿							180	60	5°	little moisture	☼		Bears solitary, hairy, scarlet flowers
C. scandens	✿	✿	✿	✿	✿	✿							460	90	5°	little moisture	☼		Named after its vine-like qualities
C. 'Stavanger'	✿	✿	✿	✿	✿	✿							15	60	5°	little moisture	☼		'Norse Fire Plant'; bright scarlet flowers

Convolvulus

Bindweed

Why not try your hand at growing colourful Convolvulus and harness the natural powers of running roots, as too often seen in the troublesome bindweed? These summer flowers make attractive punctuation marks of colour up pergolas and trellises.

Convolvulus sabatius

The world of bindweeds or Convolvulus is made up of over 250 species and their cultivars, many of which are native to the Mediterranean. The climbers among them are either perennial or annual and are not too removed from the significant weed, bindweed, that plagues gardeners' efforts. Easily grown from seed, remove all above ground foliage in the autumn and dead-head as soon as its flowering is over.

	SPRING			SUMMER			AUTUMN			WINTER			height (cm)	spread (cm)	min temp (°C)	moisture	sun/shade	colours	
Convolvulus althaeoides					✿	✿							15	15	-15°	little moisture	☼		For pots and containers
C. sabatius				✿	✿	✿	✿						60	30	-5°	little moisture	☼		Formerly called *C. mauritanicus*
C. tricolor				✿	✿	✿							30	30	-15°	little moisture	☼		Blue, white and yellow flowers
C. tricolor 'Royal Ensign'				✿	✿	✿							30	30	-15°	little moisture	☼		Ideal for hanging baskets

✿ flower | little moisture | moisture | wet

Cucurbita

Squashes and gourds

Typical members of this large group of climbers, including the Cucumis, are vigorous and produce relatively large yellow flowers. The flowers are attractive to insects which is a bonus, and the fruits are generally large and collectable, and edible in some cases. Grow over pergolas to show off their tropical fruits.

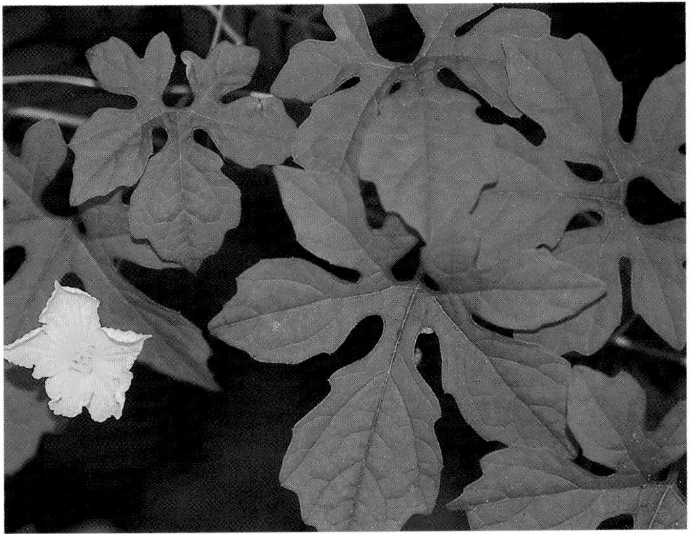

Cucurbita sp.

The gourd and pumpkin family is large and its climbing members are frequently used in the garden. The genus Cucurbita includes cucumbers, squashes, melons, vegetable marrows and courgettes. All of these are climbers that are used for food and ornaments in many gardens. Fortunately, many grow well in greenhouses or in gardens as decorative features over arches and pergolas. They prefer a good, rich soil with plenty of nutrients and in a sunny position, but not in complete shade. Water daily, but do not saturate. Attend to growing stems and make sure they are tied up if loose. Watch out for caterpillars that eat the leaves and birds that peck at the fruits.

	SPRING	SUMMER	AUTUMN	WINTER	height (cm)	spread (cm)	min temp (°C)	moisture	sun/shade	colours	
Cucurbita sp.		● ● ●	● ●		240	60	0°		sunny		Squashes, gourds, marrows
Cucumis sp.		● ● ●	● ●		240	60	0°		sunny		Melons and cucumbers

Cymbalaria

Ivy-leaved Toadflax

Belonging to the foxglove family, this is a tiny-flowered scrambler. Widely naturalized in the wild, it can be used to soften up new walls, with the foliage making them look more natural.

Wildflower gardeners will like this species that is native to southern Europe. *C. muralis* is a creeping perennial herb that has trailing or drooping stems. It roots itself in cracks between rocks and is ideal for growing on rocky walls in sunny situations. It has very attractive soft purple flowers, and as these mature they turn as fruits to dispense seeds into the wall surface. The plant will grow in all temperate climates on rocks, in rockeries and on more than imperfect brick walls. No real care is needed as it is fairly drought tolerant once established.

Cymbalaria muralis

 *sunny*  *semi-shady*  *shady*

Dioscorea

Ornamental Yam

Yams grow fast when given plenty of warmth, water and light. They have bright, lively foliage and can be grown to cover trellises and pergolas. They reproduce by producing underground tubers, which are not edible. A variegated leaf form is also available.

The South American yams, of which there are over 600 species, are a group of climbers that are much cultivated for their foliage effects. Their leaves are heart-shaped and often glossy. This attractive characteristic, combined with its propensity to grow rapidly and produce an abundance of foliage, are added features that make yams worthwhile for growing in the garden.

Dioscoreas can be grown in conservatories and greenhouses in temperate climates, and outside elsewhere. Yams grow on from shoots of tubers that are sent out. The term 'yam' also refers to members of the genus Ipomoea (see page 112) that have edible tubers. Dioscoreas grow most successfully in rich, well-drained soil in a sunny position. The sap is poisonous, so ideally plant them well away from where children play. Check the plant regularly for aphids.

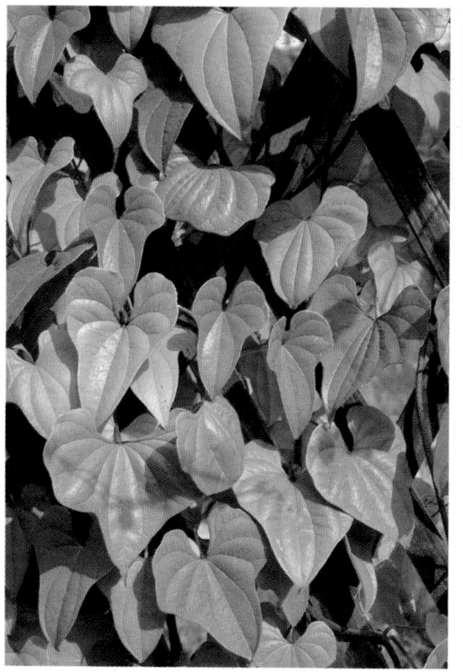

Dioscorea batatas

	SPRING	SUMMER	AUTUMN	WINTER	height (cm)	spread (cm)	min temp (°C)	moisture	sun/shade	colours	
Dioscorea batatus		● ● ●	● ●		460	60	0°	little moisture	☼		'Chinese yam', 'Cinnamon Vine'
D. batatus 'Variegata'		● ● ●	● ●		360	60	0°	little moisture	☼		A variegated leaf form
D. discolor		● ● ●			300	60	15°	little moisture	☼		Ornamental yam; inedible

Dipogon

Climbing bean

Native to South Africa, this is a twining species that has naturalized in parts of Australia. It is grown as an ornamental in Europe and North America, and is so vigorous that it can be grown as a green manure, harvested at least twice a year.

Dipogon lablab 'Ruby Moon'

Until recently this was known under a different genus, Dolichos. It is a member of the large pea family and the features of this climber, particularly *D. lablab* 'Ruby Moon' are that it has dark foliage and dark ruby beans. Each compound leaf has three leaflets. The flowers are tall upright spikes about 30cm (1ft) tall covered in pink purple flowers. Dipogon easily grows up fences and pergolas, and can also be grown up a pyramid structure to good effect.

 *flower* 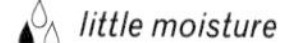 *little moisture*  *moisture*  *wet*

If you are seeking dark coloured plants as a theme in the garden, this is a colourful one to choose. Its companions might be dahlias, fuchsias and heucheras. Dipogons can be grown in most soil types and sites, and are easily grown from seed. Keep the plant well watered and watch out for moth larvae. Apart from that, these plants are fairly trouble-free from pests and diseases.

	SPRING	SUMMER	AUTUMN	WINTER	height (cm)	spread (cm)	min temp (°C)	moisture	sun/shade	colours	
Dipogon lablab		● ● ●	● ●		460	60	0°		semi-shady		A vigorous climber
D. lablab 'Ruby Moon'		● ● ●	● ●		460	60	0°		semi-shady		Dark purple pods

Distictis

Blood Trumpet *or* Royal Trumpet Vine

Another tropical climber suitable for the greenhouse or conservatory, this has red or pink flowers depending on the species and cultivar. Its punctuation points of colour on the evergreen vine make this a worthy subject outdoors in sub-tropical or tropical environments, where its vigorous growth easily covers walls and pergolas.

Distictis belongs to the Bignoniaceae family whose members are mostly powerful climbers or lianas of the rainforests of South America. Naturally inclined to vigorous growth, *D. buccinatoria*, with its red flowers, is appropriately named Blood Trumpet and comes from the Mexican rainforests. The flowers have five petals that are double-lipped and make up a trumpet shape, turning yellow or pale orange towards the base. The cultivar 'Mrs Rivers' has pink petals with a yellow throat, similar to the colours of the Mandevilla (see page 120). Leaves are oval, and the climber is evergreen, flowering during the hottest months.

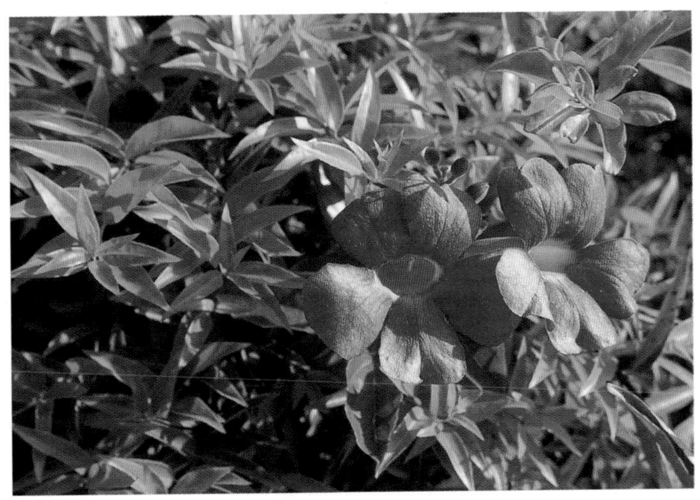

Distictis buccinatoria 'Mrs Rivers'

Generally, this is a tropical climber that needs support, grown outside in a hot site, up against a wall, in nutrient rich soil. If growing indoors, make sure the soil is loam-based and well drained. Both indoors and out, water frequently in the summer and occasionally during the winter.

	SPRING	SUMMER	AUTUMN	WINTER	height (cm)	spread (cm)	min temp (°C)	moisture	sun/shade	colours	
Distictis buccinatoria		● ● ●	● ●		2,400	150	0°		sunny		Blood Trumpet
D. buccinatoria 'Mrs Rivers'		● ● ●	● ●		1,820	150	0°		sunny		Flowers with yellow throat

 *sunny*  *semi-shady* *shady*

Dregea

Dregea has the looks, the fragrance and the scrambling ability sought in many climbers, and should be more widely grown. Easy enough to grow from seed, this attractive climber is trouble-free and frost hardy – ideal characteristics for any climber. Seeds can be propagated in a greenhouse or cold frame in the spring.

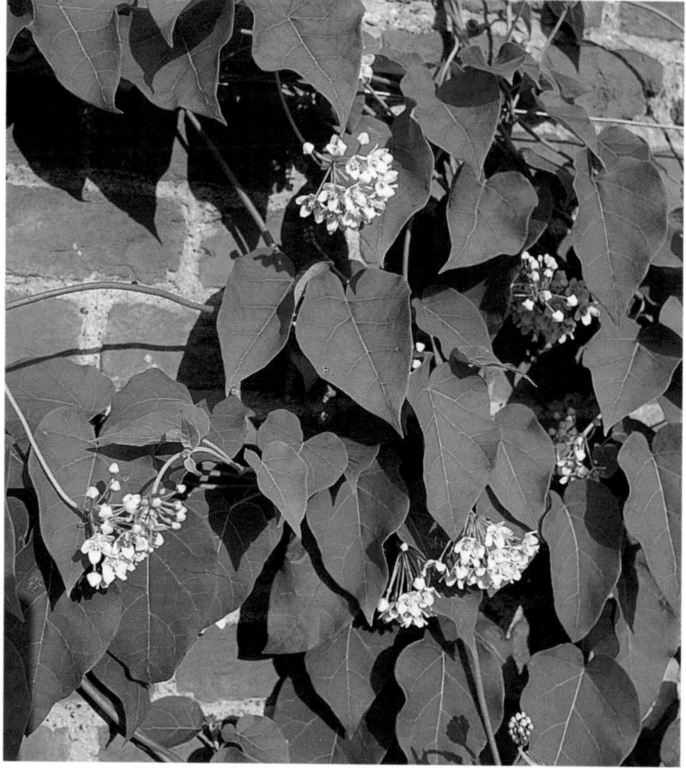

Dregea sinensis

This is a group of deciduous twining climbers native to the rainforests of South Africa and China. The genus is also known as Wattakaka. It belongs to the Milkweed family (Asclepiadaceae) that has defensive poisonous sap and therefore should not be grown where children are likely to play. The white flowers of *D. sinensis* are scented and are held in umbel bunches among the simple and entire heart-shaped leaves that are downy beneath.

D. sinensis grows well against a warm wall or on a pergola, and is frost hardy. It may also be grown in a conservatory, where its scent is better appreciated. As long as the plant is kept well watered, it grows in most soils in both sun and shade. It needs tying up securely against a wall or support in order for it to climb. Because its sap is poisonous, this plant is rarely troubled by pests and diseases. An unusual, but extremely attractive species to grow in various parts of the garden.

	SPRING	SUMMER	AUTUMN	WINTER	height (cm)	spread (cm)	min temp (°C)	moisture	sun/shade	colours	
Dregea sinensis		flower, flower, flower	flower		300	60	-5°	moisture	sun/shade	white	Scented flowers; from China
D. sinensis 'Variegata'		flower, flower, flower	flower		300	60	-5°	moisture	sun/shade	white	Variegated leaves

Eccremocarpus

Chilean Glory Vine

This is a tropical climber that is fairly hardy in temperate climates, providing a lot of foliage and colour. It dies off after a few years, which is typical of a few perennials, and it can be cut down by hard frosts, but the flowers are definitely worthwhile.

Native to Chile and Peru these Glory Vines are among about five species that are rampant around the edges of rainforests. *E. scaber* is a familiar species often grown for its forest of foliage and eccentric bunches of flowers that hang this way and that. There are many other colour forms that depart from the normal orange – yellow, rose, carmine and red. The Anglia Hybrids produce flowers in a range of these colours. A great mixer, this can be grown through white native clematis to

flower  little moisture  moisture  wet

make striking colour combinations that even Monet would have been proud of.

Eccremocarpus grows in most soil types, except chalky ones, and must be kept well watered. Prune in early spring by taking out any old woody stems.

Eccremocarpus scaber

	SPRING			SUMMER			AUTUMN			WINTER			height (cm)	spread (cm)	min temp (°C)	moisture	sun/shade	colours	
Eccremocarpus scaber			●	●	●	●	●	●					460	120	-5°		sunny		A rainforest native
E. scaber 'Carmineus'				●	●	●	●	●					460	120	-5°		sunny		One of many colour varieties

Epipremnum

Devil's Ivy *or* Golden Pothos

Grown mainly as a houseplant, this tropical evergreen climber throws out long stems with attractive alternate leaves. It flowers infrequently, if at all, and its leaves remain fairly impeccable to look at, as its poisonous sap deters leaf eaters.

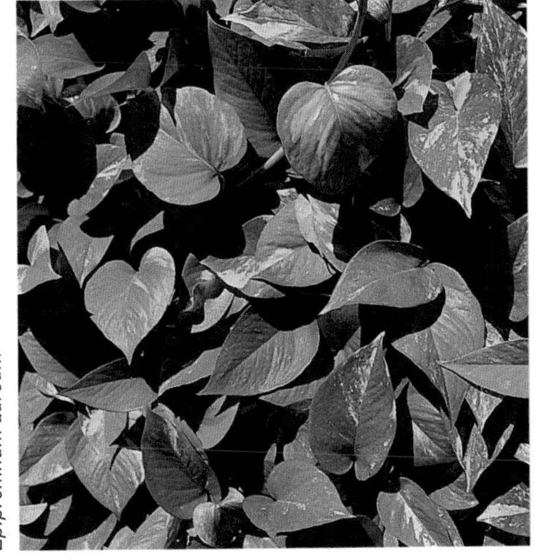
Epipremnum aureum

In the tropics, Devil's Ivy is a masterly ground cover plant that overflows paths in shady places and needs to be cut back. In temperate climates it is used more as a feature or mixer in a hanging basket where it thrives without too much attention. There are eight species of these evergreen climbers which climb using their stems. In the conservatory or home they are best seen in their different leaf coloured forms, such as *E. aureum* 'Marble Queen' or *E. pictum* 'Argyraeum'. Keep moist in containers, preferably in loam-based soil. Outside the plant prefers a rich soil, positioned in a slightly shady spot.

	SPRING			SUMMER			AUTUMN			WINTER			height (cm)	spread (cm)	min temp (°C)	moisture	sun/shade	colours	
Epipremnum aureum				●	●	●							1,200	60	15°		semi-shady		Formerly called *E. scindapsus*
E. aureum 'Marble Queen'													300	60	15°		semi-shady		More marbling on leaves than species
E. pictum 'Argyraeum'													180	60	15°		semi-shady		Spotted leaves

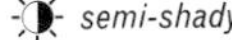 *sunny* 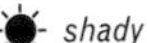 *semi-shady* *shady*

Euonymus

Wintercreeper euonymus

Worthy evergreens for the garden, euonymuses give added ornamental value on account of their colourful leaves. The tough leaves are eaten by few pests, save for a few moth larvae, and are generally pest free. Flowers are sometimes prolific and visited by insects. Fruits are colourful and seed can be sown when ripe in pots in a cold frame.

Euonymuses are not traditionally thought of as climbers, but with a little help *E. fortunei* and some of its cultivars can be encouraged up walls or fences. *E.* f. var. *radicans* in particular has a propensity to climb. They do so using aerial roots on the stem, allowing them to climb through trees to good effect. *E. fortunei* is shown here climbing 6m (20ft) up a conifer.

The great advantage of euonymuses is that they are evergreen and have some exciting leaf colours. *E.* f. var. *radicans* (formerly *E. radicans*) is from China and Japan, and is much better at withstanding sun in very hot areas than ivy. In its prostrate form, Euonymus can be useful ground cover. Plant in most soils, in shade or sun, and water only occasionally once established.

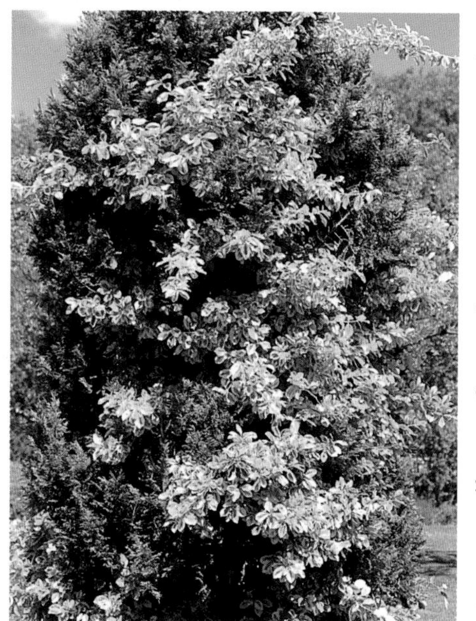

Euonymus fortunei 'Emerald Gaiety' climbing *Chamaecyparis lawsonia*

	SPRING	SUMMER	AUTUMN	WINTER	height (cm)	spread (cm)	min temp (°C)	moisture	sun/shade	colours	
Euonymus fortunei	flower				610	120	-15°	little moisture	sun/shade		'Wintercreeper Euonymus'
E. fortunei 'Emerald Gaiety'	flower				610	120	-15°	little moisture	sun/shade		One of the most attractive cultivars
E. f. var. *radicans*	flower				610	120	-15°	little moisture	sun/shade		More of a climber than the other cultivars

Fallopia

Russian Vine *or* Mile-a-minute

Whether it is an old garage or outbuilding, an unattractive wall or a jumble of gas bottles and dustbins that needs covering, this is the plant to make a quick screen. It has the added advantage of creating foliage quickly and flowers in abundance. This plant is readily available from nurseries and by mail order.

Fallopia baldschuanica

Russian Vine is native to the region of Tajikistan, Afghanistan and Pakistan, and also goes under the name of Bokhara Fleece Flower, after the similarity of its white fleece-like flowers en masse.

F. baldschuanica is a vigorous climber giving rise to its other name of Mile-a-minute, though it is only half as fast as *Clematis vitalba*. This Fallopia species is a superb climber as a screener, to make a colourful arbour or just to see the prolific

 flower  little moisture  moisture  wet

flowers borne in late summer to autumn. It was formerly put in the Polygonum genus, which are themselves very purposeful plants and good spreaders, and it retains some of its characteristics. It can be planted in any position into any soil type, but *F. baldschuanica* does flower better in full sun. Water only occasionally once the plant is established and cut away old growth and wayward stems. It generally takes care of itself and is trouble-free from most pests and diseases.

	SPRING	SUMMER	AUTUMN	WINTER	height (cm)	spread (cm)	min temp (°C)	moisture	sun/shade	colours	
Fallopia aubertii		✿ (late)	✿ ✿		1,210	180	-15°	💧	semi-shady		Heart-shaped, dark green leaves
F. baldschuanica		✿ (late)	✿ ✿		1,210	180	-15°	💧	semi-shady		Excellent for screening

Ficus

Creeping Fig

A tropical evergreen species, this grows outside in Mediterranean, sub-tropical and tropical gardens, but is confined to conservatories as houseplants elsewhere. There are two interesting cultivars, one with mini oak leaves (*F. pumila* 'Quercifolia') and one with variegated leaves (*F. pumila* 'Variegata'). Both are effectively grown in hanging baskets where they make up the foliage element.

Otherwise known as the Creeping Rubber Plant or Climbing Fig, this endearing climber is native to North Vietnam, China and Japan. *F. pumila* is a remarkable foliage plant for such a small climber. The fig family counts some of the large rainforest trees among its group, but this is a climber that climbs using aerial roots and normally in the wild would climb up other trees, perhaps its taller relatives. Grow it up white walls so that you get the intricate leaf and stem patterns, giving the enclosed garden an overall softer feel. It can be planted in most types of soil, preferably in a hot, sunny spot and kept moist at all times if grown outside. Indoors, water infrequently and check the plant for signs of rotting and insect attack.

Ficus pumila

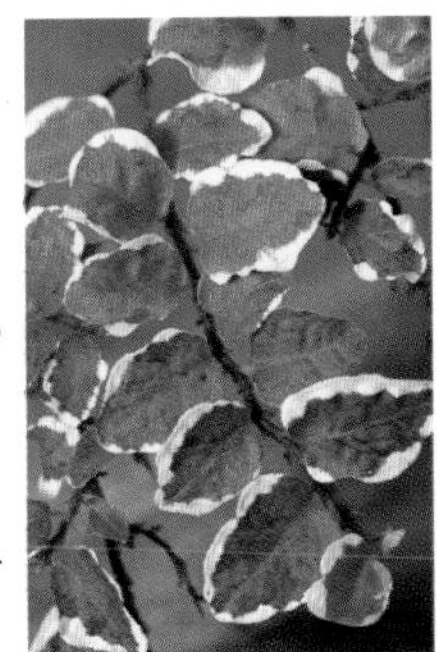

Ficus pumila 'Variegata'

	SPRING	SUMMER	AUTUMN	WINTER	height (cm)	spread (cm)	min temp (°C)	moisture	sun/shade	colours	
Ficus pumila					460	300	5°	💧	semi-shady		Abundant in tropical countries
F. p. 'Minima'					240	90	5°	💧	semi-shady		A small-leafed form
F. p. 'Quercifolia'					460	300	5°	💧	semi-shady		Leaves like oak leaves
F. p. 'Variegata'					460	300	5°	💧	semi-shady		Variegated leaves

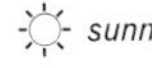 *sunny*  *semi-shady* 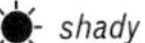 *shady*

Gelsemium

Caroline Jasmine *or* Yellow Jessamine

In warm countries this is used as a screening plant, as one might use honeysuckle or hops in milder climates. This colourful climber is also scented and it can be used to cover banks and fences. Gelsemium grows best in sunny positions. Prune after the first flowering to ensure later flowering.

Also known as Evening Trumpet Flower, or False Yellow Jasmine, the Gelsemium species *G. sempervirens* is a native to Central America. (Gelsemiums are not related to the *Jasminum* jasmines, which belong to a different plant family.) It uses twisting stems (see below) to climb and in warm climates it is grown over porches and pergolas because of its rampant growth. It can reach heights of 3–6m (10–20ft). Its 'sempervirens' name refers to its evergreen leaves and long-lasting flowers, which are produced from spring onwards, lasting throughout summer. The flowers are fragrant and when used as a bower, or grown under a window, the scents can really be appreciated.

The plant bears clusters of bright pale to deep yellow flowers, 5–8cm (2–3in) in diameter and 3cm (1in) long. There are a number of varieties, including a double flowered one (*G. s.* 'Flore Pleno').

G. sempervirens grows best in fertile soils and preferably in any hot spots in the garden, especially against sunny walls in full sun. Keep the plant moist, but refrain from watering during the winter. *G. sempervirens* is fairly frost tender, but will withstand short periods down to 0°C (32°F). As for general care, cut out old flowering stems in the spring. If grown indoors, check the plant regularly for signs of whiteflies and scale insects.

Gelsemium sempervirens

	SPRING			SUMMER			AUTUMN			WINTER			height (cm)	spread (cm)	min temp (°C)	moisture	sun/shade	colours	
Gelsemium sempervirens		flower	flower	flower	flower	flower							600	120	0°	little moisture	sun		Vigorous twining perennial
G. sempervirens 'Flore Pleno'		flower	flower	flower	flower	flower							600	120	0°	little moisture	sun		Sweetly fragrant double flowers
G. sempervirens 'Pride of Augusta'		flower	flower	flower	flower	flower							600	120	0°	little moisture	sun		Popular American variety

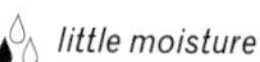 *flower* 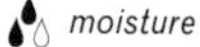 *little moisture*  *moisture* *wet*

Gloriosa

Gloriosa Lily *or* Glory Lily *or* Climbing Lily

Gloriosa lilies are always eye-stoppers. One of the best cultivars is 'Rothschildiana', which has orange along the edges of the reflexed petals and at the base of the petals. Handle its tubers with gloves and keep out of the way of children, since this is a highly toxic species. The sap may irritate the skin and all parts are toxic if ingested.

Now belonging to the Colchicaceae family, the *G. superba* species was originally part of the Lily family. As a climbing lily it is unusual. This is a spectacular species with its large red flowers, particularly when displayed in a conservatory with a mass of flowers. Each flower is made up of six wavy-edge and narrow petals that are reflexed backwards. It needs to be kept in a warm environment since it is a tropical species from Africa and India, so keep in a conservatory if the climate is temperate.

Gloriosa superba 'Rothschildiana'

Gloriosa superba

Gloriosa is a weak clamberer that needs support. It climbs using its tendril-like leaf tips. Its leaves are lily-like and pointed. Keep the plant moist but be careful not to overwater, as this could lead to a fungal attack. Watch out for signs of aphids attacking the leaves and flowers, and check regularly for any fungus.

	SPRING			SUMMER			AUTUMN			WINTER			height (cm)	spread (cm)	min temp (°C)	moisture	sun/shade	colours	
Gloriosa superba				●	●	●	●	●	●				180	90	5°				Best in a conservatory
G. superba 'Rothschildiana'				●	●	●	●	●	●				180	90	5°				Red and yellow flowers

 *sunny*  *semi-shady* *shady*

Hedera

Ivy

Ivies have many important roles in the garden, not only in the house or conservatory as foliage plants in hanging baskets, but as ground cover plants (*H. colchica* is excellent for this purpose) or for growing up pillars, walls or fences. Ivies are excellent for small, secluded and courtyard gardens which are very much in the shade. They are evergreen, with a mass of flowers in the autumn that are visited by pollinating bees and wasps. Ivy fruits are food for birds. The fruit of the species *H. h.* f. *poeticarum* are a distinctive yellow-orange. *Hedera helix* 'Oro di Bogliasco' is one of the more colourful variegated leaf ivies, more widely sold as 'Goldheart'.

Variation is best shown in the Ivy genus among the climbers, for there are currently over 300 different cultivars of the most common species – *H. helix* – available from nurseries. This is a species that is native to Europe through to Asia but has been taken to many parts of the world subsequently. In fact, *H. helix* is better known by the name Common Ivy or English Ivy. It has superb adaptations to life in the shade, and as a climber of some capabilities it has great uses in the garden. It climbs by means of aerial roots that grip on firmly to surfaces. *H. helix* cultivars are mostly to do with variations in the leaf shape or colour with some variable in overall shape of the plant. There are six other species available but they are not so versatile in cultivars. Although you can see the plant looking attractive on many an old house, do not let ivies grow up houses that have loose mortar, as they will, over time, pull it all out with their roots.

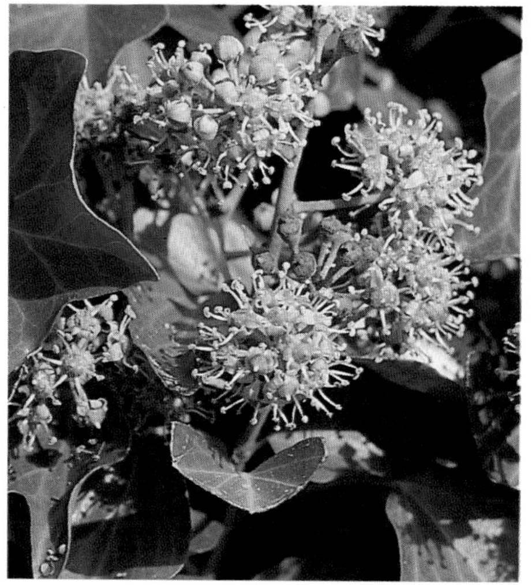

Hedera helix 'Oro di Bogliasco'

Hedera colchica 'Dentata Variegata'

Ivies are among the easiest of climbers to grow, as they are happy in any type of soil and equally at home in the sun or the shade. They are easily grown as houseplants on their own or alongside other plants for contrast in hanging baskets or containers. Ivies can also be trained on wire forms to produce topiary features. Once the plant is established, watering can be infrequent. The only care *H. helix* requires is training to grow to the required shape and cutting off wayward stems. Some ivies, especially the variegated varieties, may be damaged during severe winters, but don't worry – they will more often than not recover in the spring. If you want to encourage *H. helix* to become rapidly established as a self-climber, peg the young stems down to the soil, as they will quickly produce lateral, climbing shoots to set clambering upwards.

These plants are, in general, trouble-free from pests and diseases. All parts of ivy may cause discomfort if ingested and contact with the sap may aggravate people with skin allergies or irritate the skin.

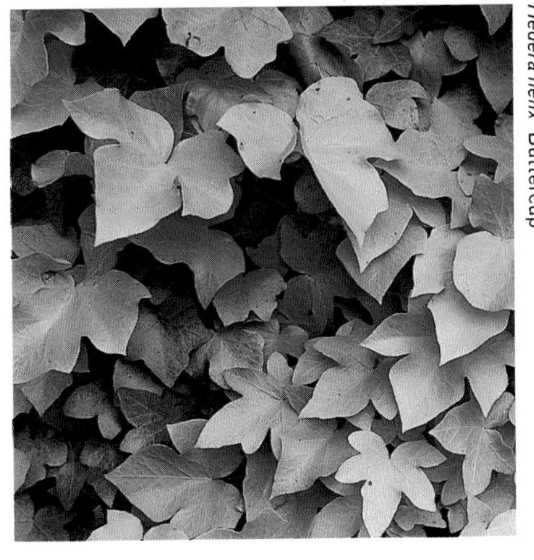
Hedera helix 'Buttercup'

H

Climbers

	SPRING	SUMMER	AUTUMN	WINTER	height (cm)	spread (cm)	min temp (°C)	moisture	sun/shade	colours	
Hedera colchica 'Dentata Variegata'		●	● ● ●	● ● ●	1,000	300	-15°		semi-shady		Good for ground cover or a large wall
H. helix		●	● ● ●	● ● ●	910	300	-15°		semi-shady		A vigorous wild species
H. helix 'Buttercup'		●	● ● ●	● ● ●	450	240	-15°		semi-shady		Buttercup yellow leaves
H. helix f. *poeticarum*		●	● ● ●	● ● ●	450	240	-15°		semi-shady		Provides autumn colour
H. helix 'Oro di Bogliasco'		●	● ● ●	● ● ●	450	240	-15°		semi-shady		An interesting variegated form

Hibbertia
Snake vine

Growing tropical climbers implies that you should always grow them in hot spots in the garden or in the conservatory. Hibbertias grow in sunny patches in rainforest areas, clambering through other vegetation. *Hibbertia scandens* will survive a short, sharp attack of frost but is best grown indoors or in a container which can then be moved.

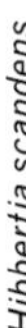
Hibbertia scandens

Grown under a variety of common names, such as Guinea Gold Vine, Snake Vine and Button Flower, *H. scandens* is native to the Northern Territories of Australia. It is best grown outside in warm environments or in conservatories, where it will do well to 7.5m (25ft), so ensure growth is kept under control! It is a vigorous, evergreen climber, liking any soil type, and can also be grown for ground cover. It has dark green leaves that are waxy – ideal for growing in coastal areas. There are over 120 related species, but they are not all climbers. The plant is peppered with yellow, button-like flowers, somewhat like roses. It can be grown in a container, it loves full sun and needs to be kept well watered. However, if grown indoors, be careful not to overwater.

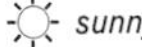 *sunny*  *semi-shady* 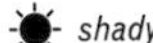 *shady*

Holboellia

In their natural habitat, holboellias are rampant climbers, clambering over small trees to get to the canopy. They are frost hardy, which is a boon to many gardeners, and reward with regular foliage each year. They come into bloom early in the year, unlike a lot of other climbers that do so in the summer.

Native to central China, *H. latifolia* is an attractive, evergreen climber. There are five species and they are generally vigorous growers, especially when established. Control might be a problem but only after the plant has become well established. It may be grown in the garden, in well drained soil with lots of humus, as a screen, or for its foliage effect over a pergola or wall. It fruits only infrequently. Generally, these plants do not require any attention, apart from watering on demand in hot weather.

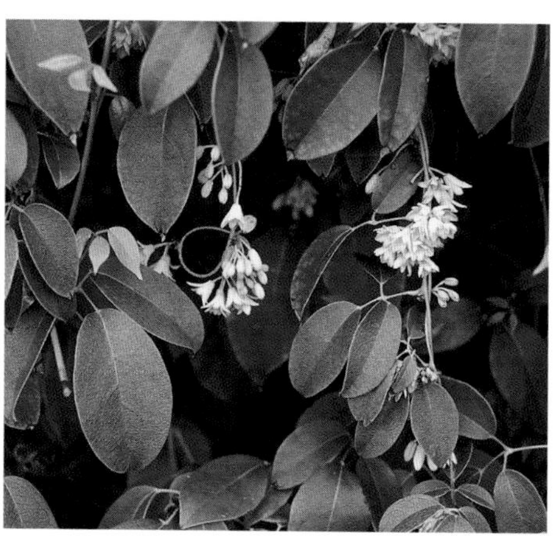

Holboellia latifolia

	SPRING			SUMMER			AUTUMN			WINTER			height (cm)	spread (cm)	min temp (°C)	moisture	sun/shade	colours	
Holboellia coriacea		●	●	●									670	90	-5°				Purple fruit; sweetly fragrant
H. latifolia		●	●	●									500	90	-5°				Red to purple fruit; sweetly fragrant

Hoya

The Wax Plant

Hoyas can be grown either indoors as a houseplant or outdoors over arches and pergolas – or even through trees in more tropical climates. Their attractive flowers and fragrance make them ideal for growing in hanging baskets in conservatories.

Hoya carnosa

Native to the hotter regions of the Himalayas to Burma, the Hoyas are rainforest climbers that scramble around clearings and coastal areas. There are over 200 species but only a handful are cultivated for the garden. Among these are *H. lanceolata* subsp. *bella* (*H. bella*). They are pure white and fragrant and, of course, waxy, which is the reason for this plant's common name. Plant in fertile soil, in partial shade with some full sun, and keep moist.

	SPRING			SUMMER			AUTUMN			WINTER			height (cm)	spread (cm)	min temp (°C)	moisture	sun/shade	colours	
Hoya lanceolata subsp. *bella*				●	●	●							45	30	5°				Scented flowers
H. carnosa			●	●	●	●	●	●	●				610	90	5°				Scented flowers
H. carnosa 'Exotica'			●	●	●	●	●	●	●				610	90	5°				Yellow and pink foliage

● *flower*  *little moisture* *moisture* *wet*

Humulus lupulus

Hop

Once established, hops reward with enormous growth in the spring and reliable foliage and fruits in the autumn. The foliage and stems die down to ground level over winter and must be pruned away to keep the plant healthy.

Hops are now widely grown in gardens. There are just two species, *H. lupulus*, which is used commercially in brewing, and *H. japonicus*. About a dozen forms of *H. lupulus* are known. Hop plants come in different sexed plants (N.B. for the flowers used in brewing, you need the female plant), but it is hard to know what you are buying when the plants are young. However, they grow rapidly, making their first 1.8m (6ft) in about two weeks. Most soil types are suitable for growing the plant.

An attractive variety is *H. lupulus* 'Aureus', or the Golden hop, that does so much better in full sun. Allow plenty of space for hops to grow, and give them sides of buildings, tall fences and pergolas on which to climb.

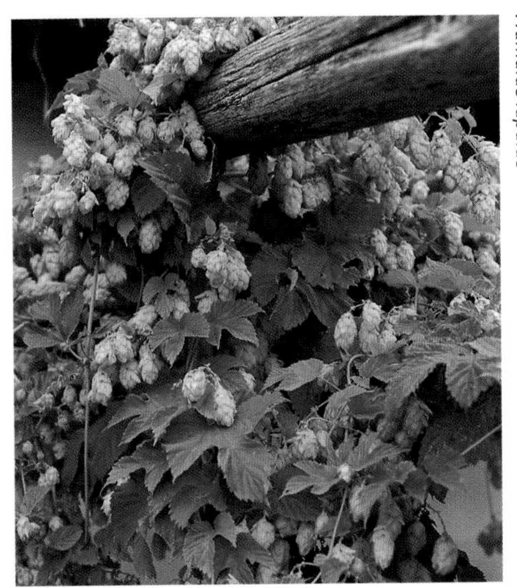

Humulus lupulus

	SPRING	SUMMER	AUTUMN	WINTER	height (cm)	spread (cm)	min temp (°C)	moisture	sun/shade	colours	
Humulus japonicus 'Variegatus'		● ●			460	90	-15°		sunny		Green and white foliage
H. lupulus		● ● ●			610	150	-15°		sunny		A fast climber
H. lupulus 'Aureus'		● ● ●			610	150	-15°		sunny		Superb yellow foliage

Hydrangea

Climbing Hydrangea

The autumn foliage of *H. petiolaris* produces a warm autumn glow of orange. As a deciduous climber it sheds all its leaves, but keeps its thick, woody stems alive. It is very hardy and makes a good screener or background of autumn colour.

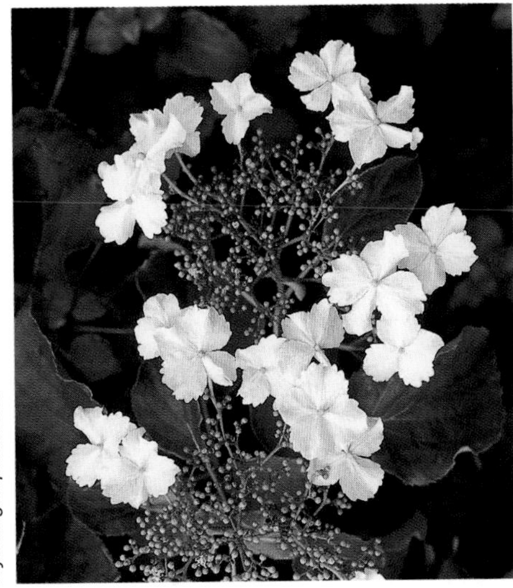

Hydrangea petiolaris

Unusual among the world of hardy shrubs, *H. petiolaris* is one of the few hydrangeas that are climbing. It originates from the east, particularly from Korea and Japan as well as Russia and Taiwan. It climbs using aerial roots. Tolerant of a lot of shade, it is ideal for growing in very shady parts of the garden, up trees and up walls of houses. During the summer, it produces lots of big, white trusses (corymbs) of flowers that have both fertile and sterile flowers. This can be particularly useful in dark areas of the garden that can be lightened up with this species. It can tolerate most soils, but prefers soils with rich humus. Generally, *H. petiolaris* takes care of itself.

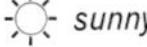 sunny  semi-shady 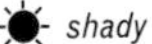 shady

Ipomoea
Morning Glory

Morning Glories have lots of twining stems and so a wire or netting fence is ideal for them to reach their flowering position. The most common species is *I. purpurea*, with purple flowers and heart-shaped leaves, known as Common Morning Glory.

As their name suggests these plants produce their flowers in the morning and by evening they are gone. During the morning they are visited by insects, especially bumblebees, that pollinate them. Colourful flowers are produced in large quantities throughout the summer when the plant gets established.

Growing ipomoeas from seed is easy enough and training them up a trellis or fence in full sun is aided by their twining stems. There are a number of different coloured varieties and species of these rapid-growing climbers and sprawlers, including red (*I. nil* 'Scarlett O'Hara'), white ('Pearly Gates') and pink varieties ('Festival de Chaumont'). The Red Morning Glory or Star Morning Glory – *I. coccinea* – has much smaller flowers, but of an intense, vibrant red, with finely-divided leaves, like fern fronds. Slightly different, but also quite attractive, is *I. lobata*, with rows of orangey-white flowers that thrust out of the plant.

Grow in rich soil or potting compost in a large pot, preferably in full sun, and water daily. Beware of large moth larvae on the plant.

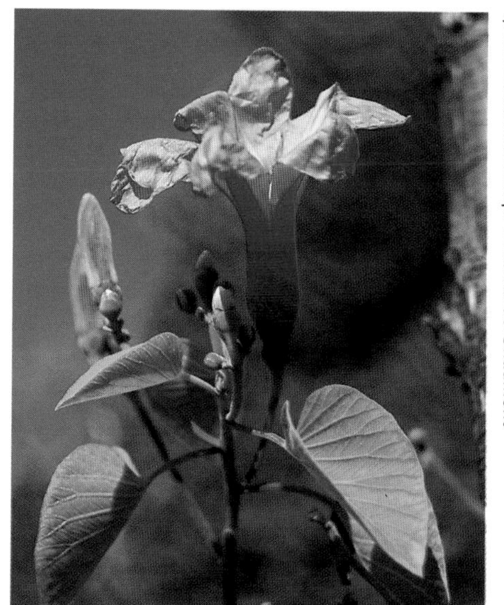
Ipomoea carnea subsp. 'Festival de Chaumont'

Ipomoea nil 'Scarlett O'Hara' showing flower and fruit

	SPRING			SUMMER			AUTUMN			WINTER			height (cm)	spread (cm)	min temp (°C)	moisture	sun/shade	colours	
I. carnea subsp. 'Festival de Chaumont'				●	●	●	●	●	●	●	●		270	60	5°	moisture	sun		Named after the French flower festival
I. coccinea				●	●	●							460	90	5°	moisture	sun		Bright red flowers and divided leaves
I. lobata				●	●	●	●	●	●				460	90	5°	moisture	sun		Spanish national flag colours
I. nil 'Scarlett O'Hara'				●	●	●	●	●	●				460	90	5°	moisture	sun		Vivid red colours
I. purpurea				●	●	●							460	90	5°	moisture	sun		The regular species to grow
I. quamoclit				●	●	●							460	90	5°	moisture	sun		Fine foliage, ideal for conservatory
I. tricolor 'Pearly Gates'				●	●	●							460	90	5°	moisture	sun		Almost a transparent white

● *flower*  *little moisture* *moisture* *wet*

Jasminum

Jasmine

Jasmines are easy to grow as they are generally self-sufficient, and reliably appear year after year. Some do not put on much growth, and this may be a fault with the stock. If this happens, they are relatively cheap to replace. Others can be grown over pergolas or up pillars, or next to gates and doors for their scent. Jasmines are fairly tolerant of shady places. Old jasmines produce a lot of thatch and this needs to be removed after flowering to allow new growth to prosper.

Jasmines come in a variety of colours and forms and make excellent subjects for the garden. They are readily available all year round as container plants and their scent is particularly attractive, although not all jasmines are fragrant. Jasmines produce lots of flowers – in white, pink or yellow – and their foliage is frequently mottled yellow and green, according to the variety. During the spring and summer the reflexed yellow flowers of the Primrose Jasmine, *J. mesnyi*, are produced. Variegated yellow and green leaves can be seen in *J. officinale* 'Argenteovariegatum' or in 'Aureovariegatum' that has more yellow in the leaves. Completely yellow leaves are to be found in *J. officinale* 'Fiona Sunrise'. The winter- flowering jasmine, *J. nudiflorum*, has bright yellow flowers that are produced over winter and into spring. Typical of the jasmines, the common jasmine, *J. officinale*, has trusses of white scented flowers borne from its semi-deciduous and twining stems. The colour of some jasmines changes from bud to flower, and so it is with *J. polyanthum*, that has masses of pink buds followed by white flowers. Plant in semi-shade and keep well watered. Prune out old wood and any dead stems.

Jasminum officinale

Jasminum polyanthum

J

Climbers

	SPRING			SUMMER			AUTUMN			WINTER			height (cm)	spread (cm)	min temp (°C)	moisture	sun/shade	colours	
Jasminum mesnyi	●	●	●	●	●	●							370	120	0°		semi-shady		Also known as 'Primrose Jasmine'
J. nudiflorum	●									●	●	●	300	300	-15°		semi-shady		Winter-flowering jasmine
J. officinale				●	●	●	●						1,200	120	-5°		semi-shady		Scented flowers
J. officinale 'Argenteovariegatum'				●	●	●	●						1,200	120	-5°		semi-shady		Silver variegated leaves
J. officinale 'Aureovariegatum'				●	●	●	●						1,200	120	-5°		semi-shady		Yellow variegated leaves
J. officinale 'Fiona Sunrise'				●	●	●	●						120	30	-5°		semi-shady		A foliage plant
J. polyanthum	●										●	●	300	90	0°		semi-shady		Lots of scented flowers

 *sunny* 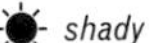 *semi-shady* *shady*

Kalanchoe

Kalanchoes are easy to keep, since they have thick and shiny leaves that are resistant to intense heat and a certain amount of drought. They can survive some neglect and in this respect they are useful as houseplants. Put them out into a sunny position during the summer, but out of cold winds and drafts.

Otherwise known as Palm-Beach-Bells, kalanchoes are often grown as houseplants in temperate climates and outside in warmer climates. They do well in hanging baskets and are pendant, reflecting the environment in which they live in South Africa and Madagascar, within and around the margins of rainforests. Hanging downwards rather than climbing upwards, although some species are climbers, kalanchoes have attractive flowers that are bell-shaped, with a number of colour varieties available.

Kalanchoes are succulent perennials that require very little attention in the garden or in an indoor environment. The plants do well in most soil types and, although they tend to look after themselves in general, should be positioned in a fairly sunny location, preferably against a warm, sun-drenched wall if kept outdoors. Keep the soil moist but take care not to overwater. Watch out for aphids and mildew, which can be problematic for kalanchoes that are grown indoors.

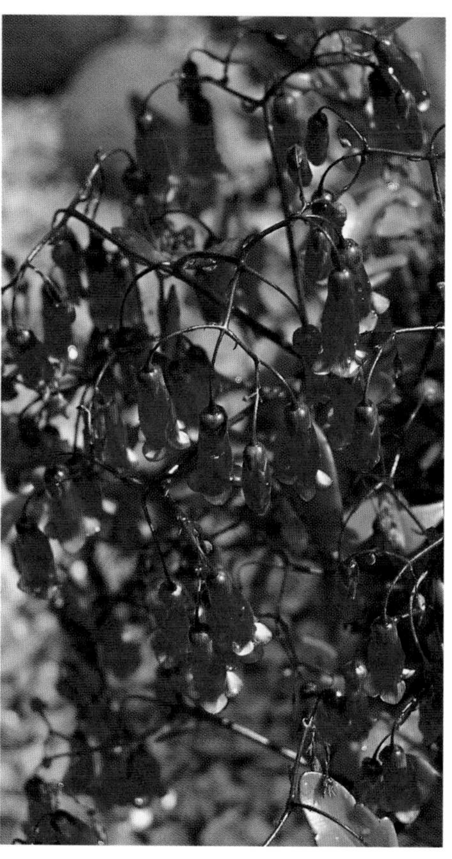

Kalanchoe 'Tessa'

K

Climbers

Kennedia

Coral Pea

Coral peas or vines are extremely versatile in the garden, as they can be trained over pergolas and arches, or else grown as ground cover in warmer environments. In more frost-prone areas they are great plants to grow in the conservatory, most typically for their pretty, pea-like flowers.

As their common name suggests, kennedias are members of the pea family, and they grow like peas with long stems, climbing up to 6.1m (20ft) in some species, such as the Black coral pea, *K. nigricans*. This species is unusual because – as its name suggests – it produces black flowers (quite rare in the flower world), each dressed with a splash of yellow. These 15cm (6in) long, purple-black flowers are produced from late winter to late spring or even early summer – providing a great touch of early colour for the garden. *K. nigricans* thrives in sandy soil and would tolerate coastal sites.

Another twining climber from the genus is the Common coral vine, *K. coccinea*. This plant enjoys regular garden soil, as long as it is not too impoverished. Kennedias are native to relatively dry areas of forest, semi-desert and rainforests in Australia and have developed some adaptations which insure them against drought. However, it would be wise,

flower  little moisture  moisture  wet

particularly in the conservatory or greenhouse, to keep the plants moist – although not oversaturated. In the growing season, a balanced liquid fertilizer will improve kennedias' quality. During the winter months, water these plants only sparingly.

Generally, kennedias need very little looking after. If a variety is to be trained over a pergola or archway, keep any wayward stems tied up and under control. Any pruning should be done after flowering or in late winter, as long as it is not a variety that flowers during the late winter months. Keep a watchful eye out for aphids and moth larvae, particularly for plants kept under glass in a greenhouse or conservatory.

Kennedia nigricans

	SPRING			SUMMER			AUTUMN			WINTER			height (cm)	spread (cm)	min temp (°C)	moisture	sun/shade	colours	
K. coccinea		●	●	●									180	90	5°		semi-shady		'Common Coral Vine"
K. nigricans	●	●	●	●								●	610	120	5°		sunny		'Black Coral Pea'

Lapageria
Chilean Bellflower

This beautiful climber should ideally be grown in a high humidity environment or else sprayed daily. It grows best in partial shade and kept out of the wind. It climbs using suckers, but will need some support on a conservatory wall.

So resplendent is Lapageria that it is the national flower of Chile. *L. rosea* is a native of that country and very beautiful with its big, pinkish-red bells. In many countries it is best grown in a conservatory against a white wall to maximize the elegant display of the flowers.

Lapageria rosea

In the wild, the species grows in moist woodland so it is tolerant to partially shady conditions but needs regular watering. The Chilean Bellflower flowers on and off from spring to autumn, and its pink flowers are sometimes spotted with white. The large leaves are oval, glossy and leathery.

Lapageria grows best in loose, rich soil, preferably augmented with moss and leaf mould. Check that its roots and foliage are kept moist – never allow the plant to dry out. Generally, prune well after flowering and check for slugs and snails, which are rather partial to the Lapageria.

Lathyrus

Sweet peas

Sweet or everlasting peas are a hugely popular group of garden plants that are grown especially for their fragrant flowers and incredible display of multi-coloured flowers. They are easy to grow, too. There are over 80 species and cultivars on the market, offering a big choice – and far too many to discuss in detail here. Cutting the flowers regularly encourages many more to follow on. There are a large number of varieties to choose from to satisfy many colour combinations. Sweet peas grow well in full sunny conditions and in a fertile soil. Their seed can be collected from their little pea pods and sown the following spring. Clump-forming species and cultivars are good for rock gardens, woodland areas in the garden or in an herbaceous border.

One of the easiest of the everlasting peas to grow for long-lasting, year-on-year effect is *L. grandiflorus*. This variety produces a mound of vegetation punctuated with pink pea flowers. This plant will come up as high as a first-floor window and amaze by its perennial persistence. Virtually nothing has to be done to encourage this species, for it will spring out of the ground from where it vanished when it died down in winter. The more delicate sweet peas (*L. odoratus*) that people grow for cutting are easy enough to grow from seed, and then are grown up canes.

There are many different groups of sweet peas, each of which have certain gardening qualities. For instance, among the best for cutting are Multiflora cultivars, the Explorer Group or 'White Supreme'. Members of the Bijou Group hardly need any support and are ideal grown as a bush. 'Jayne Amanda' can be grown as a bush or a cordon (a specially trained plant). If ground cover is needed then try the Snoopea Group, or for hanging baskets try 'Pink Cupid'.

Lathyrus 'Alistair'

Lathyrus Explorer Group

L

Climbers

 *flower*

 *little moisture*

 *moisture*

 *wet*

Lathyrus grandiflorus with curvaceous flowers

To grow plants from seed, leave a few flowers on last year's stems to set seed, or buy new seeds. Sow them in small pots, rather than outside where they may get swamped. Transfer them to their position, already staked. Protect from slugs and mice, and tie the stems up stakes while the plant is ascending. Pests can be a problem when growing sweet peas, as they produce lots of foliage. The leaves are thin and not protected by natural chemicals, so aphids and thrips (plant-loving insects) can be a problem, and slugs and snails will eat seedlings. Check for powdery mildew and try not to overwater as this may encourage fungal attack.

TIP

Make sure, when growing sweet peas from seed, that you place tall enough stakes in the ground for the rapid-growing plants to climb up. Stakes no less than 2.1m (7ft) high should be used to tie up the growing stems.

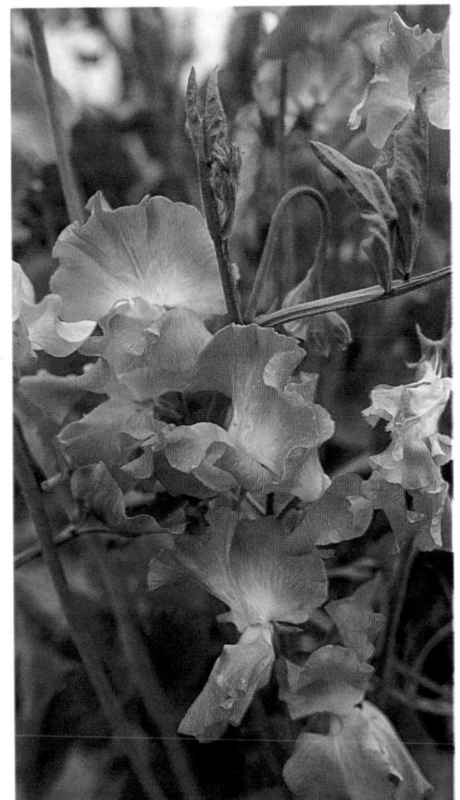

Lathyrus odoratus

	SPRING	SUMMER	AUTUMN	WINTER	height (cm)	spread (cm)	min temp (°C)	moisture	sun/shade	colours	
L. grandiflorus		● ● ●			120	30	-15°		sunny		Perennial everlasting pea
L. latifolius		● ● ●	● ●		150	30	-15°		sunny		Another perennial pea
L. odoratus		● ● ●	● ●		150	30	-15°		sunny		Grow for many colours

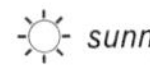 *sunny*  *semi-shady*  *shady*

Lonicera
Honeysuckle

Honeysuckles can be grown from seed or from cuttings. Ripe seeds can be sown in the autumn, with others such as *L. hildebrandiana* in the spring. When making cuttings use new green wood in the spring or older darker wood in the autumn and propagate accordingly. Honeysuckles are attacked by aphids from time to time, but generally the plant grows so rapidly that it can sustain localized attacks. If the honeysuckle is grown in partial shade, attacks from aphids are minimized. Honeysuckles get so thick that birds nest in them, but this shouldn't be a problem.

Honeysuckles are some of the easiest climbers to raise. They are readily available from nurseries and require very little assistance in growing. They are also very hardy and not particularly bothered by pests. Their scented flowers, on the other hand, are just what you might want from a climber. Honeysuckles are big, bold plants and their heavy scents are produced particularly at night, wafting into hollows and paths, and contributing strongly to a very agreeable scented garden. The large flowers of honeysuckles attract pollinating insects and night-flying moths, but these are beneficial insects and not pests. The stems of older honeysuckles become large, very woody and twisted around each other. It is useful, every few years, to cut back the plant during the winter, getting rid of any knotted wood and branches, and keeping the plant within bounds. There are many places to grow honeysuckles, such as over a porch or arbour where the scents can be best appreciated. Alternatively, try up a pergola, or in a hedge, where it can grow unrestrained and mingle with other vegetation such as Clematis and Wisteria, perhaps popping out flowers 6m (20ft) up.

Lonicera japonica 'Halliana'

Lonicera periclymenum

There are very many species and varieties of honeysuckle to choose from, only a few of which are listed in the table opposite. During the winter months the highly scented flowers of *L. fragrantissima* burst from the stems in a great display. This is followed by the cream flowers of *L. pileata* that has the advantage of providing evergreen foliage all year round. This Chinese species also has a number of different coloured leaf cultivars. For a kind of speckled leaf appearance, try

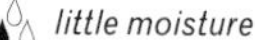

flower little moisture moisture wet

Lonicera x tellmanniana

L. japonica 'Aureoreticulata', that has intricate map-like markings on its green leaves. Appealing variegated foliage is also seen in *L. periclymenum* 'Harlequin'. For sheer size and beauty it is hard to beat the Giant Burmese honeysuckle, *L. hildebrandiana*, that has the longest flowers of all honeysuckles, 8–15cm (3–6in) long, but this is grown best in warmer climates outside, or else indoors in conservatories. Most soil types are fine for honeysuckles, which should be watered regularly until established, and then checked during drought periods. Prune only to keep in check and to remove any old, woody stems.

	SPRING			SUMMER			AUTUMN			WINTER			height (cm)	spread (cm)	min temp (°C)	moisture	sun/shade	colours	
Lonicera hildebrandiana				●	●	●							910	150	0°				Giant Burmese Honeysuckle
L. japonica 'Halliana'	●	●	●	●	●	●							460	90	-15°				White and soft yellow flowers
L. periclymenum					●	●							670	90	-15°				Also called woodbine
L. p. 'Graham Thomas'					●	●							460	90	-15°				A popular variety; white and yellow flowers
L. p. 'Serotina'					●	●							460	90	-15°				Late Dutch honeysuckle
L. x tellmanniana			●	●	●								460	90	-15°				Hybrid of garden origin
L. tragophylla					●	●							610	90	-15°				A Chinese species

Lophospermum

Creeping Gloxinia

Lophospermum is a useful climber to have close at hand on a patio or courtyard, where its progress through a bush or small tree will be rewarded by pink tubular flowers like those of foxgloves, to whose family it belongs.

Coming from tropical Mexico, Lophospermum needs to grow as an annual outside in temperate regions, or inside in a conservatory. The more fertile and drained the soil, the better. It is a delicate climber with broad, heart-shaped leaves that are toothed and its upwardly pointing shoots bear soft pink flowers with yellowy-white throats. *L. erubescens* is a perennial climber with trumpet-shaped, rose-pink flowers.

Lophospermum scandens

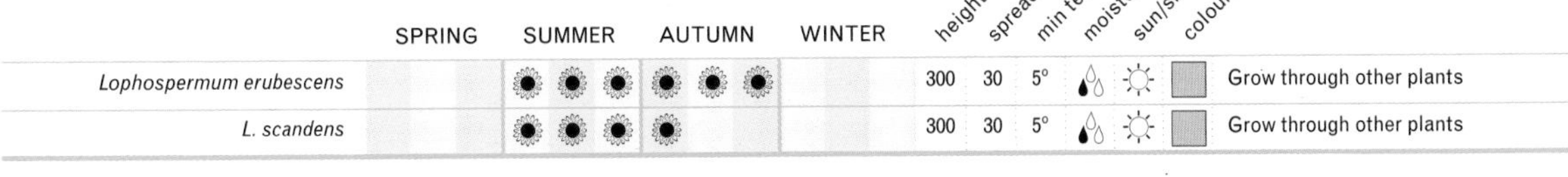

	SPRING			SUMMER			AUTUMN			WINTER			height (cm)	spread (cm)	min temp (°C)	moisture	sun/shade	colours	
Lophospermum erubescens				●	●	●	●	●	●				300	30	5°				Grow through other plants
L. scandens				●	●	●	●						300	30	5°				Grow through other plants

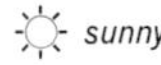 *sunny*  *semi-shady*  *shady*

Mandevilla

Chilean Jasmine

An eye-catching vine from Brazil, mandevillas are grown a lot for decoration and ornamentation. They can be grown along railings and fences in warmer climates, or as a special plant in a hanging basket. They have a certain amount of sophistication because their petals are so beautiful, ranging from white and pink to red. They are also easily grown as houseplants or in the conservatory.

There are two species of Mandevilla commonly grown, *M. laxa* that usually has white flowers, and *M. splendens* that has rose pink flowers. They are twining climbers that have tuberous roots. Species belonging to the Dipladenia are now classified as mandevillas.

One of the best varieties of Mandevilla to grow is 'Alice du Pont', which has pale pink flowers. Rich soil is required for hanging baskets, or growing outside in a warm spot against a wall or in a conservatory. Propagation can be achieved by sowing seed, or taking spring or summer cuttings from softwood and hardwood stems. Keep plants moist but do not overwater. For best results, fertilize monthly.

Mandevilla splendens

Mandevillas are susceptible to red spider mite outdoors and mealybugs if grown in a greenhouse or a conservatory. Grow out of the reach of children, since this tropical climber has sap that is an irritant.

Mandevilla laxa

	SPRING			SUMMER			AUTUMN			WINTER			height (cm)	spread (cm)	min temp (°C)	moisture	sun/shade	colours	
M. x *amabilis* 'Alice du Pont'				●	●	●							670	90	5°	little moisture	sun		Popular plant for pots, hanging baskets
M. laxa				●	●	●	●						460	60	5°	little moisture	sun		Chilean jasmine
M. splendens				●	●	●							610	120	5°	little moisture	sun		The regular species of Mandevilla

● *flower*  *little moisture*  *moisture* 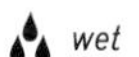 *wet*

M

Climbers

Millettia

Evergreen wisteria

Whether it is in climbing or scandent mode, the Millettia genus tends to be vigorous, producing a mass of leaves. Each leaf is compound with leaflets (pinnate) and each leaflet is elliptical. It can be grown over pergolas, arches and arbours, and its purple-red flowers can be produced in large numbers.

Belonging to the same family as wisteria, namely the pea family, this is distinguished from wisteria in having evergreen leaves, which gives rise to its common name. The genus is a tropical one, living in the wild in Africa and Madagascar, so if you are growing it in temperate climates, it is best to grow it in a conservatory. In warmer climates it is easily grown outside up ironwork grilles and fences, and as an effective foliage plant to make a screener. Grow in fairly fertile soil and keep quite moist to start with, watering after only when needed. Cut out old growth and any dead branches, and keep tied up. Indoors it is prone to insect attack. Like wisteria, *M. reticulata*, from China and Taiwan, has long panicles of flowers, coloured deep purple, and up to 20cm (8in) long. The flowers are of a particular shade of deep purple that is shared with few other plants.

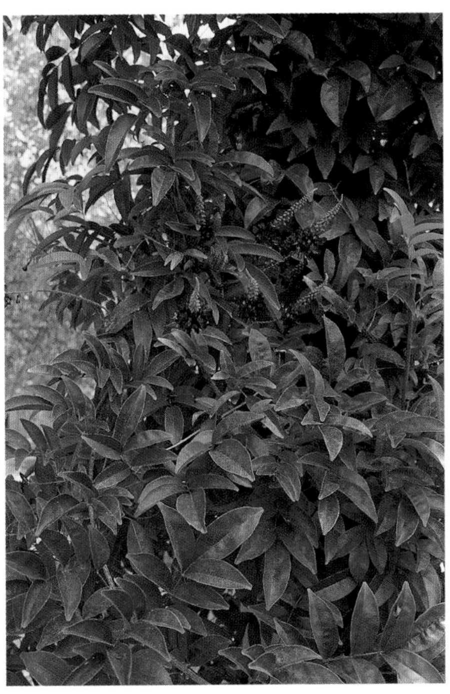

Millettia reticulata

Monstera

Swiss Cheese Plant

Ubiquitous as a houseplant, this performs like a completely different plant outside in warm climates. In the house, the Swiss cheese plant is a relatively slow grower, but outside it can reach 21m (70ft), scaling fences, trees and houses.

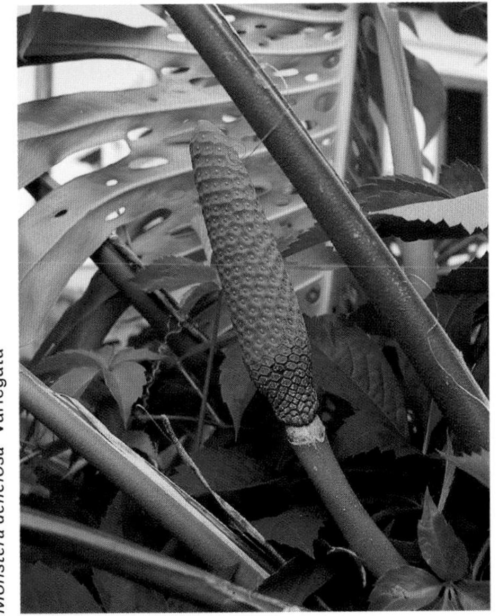

Monstera deliciosa 'Variegata'

It is called the Swiss Cheese Plant because of the indentations in the leaf and occasional holes that distinguish it from Philodendron (see page 128). The plant is not demanding and will grow at its leisure indoors, but outside it will put on an extra leaf every ten days. Its success indoors or outdoors is that it grows well in partial shade. Only in warmer climates does it produce fruit. As an evergreen climber, Monstera thrives in semi-shade and is not often attacked by insects. Occasionally there are attacks by red spider mite and scale insects, but these can be removed by cleaning the large leaves regularly. For propagation, seeds can be sown or cuttings can be made from root tips or from layering stems.

Mucuna

Itch Plant *or* New Guinea Creeper

In temperate zones, grow the Mucuna genus indoors; elsewhere, in tropical and sub-tropical zones, grow it outside as a decorative species against a wall. The curved or beaked flowers are superb. Protect the plants from frosts. New stems need propping up and adequate support is also required for the heavy, pendulous flowers. As it matures, old woody stems need to be cut back.

Mucuna is a long-lived, perennial vine. It is a bold, woody vine that will travel far along a wall. Its pendulous collection of spectacular flowers are also bold in a deep purple colour and hang in large tussles from the stems. The common name for *M. sempervirens* – Florida Velvet Bean – refers both to its flowers and fruits. It is a member of the pea family. Other species such as *M. bennettii* – the New Guinea Creeper – have red flowers. Plant mucunas in well-drained, fertile soil outside or in loam-based compost indoors. Water freely until established and thereafter water occasionally, ensuring not to overwater. Prune plants back after flowering. Indoors, mucunas are susceptible to whitefly and red spider mites.

There are over 100 species of Mucuna to choose from, but they are generally frost tender and need to be grown in a sheltered hot spot against a wall or in a conservatory. Only the hardiest are listed here.

Mucuna sempervirens

	SPRING			SUMMER			AUTUMN			WINTER			height (cm)	spread (cm)	min temp (°C)	moisture	sun/shade	colours	
Mucuna bennettii				●	●	●							2,130	150	5°	little moisture	◐		New Guinea Creeper
M. pruriens			●	●	●	●							370	90	5°	little moisture	◐		Vigorous climber
M. sempervirens				●	●	●	●						370	300	5°	little moisture	◐		Itch plant

● *flower* | *little moisture* | *moisture* | 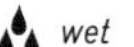 *wet*

Muehlenbeckia

Wire Plant *or* Macquarine Vine *or* Climbing Lignum

Versatile outdoors and indoors, this climber can be a great 'smotherer' plant in warm and humid locations where it is excellent grown over walls and around the bottom of trees. Its wiry growth and close-knit structure can be used to cover, smother and screen objects. In the house it can be grown effectively in a container or hanging basket.

Compared with most climbers, the form of Muelenbeckia is quite extraordinary. There are about four species in cultivation, and a number of varieties, and they have long trailing stems with the tiniest leaves arranged alternately along the thin stems. Some are even devoid of leaves completely. It is a creeping and scandent climber that can trail over the ground (it comes from rocky environments in Australia) or shin up pillars and surround the base of trees. This is all very effective and gives rise to *M. adpressa*'s name of Climbing Lignum, for its dense mass does look like a separate plant. *M. complexa* is particularly useful as ground cover.

This reasonably trouble-free plant is best grown in well-drained, fertile soil in warm, partially shaded areas outdoors. Provide muelenbeckias with shelter from cold, drying winds and give the plant suitable support where required.

Muehlenbeckia complexa

Muehlenbeckia complexa

Muelenbeckias can also be grown in pots or containers, indoors in a conservatory or outside. Keep the plant moist but not saturated. Prune out any dead stems to maintain a healthy look.

	SPRING			SUMMER			AUTUMN			WINTER			height (cm)	spread (cm)	min temp (°C)	moisture	sun/shade	colours	
Muehlenbeckia adpressa	●	●	●	●	●	●							180	60	0°		sunny		Climbing Lignum
M. axillaris				●	●	●	●						30	60	-5°		sunny		Tiny yellowish green flowers, scented
M. complexa				●	●	●							300	80	-5°		sunny		Tiny greenish white flowers, scented

 *sunny*  *semi-shady* *shady*

M

Climbers

Parthenocissus

Virginia Creeper

Virginia creepers are readily available from nurseries, and a good specimen will have a number of long, thin shoots. The plants need to be supported until established when they will find their own way. They can be propagated by growing seed, taking cuttings of either young stems in summer or old stems in autumn, or by layering. They are very vigorous and are only advised to be grown in larger gardens or on house walls. They are good climbers to grow since they are relatively trouble-free.

The Parthenocissus genus is a mixture of vines originating from various parts of the world. The five-leafed *P. quinquefolia* is the true Virginia Creeper native to Florida, Texas and Mexico in North America. It is also called the Woodbine, American Ivy and Five-leaved Ivy (not to be confused with Hedera, see page 108–109). Boston Ivy, or *P. tricuspidata*, is not from Boston, USA, but from China and Japan, and is also known as Japanese Ivy. Two other species are widely cultivated (there are ten species): *P. henryana* that has a whitish bloom over its leaves and *P. thomsonii*, both from China. All species are vigorous growers. Gardeners use Virginia creepers for climbing up walls, efficiently covering vertical surfaces and producing lots of leaves. They are also effectively grown through trees, over arbours and even over small buildings. They are deciduous climbers and because their leaves change to autumn colours before leaf fall, they are used decoratively on houses.

Easy enough to grow – they like most garden soils and will tolerate either sun or shade – they need to be cut back to the area they should occupy on a house and have any wayward stems cut out. Apart from watering to begin with, this climber generally takes care of itself.

Parthenocissus thomsonii

Parthenocissus henryana with its dusty white veins

	SPRING	SUMMER	AUTUMN	WINTER	height (cm)	spread (cm)	min temp (°C)	moisture	sun/shade	colours	
Parthenocissus henryana		flower flower flower			910	180	-15°	little moisture	sun/shade		Chinese Virginia Creeper
P. quinquefolia		flower flower flower			1,520	240	-15°	little moisture	sun/shade		Virginia Creeper
P. thomsonii		flower flower flower			910	180	-15°	little moisture	sun/shade		A woody climber
P. tricuspidata		flower flower flower			2,130	300	-15°	little moisture	sun/shade		Boston Ivy, but from China

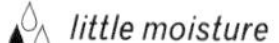 *flower*  *little moisture* 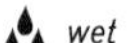 *moisture* *wet*

Passiflora

Passion Flower
or Granadilla

The best way to get started with passifloras is to buy a potted plant, of which there are many species and cultivars widely available. They are best grown in dappled light or in a place where only weak sun strikes the plant for a short period each day. They need water to get established and while flowering, but during the winter they only need occasional watering. Grown indoors, they are susceptible to virus attack of the leaves and red spider mite. They can be grown from seed, or from semi-ripe wood in the summer, or from layering in summer or autumn.

Passion flowers are well worth growing as a talking point in the garden, since the unique flowers are fascinating in all their fine detail. They also have a religious significance and have often been grown in gardens for their masses of flowers. Once established, passion flower plants can grow up to 4.6m (15ft) in height. They do need support and possibly require controlling, depending on the area wanted for coverage. They can be grown outdoors in very warm regions where they may even be evergreen, but in temperate climates they are really deciduous. Reasonably frost hardy, they may have to have their roots protected by a mulch during the coldest months.

The flowers are intricate, including ten radiating petals, five stamens and three stigmas. Among the 400 species of passifloras, there are many different coloured Passiflora species to choose from for the garden, and enough to complement any colour scheme. Only a few are listed here. There are bright reds (*P. coccinea*, *P. manicata*), sumptuous pinks (*P. antioquiensis*), along with whites and purples. The degree to which the flower has a tendency to produce masses of wavy filaments around the edge of the flower is best seen in *P. quadrangularis* or Giant Granadilla, whose large flowers are also scented. Passifloras are versatile as screeners and will readily cover a wall, especially in warmer areas, always with the added bonus of spectacular flowers. Many passifloras also produce fruits, most of which are edible.

Passiflora quadrangularis

Passiflora 'Amethyst'

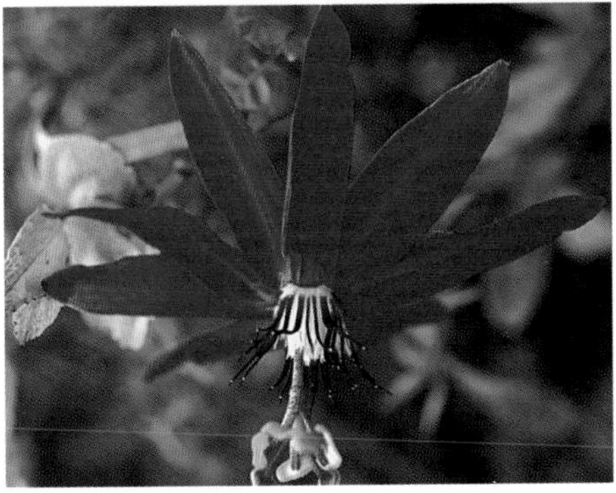
Passiflora coccinea

P

Climbers

	SPRING			SUMMER			AUTUMN			WINTER			height (cm)	spread (cm)	min temp (°C)	moisture	sun/shade	colours	
Passiflora 'Amethyst'				●	●	●	●	●					410	150	5°		semi-shady		A popular variety
P. antioquiensis				●	●	●							500	180	-5°		semi-shady		Sumptuous pink flowers
P. coccinea					●	●	●	●					370	150	5°		semi-shady		Red Granadilla
P. manicata		●	●	●	●	●	●	●					300	90	5°		semi-shady		Bright red flowers
P. quadrangularis					●	●	●	●	●				1,520	240	5°		semi-shady		Giant Granadilla

 *sunny* 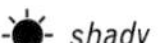 *semi-shady* *shady*

Periploca

Silk Vine

The Silk Vine is so named because of the lustrous allure of its glossy leaves. *P. graeca* is the usual periploca grown in gardens and it fills up a space rapidly with its attractive foliage. Cuttings can be taken of semi-ripe stems during the summer, and propagation can also be done by sowing seeds in a propagator in the spring.

Periploca graeca

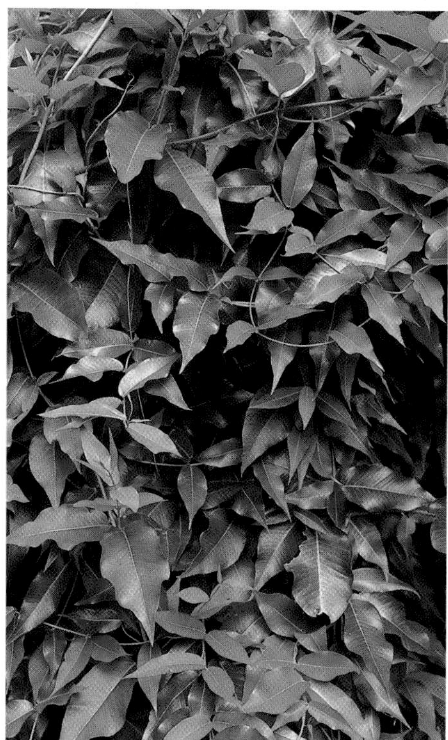

Periplocas are very good for foliage screening, but not so hot for the scent of the flowers. The green, yellow and purple flowers have quite an unpleasant smell. The leaves are very attractive, being a glossy green, pointed and lance-shaped, and can reach about 10cm (4in) in length. There are 11 species of periplocas and they come from the Mediterranean, Africa and Asia where they scramble through vegetation. Thus, in the garden, they should be grown in warm locations, and given some root protection during the winter. They grow well in full sun and in most sorts of garden soil, so long as the soil is well drained. Water well until the plant is established, and then sparingly on demand. They can be grown over trellises, arbours and over walls, and do require some sort of support to carry them. Prune out any old stems in the spring before major growth takes place. Luckily they are generally trouble-free from pests and diseases.

Petrea

Petrea

An exciting climber with unusual flowers, the Petrea has great versatility. It is both a climber, intermingling with trees and shrubs, and also a border and ground cover plant. It needs to be grown in a warm position, since petreas originate from the tropics. It can be propagated from semi-ripe cuttings or from layering.

Yet another tropical climber that is cultivated in the garden, petreas are grown indoors in cooler climates and outdoors in warmer ones. Outside, most garden soils are sufficient, although Petrea grows best in well-drained, fertile soil. In an indoor environment, plant in loam-based potting compost. When grown in a conservatory or greenhouse, watch out for mites and aphids attacking the plant. Once this plant

Petrea volubilis

 flower 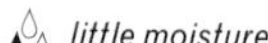  moisture  wet

is properly established, take care not to overwater it.

This climber has attracted a number of names that it can be bought by, including the Blue Bird Vine, the Queen's Wreath and the Purple Wreath. These names refer to the effervescent nature of the flowers, that are lavender fading to cream in colour. As climbers, petreas tend to sprawl around over the ground, so they can be useful for ground cover in warmer climates. Conversely, they can also be effectively trained up a tree, where they can look most spectacular cascading from the canopy. Petrea has semi-evergreen opposite leaves, but it is frost tender, so take care in more temperate climates. In fact, where temperatures fall below 10–13°C (50–55°F), it is best grown under glass.

	SPRING			SUMMER			AUTUMN			WINTER			height (cm)	spread (cm)	min temp (°C)	moisture	sun/shade	colours	
Petrea kohautiana	●	●	●	●	●	●						●	910	180	5°				Semi-evergreen
P. volubilis	●	●	●	●	●	●						●	1,210	150	5°				Also known as Purple Wreath

Phaseolus

Beans

Gardeners use Phaseolus beans both in the kitchen garden as food, and decoratively for their colourful flowers and pods. They have a propensity to climb up tripods and canes with ease. Although these plants – variously named runner beans, scarlet runners, French or Kidney beans – originate from South America, they are easily grown outdoors in temperate climates during the spring and summer.

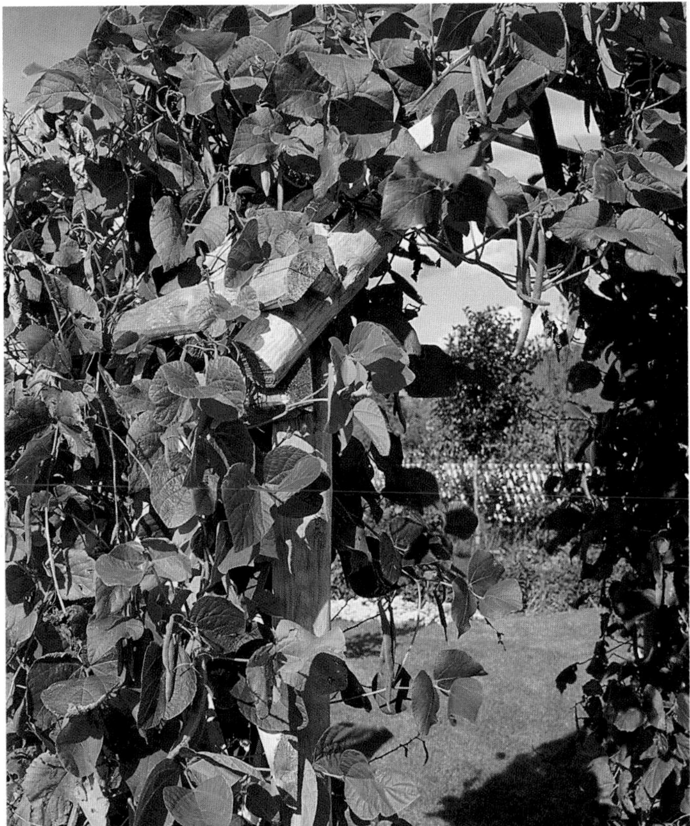

Phaseolus coccineus

Grown as annuals, the Phaseolus genera germinate rapidly and climb using twining stems. Being members of the pea family, they produce assymetrical flowers in various shades of white, cream and rose red, followed by pods containing seeds. Decorative species with colourful flowers make ideal foliage and colour on a small tripod set in an herbaceous border, and in combination with other climbers, such as clematis.

Most garden soils are fine, but Phaseolus thrives best in fertile compost. Keep the plant well watered at all times. Propagation is fairly straightforward. Collect seed from pods left to dry on old plants, or dry indoors. Sow in individual pots in early spring, in a propagator prior to planting out, or plant directly into ground in late spring. Tie up lead shoots to support and speed up the climbing behaviour of the plant. Various insects eat the leaves and both birds and insects attack the fruit, so continually check your plants.

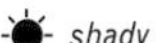

Philodendron

Readily available from nurseries and mail order, there are among 500 different species of Philodendron that come mainly from the rainforests of Central and South America. This explains why they are kept as houseplants in temperate climates and grown outdoors elsewhere.

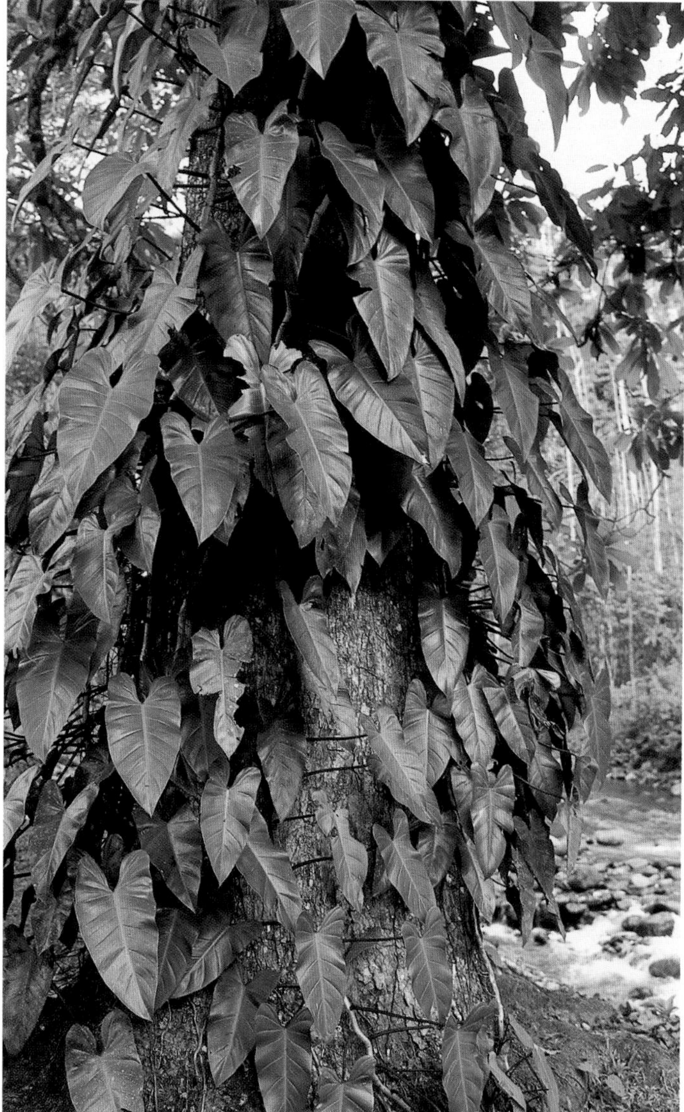

Philodendron scandens

Despite their widespread use as houseplants, Philodendrons are poisonous plants. They are very vigorous climbers, well able to scale a tree or fence. Their leaves are usually simple, but not in the case of the Tree Philodendron (*P. bipinnatifidum*), which is heavily divided. With thick glossy leaves, able to withstand tropical downpours, these are among some of the hardiest of all houseplant climbers, being able to withstand a lot of bashing from people passing by. Inside, grow in potting compost without loam, but outdoors the plants are generally happy in most garden soil types. Philodendrons prefer partial sun and shade, and once established, need watering only when required. Lead shoots need support to grow up. Indoors in the house or conservatory, check the plant regularly for mites and scale insects.

Philodendrons can be increased either by growing seeds in an incubator, taking cuttings of leaf tips or stem tips during the summer, or by layering a long stem into the compost or ground. Either way the plant grows on with long stems, using aerial roots for attachments.

Philodendron scandens

P

Climbers

	SPRING			SUMMER			AUTUMN			WINTER			height (cm)	spread (cm)	min temp (°C)	moisture	sun/shade	colours	
Philodendron angustisectum				flower	flower	flower	flower	flower	flower				460	60	5°	little moisture	sun/shade		Reflexed leaves
P. bipennifolium				flower	flower	flower	flower	flower	flower				610	90	5°	little moisture	sun/shade		Also known as Panda Plant, Fiddleleaf
P. bipinnatifidum				flower	flower	flower	flower	flower	flower				460	60	5°	little moisture	sun/shade		Also known as Tree Philodendron
P. cordatum				flower	flower	flower	flower	flower	flower				610	90	5°	little moisture	sun/shade		Also known as Heart Leaf
P. scandens				flower	flower	flower	flower	flower	flower				610	90	5°	little moisture	sun/shade		Heart Leaf or Sweetheart Plant

flower

little moisture

moisture

wet

Plectranthus

Swedish Ivy *or* Swedish Begonia

Mixed with other species, Plectranthus makes a good foliage plant that is appealing thanks to its long trailing stems that flow out and downwards from the basket. It can be increased by dividing the plant during the summer, growing seeds or growing on stem cuttings all year round.

Usually referred to by its Latin name, rather than by its common name of Swedish Ivy, Plectranthus is a trailing and spreading plant that is best grown in hanging baskets. It is also widely grown as a houseplant, with a huge number of species and forms from which to choose – there are 350 species of African and Asian origin.

During the summer this plant can be taken outdoors. In warmer climates, however, it can be grown outdoors permanently and can be encouraged to become a ground cover plant. Its patterned ovate leaves do look very appealing en masse. Plectranthus belongs to the Deadnettle family, and typically has soft leaves, which are also scented.

Plectranthus madagascariensis

Plectranthus forsteri 'Marginatus'

Indoors, grow this plant in a loam-based compost in full light but ensure that it has some protection from direct sunlight. Outside in warmer areas, grow in moderately fertile, well-drained soil in partial shade. Plectranthus is frost-tender, so take care if you plan to grow it outside permanently in cooler climates. Water daily in summer, but only sparingly in winter. During the growing season, a balanced liquid fertilizer should be applied once a month for the best results.

	SPRING	SUMMER	AUTUMN	WINTER	height (cm)	spread (cm)	min temp (°C)	moisture	sun/shade	colours	
Plectranthus forsteri 'Marginatus'		✹ ✹ ✹			30	90	5°		semi-shady		Creamy white margins to leaves
P. madagascariensis		✹			30	15	5°		semi-shady		Crush leaf to release mint scent
P. verticillatus (= P. australis)		✹ ✹ ✹			90	30	5°		semi-shady		Also known as Swedish Ivy

 *sunny*  *semi-shady* 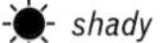 *shady*

Plumbago

Leadwort

Leadworts are some of the most versatile plants around: they are often used in hanging baskets for their trailing nature; they are used up and over walls in semi-tropical and tropical gardens; and in warmer climates, plumbagos are often used to create magnificently coloured hedges.

In tropical climates, leadworts are very vigorous growing plants that will easily cover a long wall from top to bottom. They can also form big bushes that need to be clipped regularly. Their pale, lead-like blue is appealing and highly characteristic. However, there is a red species, *P. indica*, called Scarlet Leadwort, which originates from Asia. The species most commonly grown in gardens is *P. auriculata*, from South Africa. Normally light blue in colour, there is also a white variety, *P. auriculata* var. *alba*. If plumbagos are grown indoors, they can be moved outside during the summer.

Leadworts should be grown in a conservatory or cool greenhouse where temperatures fall below 7°C (45°F). Plant in loam-based compost indoors or any general garden soil outside, ensuring that the plant is sited in a sunny position.

Water regularly until established. Semi-ripe stems are the best from which to take cuttings and to grow them on in the summer. Root cuttings can also be made. Propagation can also be achieved by sowing seeds in a propagator. When growing in a greenhouse it may be necessary to cut back the plant regularly to stop it becoming rampant. Indoors, there may be problems with red spider mite and whiteflies.

Plumbago mixed in with Bougainvillea

Plumbago auriculata

	SPRING			SUMMER			AUTUMN			WINTER			height (cm)	spread (cm)	min temp (°C)	moisture	sun/shade	colours	
Plumbago auriculata				flower	flower	flower	flower	flower	flower				610	300	0°	moisture	sun	blue	Vigorous when given heat
P. a. var. *alba*				flower	flower	flower	flower	flower	flower				610	300	0°	moisture	sun	white	White variety of above
P. indica								flower	flower	flower	flower	flower	180	90	0°	moisture	sun	red	An untypical red species

 *flower*  *little moisture*  *moisture* *wet*

Climbers

Pyrostegia

Flame Vine *or* Golden Shower

Grown outdoors in hot countries, Pyrostegia makes a perfect climber for a hot and sunny situation. In temperate climates it can only be grown in a conservatory since it is frost tender. Propagation can be achieved by growing seeds or taking cuttings of semi-ripe stems and growing them on in a propagator.

The name of Flame Vine is more appropriate for this vine with its garlands of vivid orange flowers hanging between its long green leaves. The colour is more pronounced in the sunshine, for this is a species native to the rainforests of South America. There are four species of this genus of evergreen woody climbers, that climb using tendrils. They are best grown outside over a wall or fence in full sun, where they will grow up to 9m (30ft). They look particularly stunning cascading from the canopy of a tree. Flame Vines are members of the Bignoniaceae family, noted for their climbing vigour. Their brilliant flowers are tubular and borne in tight clusters.

Plant outdoors, in full sun, in most soil types, although well-drained, fertile soil will produce best results.

Pyrostegia venusta

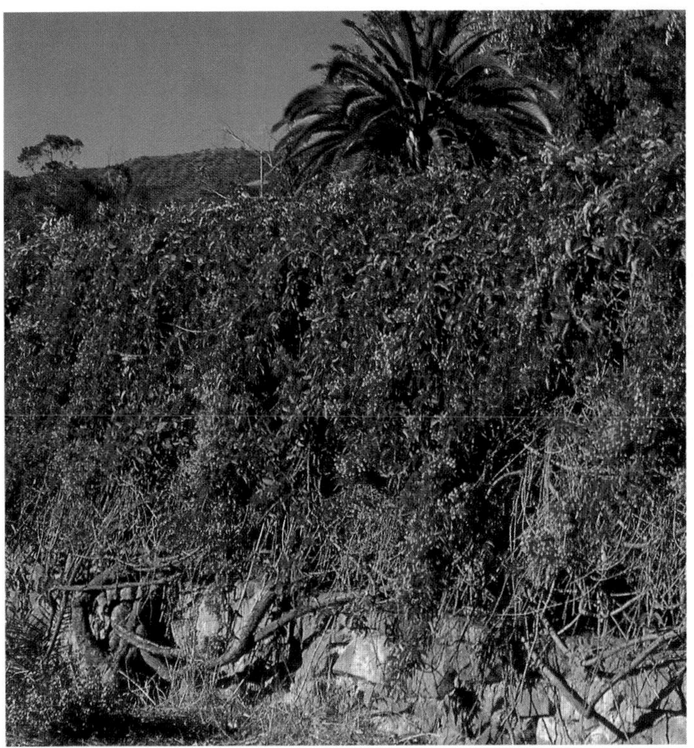

Pyrostegia venusta

Give plenty of water to begin with and then keep the plant moist, watering less frequently during winter months. Indoors, grow Pyrostegia in loam-based potting compost with added leaf mould and sharp sand for drainage. Once a month apply a balanced liquid fertilizer. Check regularly for signs of scale insects and mites, particularly indoors.

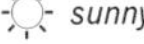 *sunny*  *semi-shady* 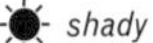 *shady*

Rhodochiton

Readily available from nurseries, Rhodochiton can be grown on to flower during the summer months. It can also be grown from seed using a propagator, and can be treated as an annual, even though it is a perennial. Hot spots in the garden are ideal for this colourful climber, clinging on by using its twining leaf stalks.

Rhodochitons are very popular climbers in temperate climates, even though they come from the warmth of Mexico, where they are woodland scramblers. They do not mind full sun or partial shade, and they are profligate with their intriguing flowers. The flower colour itself is fairly unusual and the plant therefore has a useful place as a part of a colour-managed garden. The shape of the flower is unusual, with a large tube protruding from its base. Grown in an herbaceous border to climb through adjacent plants, or grown in a hanging basket, this is an eye-catching species worthy of display.

The best site outside for Rhodochiton is humus-rich, fertile and well-drained soil in a hot, sunny spot. (Because these plants are frost tender, decide whether to risk planting outdoors if you live in a more temperate climate.) Indoors, grow in loam-based potting compost for best results. Indoors and out, water regularly at first, then refrain from regular watering once the plant is fully established. Feed a balanced, liquid fertilizer monthly. Watch out for mites and scale insects, which can be a problem for Rhodochiton if grown inside in a conservatory or greenhouse.

Rhodochiton atrosanguineus is a good foliage plant

Rhodochiton atrosanguineus

flower | 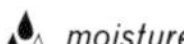 little moisture | moisture |  wet

Rosa

Rose

Colourful roses assert themselves in the garden in many ways, not least as climbers and ramblers. They can be major eye-catchers – such as 'Kiftsgate', 'Seagull' or 'Rambling Rector', which can all take over trees – or they can be more modest climbers up walls and over fences. In their natural environment, roses climb and ramble over other vegetation, and this can be put to good use in the herbaceous border or over bare ground where the natural tendency of roses to cover ground can be exploited. With their long stems, wickedly barbed with thorns, roses produce lots of colourful flowers in trusses or as single flowers, especially in more modern varieties.

Climbing and rambling roses are just two different types of Rosa, but they have slightly different characteristics, which can affect your choices. Ramblers are naturally very vigorous and will produce lots of long, bendy stems. They can produce masses of small flowers in large trusses, but ramblers only flower once in the year. They are also susceptible to mildew.

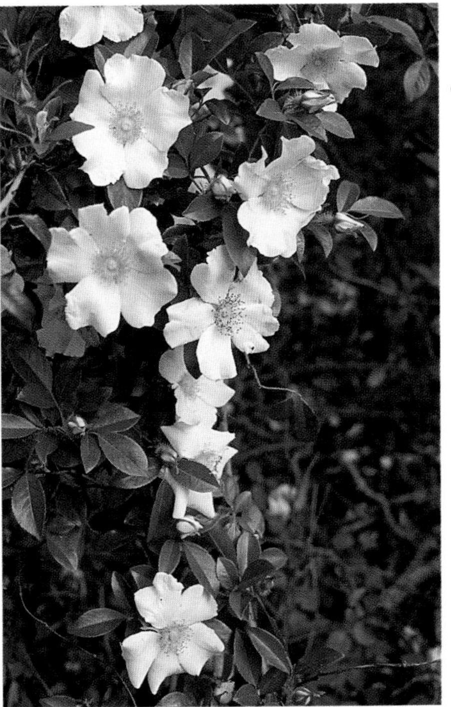

Rosa laevigata is a vigorous climber

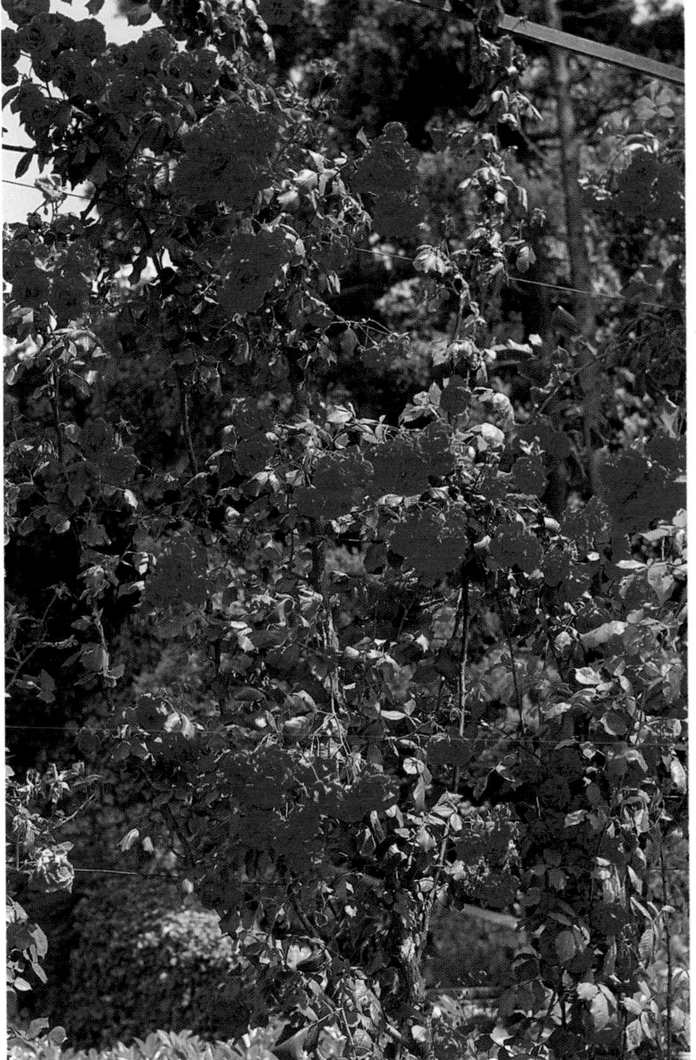

Rosa excelsa

Climbers are the opposite of ramblers in many ways; they have larger flowers but in small trusses, and they flower more than once during the season. Their stems are firmer than those of ramblers, they are more resistant to disease and their flowers are borne on old wood instead of new growth.

Some of the best varieties of climbers to buy are the Climbing Bourbons (such as 'Zéphirine Drouhin'),

Rosa 'Danse du Feu'

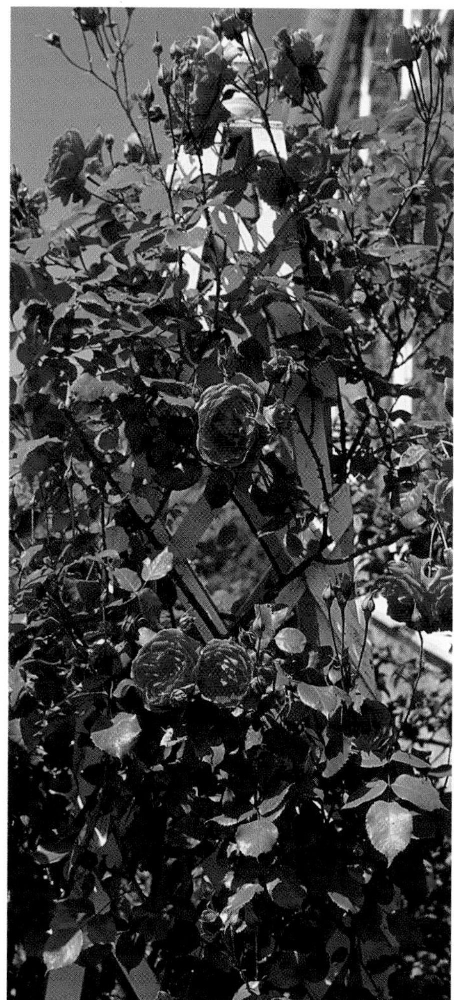
Climbing roses do well on decorative pyramids

Climbing Tea Roses and large-flowered climbers. Special delights can be had from species climbers and ramblers such as *R. banksiae*, *excelsa* and *laevigata* that come with vigour and a certain amount of natural hardiness and resistance to diseases and pests. On the subject of pests and diseases, there are quite a few to watch out for, depending on the species and variety. Keep a particular eye out for aphids, red spider mites, caterpillars scale insects and mildew.

Rosa 'American Pillar'

flower | little moisture | moisture | wet

To propagate roses you can take the seeds from the hips. Take care when doing this, since the tiny hairs protecting the seeds are like natural itching powder, so do not get these on your skin. Germinate the seeds in a propagator. Roses are equally easy to propagate from cuttings. These can be made from semi-ripe and woody stems, dipped in hormone powder and grown on in compost, outside in summer, or in a propagator.

Rose cuttings grow fast. Prune ramblers soon after flowering since they only flower on new wood. Therefore, the earlier you do this, the longer the resultant wands will be. These will bear flowers for the following year. Prune climbers back to the old wood on which they will flower next year. Climbers are easier to keep within the confines of a smaller garden.

TIP

Planting in the same soil in which roses have recently been grown is unsuitable for new rose specimens, due to the build-up of harmful soil organisms. Exchange the soil, which can be used elsewhere in the garden, or choose a fresh site!

Rosa 'Pink Perpetue'

Rosa 'Zéphirine Drouhin'

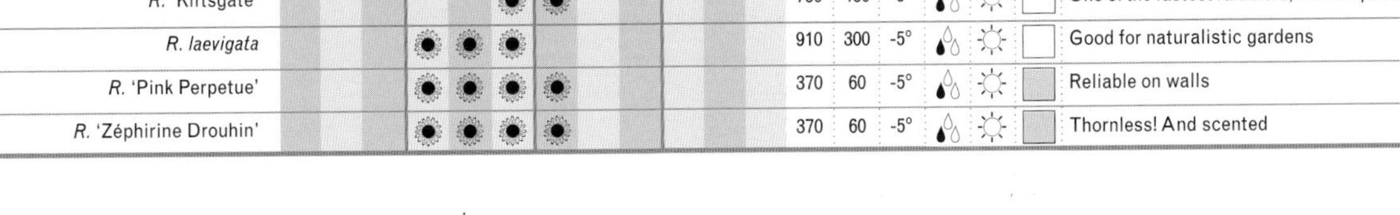

	SPRING			SUMMER			AUTUMN			WINTER			height (cm)	spread (cm)	min temp (°C)	moisture	sun/shade	colours	
Rosa 'American Pillar'					●	●							460	120	-5°		sunny		Popular variety, good for pergolas
R. banksiae			●	●									300	240	-5°		sunny		Long drooping wands
R. 'Danse du Feu'				●	●	●	●	●	●				350	250	-15°		sunny		Excellent climber for colour
R. 'Kiftsgate'						●	●						760	460	-5°		sunny		One of the fastest ramblers, needs space
R. laevigata				●	●	●							910	300	-5°		sunny		Good for naturalistic gardens
R. 'Pink Perpetue'				●	●	●	●						370	60	-5°		sunny		Reliable on walls
R. 'Zéphirine Drouhin'				●	●	●	●						370	60	-5°		sunny		Thornless! And scented

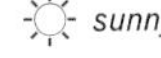 sunny 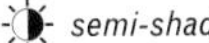 semi-shady 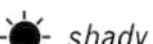 shady

R

Climbers

Rubus

Bramble

Members of the Rubus genus have a natural tendency to climb. They are great exploiters of the environment and their long exploratory stems always need to be kept in check. Apart from the familiar raspberries and brambles, there are a number of colourful relations worth growing decoratively.

Brambles are, after all, members of the rose family. They produce tiny, rose-like flowers, except the 'beautiful-flowered' *R. ulmifolius* 'Bellidiflorus' that has finely divided flowers and elm-like leaves. Another favourite for the garden is *R. cockburnianus*, with pale pink and white flowers, and its 'Goldenvale' cultivar that has golden leaves. These can be grown to trail across the ground as cover.

Brambles can grow in most soils in the garden and enjoy a situation in partial shade in a sunny spot. Water regularly until they are established. Generally these are fairly easy plants to grow, as they tend to look after themselves once established. Keep an eye out, however, for moth larvae as these love eating the leaves of brambles. Just remove them from the plant to prevent leaf-munching.

Ornamental 'brambles' are relatively easy to propagate since they already have a vigorous disposition. They can be easily propagated by taking semi-ripe cuttings and simply planting them outdoors in a nursery bed of sand and compost, or they can be layered wherever they throw out long stems. Vigorous growing species are best planted out in a wild or woodland garden, where they can roam free, as they do in any number of natural, uncultivated situations. *R. squarrosus* is an interesting newcomer, but it has ferociously barbed stems.

Rubus ulmifolius 'Bellidiflorus'

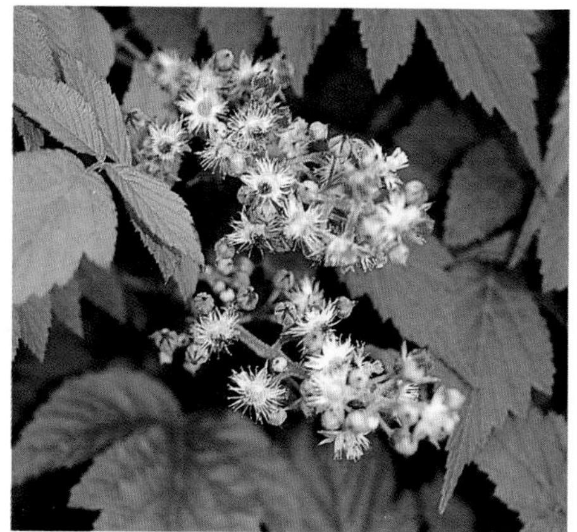

Rubus cockburnianus

	SPRING			SUMMER			AUTUMN			WINTER			height (cm)	spread (cm)	min temp (°C)	moisture	sun/shade	colours	
Rubus 'Benenden'			flower	flower									300	90	-15°	little moisture			Also known as Tridel
R. cockburnianus				flower	flower	flower							240	240	-15°	little moisture			Try the yellow leaved variety
R. squarrosus				flower	flower	flower							90	90	0°	little moisture			Delicate and spectacular
R. ulmifolius 'Bellidiflorus'					flower	flower							240	370	-15°	little moisture			Double flowers

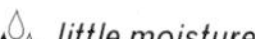 *flower* | *little moisture* | *moisture* | *wet*

R

Climbers

Schisandra

Schisandras are woodland species that come mostly from Asia, with one species from North America. They are best grown in semi-shady positions, as well as growing up walls, arbours and in small courtyard gardens. There are about 25 species of this genus and they have white and red flowers.

To get the fleshy red or pink fruit of the Schisandra you need a plant of each sex. A good species to start with is *S. chinensis*, which is a deciduous climber that has scented cream flowers, or *S. rubriflora* that has red flowers.

Plant in reasonably fertile but well-drained soil, in partial shade or dappled light. Water to start with, then sparingly once it is established. Generally, these plants are easy to grow and fairly trouble-free from pests and diseases. You can propagate these plants from their seeds or by taking cuttings of the semi-ripe wood in the summer or the older wood in the autumn. Grow them on in propagators or in nursery beds. The plant is very versatile since it can be used as a climber over frames and trellises, and grows well planted in light woodland.

Schisandra chinensis

Schisandra rubriflora

	SPRING			SUMMER			AUTUMN			WINTER			height (cm)	spread (cm)	min temp (°C)	moisture	sun/shade	colours	
Schisandra chinensis			●	●	●	●							910	120	-15°				Good for a shady spot; fragrant flowers
S. henryi	●	●	●										370	60	-15°				Red fruits
S. rubriflora			●	●	●	●							910	120	-15°				Good for foliage and flowers

 *sunny*  *semi-shady*  *shady*

Smilax
Smilax

Wild or less structured gardens should not be without smilaxes. They give excellent value as foliage plants, and if an intruder-deterring hedge is needed, the spines of Smilax might be useful. Climbing in semi-shade, smilaxes are useful in overshadowed gardens, woodland gardens and hedgerows.

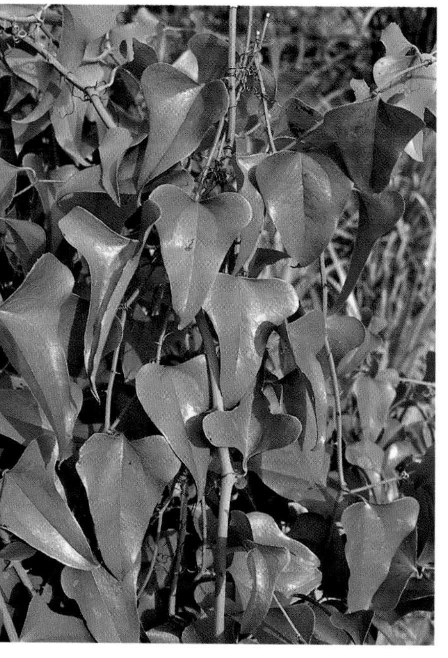
Smilax aspersa

Smilaxes are an interesting group of natural born climbers. They may be found in the wild scrambling effortlessly through hedgerows and thickets. They climb using tendrils and are sometimes very prickly, often producing lots of leaves rather than flowers. As foliage plants in a more natural garden, smilaxes would be good choices. There are over 200 species from which to choose. The shapes of the leaves, heart-shaped to dagger-shaped, are interesting features. They are sold under a variety of names, such as Greenbrier, Sawbrier and Horsebrier, and belong to the Lily family.

Ordinary garden soil is fine for smilaxes, positioned in partial to full sun. Water regularly to start off with, then less frequently once the plant has become properly established.

	SPRING	SUMMER	AUTUMN	WINTER	height (cm)	spread (cm)	min temp (°C)	moisture	sun/shade	colours	
Smilax aspersa		flower flower flower			300	90	-5°	little moisture			Natural born climber
S. china	flower flower flower				460	120	-5°	little moisture			Separate sexed plants

S

Climbers

Solandra
Chalice Vine *or* Cup of Gold

Being scandent plants, solandras need to be given support whenever possible. Stock can be brought on by growing the seed, taking cuttings or by layering. Plants need to be watered regularly to start with, then sparingly during the winter period. Grown outside there are not many problems, but inside the plants are frequently attacked by mites and scale insects.

Chalice Vines are so named after the large chalice-like flowers produced by this woody vine. There are eight species, half of which are in cultivation, and they belong to the potato family that gives them their climbing characteristics. Coming from the rainforests of Mexico, these are plants that are best grown in a greenhouse, or in tropical and sub-tropical climates outdoors in plenty of sun. They are naturally frost-tender plants and can be grown over pergolas, arches and walls. The leaves are simple and ovate and the plant makes a good foliage plant in its own right.

Solandra prefers reasonably fertile garden soil, or loam-based potting compost if grown indoors. They are best positioned outside in a sunny site or, if temperatures are likely to fall

 *flower* 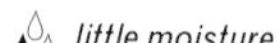 *moisture* 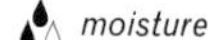 

little moisture · *moisture* · *wet*

Solandra maxima

below 7–10°C (45–50°F), bring them indoors to a conservatory.

Water regularly to start with and add a balanced liquid fertilizer every four weeks if indoors. Water more sparingly during the winter months. Generally, this plant is fairly trouble-free, but be on the look out for red spider mites and scale insects if growing inside, as these can prove troublesome. Provide support for the climbing stems and prune back in late winter or early spring if necessary to restrict its size.

	SPRING	SUMMER	AUTUMN	WINTER	height (cm)	spread (cm)	min temp (°C)	moisture	sun/shade	colours	
Solandra grandiflora	● ● ●				1,210	120	5°		sunny		Frost sensitive
S. maxima		● ● ●			1,210	120	5°		sunny		Frost sensitive

Solanum

Climbing Potato *or* Climbing Solanums

Support is needed regularly for these climbers since they move fast and must have artifical purchase points or have other plants to ramble through.

The term 'climbing potato' or Solanum covers hundreds of species and cultivars that belong to the potato family. They are all usually vigorous and are reasonably well protected from insect attacks as they have natural feeding deterrents in their leaves.

Among the most popular of the solanums is *S. crispin* 'Glasnevin', which features great trusses of purple flowers. There are many white-flowered climbing potatoes, such as *S. laxum (=jasminoides)* with fragrant blossoms. The fruits of climbing solanums may be green, red or black and are usually poisonous. Grow in fertile soil and keep watered in summer.

Solanum wendlandii

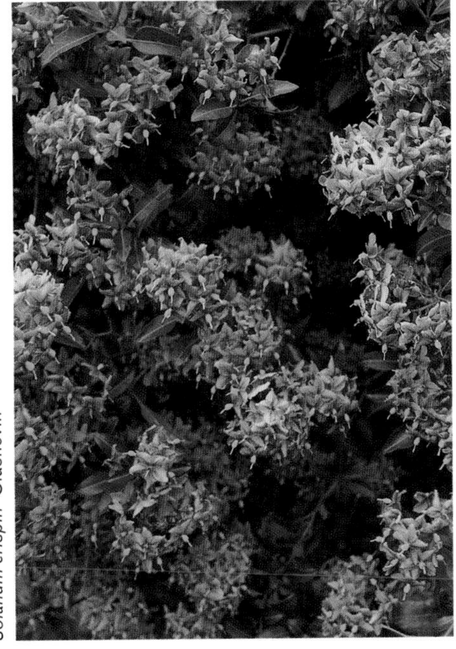
Solanum crispin 'Glasnevin'

	SPRING	SUMMER	AUTUMN	WINTER	height (cm)	spread (cm)	min temp (°C)	moisture	sun/shade	colours	
Solanum crispum 'Glasnevin'		● ● ●	● ●		600	90	-5°		sunny		Chilean Potato Vine
S. laxum (=jasminoides)		● ● ●	● ●		600	90	0°		sunny		Potato Vine
S. wendlandii		● ● ●			480	60	5°		sunny		Potato Vine, Paradise Flower

 *sunny*  *semi-shady* 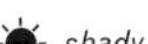 *shady*

S

Climbers

Sollya

Bluebell Creeper

Sollya grows more like a bush than a climber with long stems. It produces huge numbers of tiny thin leaves that are evergreen, and from the mass of the plant, new shoots of lighter green leaves are produced. The plant needs to be protected from weather colder than 5°C (41°F) or brought indoors.

Sollyas belong to the Pittosporum family and are native to light woodland in Australia. Called the Bluebell Creeper, it does creep around (albeit rather slowly) and it is more scandent than a full blown climber. Its flowers are a soft blue colour (slightly reminiscent of bluebells) and the plant stays in flower for the whole of the summer, which is unusual for many climbers. As Sollya is an evergreen, it gains extra marks as it gives more to foliage than a lot of other climbers. Altogether this is a plant that has a lot of useful gardening qualities. It is becoming more widely grown, and what it loses in vigour, it gains in beauty.

It thrives in well-drained, humus-rich soil outdoors, or else loam-based compost inside. Place in the hottest spot in the garden for best results. Watch out for red spider mites if grown indoors.

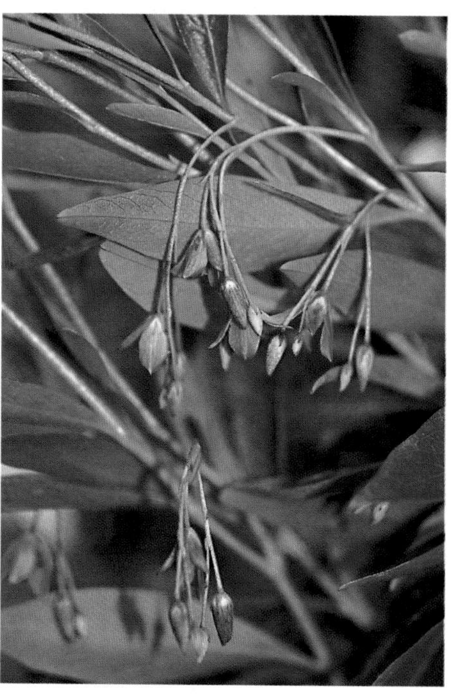

Sollya heterophylla

S

Climbers

Stephanotis

Otherwise known as the Madagascar jasmine, indicating where it comes from as a native plant, Stephanotis is a widely available climber that is noted for its fragrant flowers. It is also called Bridal Wreath and Floradora. It is frost tender and should be grown indoors if temperatures fall lower than 15°C (59°F).

Stephanotis floribunda

A very successful conservatory plant, or a house plant, Stephanotis does very well outdoors over arches and arbours in tropical and semi-tropical gardens. The flowers are relatively tough and waxy, and produce plenty of scent in the evening. The purpose of the scent is really to attract pollinators, but the species has captured the heart of many a gardener and houseplant arranger.

Propagation can be done by germinating seeds in a propagator with bottom heat, or by growing on cuttings taken from semi-ripe wood. Outside there are few problems from pests and diseases, but inside various insect pests attack the plant, including red spider mites, mealybugs and scale insects. Grow in rich, moist, fertile soil for best results.

 *flower*  *little moisture*  *moisture*  *wet*

Stigmaphyllon

Butterfly Vine

Stigmaphyllon is grown widely in the warmer states of the USA, as well as in South America, the Caribbean and West Africa. This plant has delightful yellow flowers, the fruit of which have two wings that resemble those of butterflies, hence its common name.

Able to climb up a pillar or fence to over 9m (30ft) in height, Stigmaphyllon has long, evergreen leaves (sometimes toothed, sometimes not) and is therefore invaluable as a foliage plant. The yellow flowers, which bloom from spring to autumn, hang in clusters, giving rise to its other name of the Orchid Vine. There are over 110 species of Stigmaphyllon and they deserve to be more widely grown, if only in conservatories in temperate climates.

Stigmaphyllon ciliatum showing its 'butterfly wings'

Grow outside in tropical and sub-tropical climates up a tree or over a garden structure. In temperate climates, as the plant is frost tender, grow as a houseplant or up a wall of a conservatory. Stigmaphyllon enjoys fertile, well-drained soil outside or loam-based potting compost in full light, but shaded from the hot sun if grown indoors. During growth, water freely and apply a liquid fertilizer every four weeks for the best results, particularly if grown indoors under glass. Support any climbing stems and prune back to maintain the desired size. Stigmaphyllon can be propagated by growing the seed in a propagator, or by growing cuttings made from semi-ripe wood.

Stigmaphyllon ciliatum

Streptosolen
Marmalade Bush

A native of tropical South America, in the wild this species scrambles happily among other plants that it uses for support. In the garden, however, it needs to be given full support, as otherwise it will fall around and not grow properly. Grown best in a hot spot in full sun, Streptosolen will become an eye-catcher with its striking yellow and orange flowers.

The Marmalade Bush is very appropriately named. There can hardly be any other widespread plant that approximates to the bright colour of this climber. The flowers, seen en masse, or in combination with others, are always special. For its unique colours, Streptosolen makes a valuable contribution to colour-themed gardens. Grown best outdoors in a Mediterranean climate they can be grown backed up to a wall where they perform well. In temperate climates it can be grown in a conservatory. It is a scrambling climber and therefore needs support to keep it climbing.

Plant in fertile, moist but well-drained soil outdoors. Inside, grow in loam-based potting compost in full light with shade to protect it from the hot sun. Water regularly before the plant is established and then later only when needed. Indoors, apply a balanced liquid fertilizer once a month. Water sparingly during the winter. Prune back in late winter or the early spring. Streptosolen may well need restrictive pruning if grown under glass. Generally the plant is trouble-free if grown outdoors, but inside check regularly for whiteflies, red spider mites and aphids if kept in a greenhouse or conservatory.

Streptosolen sp. solanaceae

Streptosolen jamesonii

flower 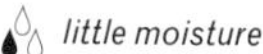 little moisture 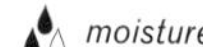 moisture  wet

Tecoma

Cape Honeysuckle

Best grown outdoors in tropical and semi-tropical countries, where it will reach up to about 6m (20ft) depending on the species, Tecoma is a vigorous group of climbers that are excellent for foliage effects and, of course, their yellow, red and orange flowers. In temperate climates, grow it as a conservatory plant. Tecoma can be grown from seeds or cuttings.

Tecoma has been formerly called Tecomaria and Bignonia, the latter referring to the plant family to which they belong, noted for its vigorous climbers. There are about a dozen species and they generally have orange to red flowers, though *T. capensis* has at least three named colour variants. In a sense the tecomas behave in a similar way to Loniceras (honeysuckles – see pages 110–11) in that they scramble over vegetation and up trees and shrubs. They also have long, trumpet-like flowers similar to those of Lonicera, with the male and female flower parts prominently protruding. They have evergreen leaves that are sub-divided (pinnate).

Grow outdoors in moist but well-drained fertile soil in the full sun. Inside, in a conservatory or greenhouse, plant directly into a border or large tub of loam-based potting compost in the full light. During its growing season, water regularly and apply a half-strength liquid fertilizer once a month. During the winter months, water sparingly. Tecomas are fairly trouble-free climbers, but indoors it may be wise to check for red spider mites and whiteflies from time to time, as these pests can be a problem if the plant is kept under glass.

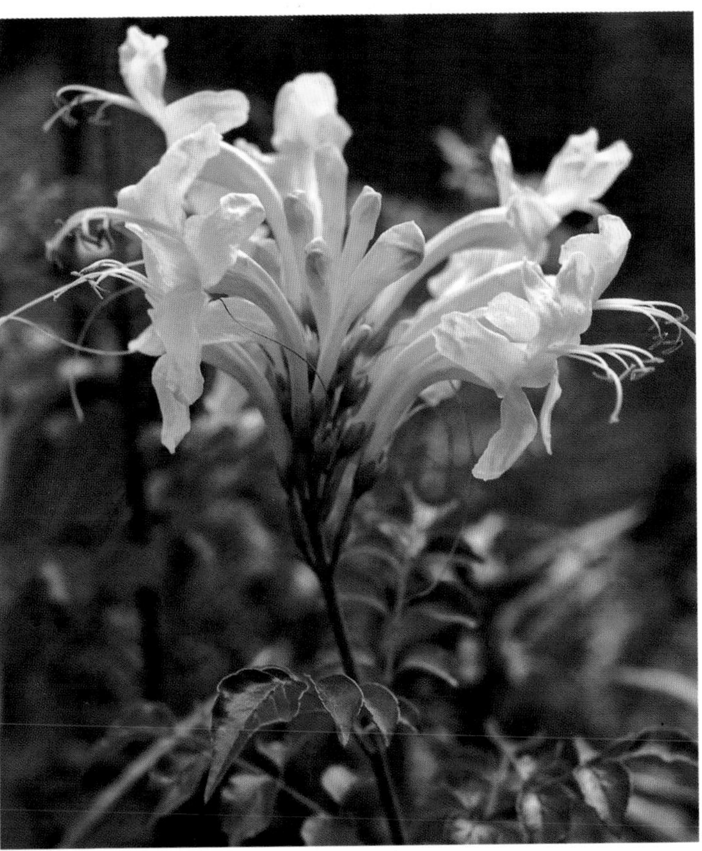

Tecoma capensis 'Aurea'

Climbers

	SPRING			SUMMER			AUTUMN			WINTER			height (cm)	spread (cm)	min temp (°C)	moisture	sun/shade	colours	
Tecoma capensis 'Aurea'				●	●	●	●						370	180	5°		☼		Large yellow flowers
T. stans	●	●	●	●	●	●						●	850	460	5°		☼		Also known as Yellow Bells

☼ *sunny*  *semi-shady*  *shady*

Thunbergia

Black-eyed Susan

A most delightful group of climbers, and of great versatility, ranging from the conservatory-friendly Black-eyed Susan to the towering Bengal Clock Vine. Yellows, blues and reds are exhibited by this group of climbers that originates from Africa and Asia. Most of them are suited for tropical and semi-tropical climates, or for growing in a conservatory in temperate climates.

Black-eyed Susans are named after the dark centres of the delightful yellow and symmetrical flowers. These plants are easy to grow, ideal outside on a small tripod or in a conservatory on a pillar or wall. They are not overpowering and vigorous plants, but are delicate and manageable in small places. There are, however, over 100 species, and some of them are very vigorous growing. Another yellow-flowered, but much bigger, Thunbergia is *T. gregorii*, which is woody and evergreen. The Bengal Clock Vine, *T. grandiflora*, will grow to over 9m (30ft) and will cover the side of buildings with its gorgeous-looking mauve flowers. *T. mysorensis* is one for the conservatory and has long pendulous flowers in yellow and red.

Grow in fertile, well-drained soil in a hot, sunny spot or under glass in a conservatory or greenhouse and keep well watered, ensuring that the plant does not become saturated. Inside, check for red spider mites, scale insects and whiteflies.

Thunbergia mysorensis

Thunbergia gregorii

	SPRING			SUMMER			AUTUMN			WINTER			height (cm)	spread (cm)	min temp (°C)	moisture	sun/shade	colours	
Thunbergia alata				flower	flower	flower	flower	flower	flower				240	60	5°	little moisture	sun		The best for a conservatory
T. grandiflora				flower	flower	flower							910	120	5°	little moisture	sun		Outdoors only in warmer areas
T. gregorii				flower	flower	flower							370	120	5°	little moisture	sun		Outdoors only in warmer areas
T. mysorensis	flower	flower	flower										610	120	5°	little moisture	sun		Suitable for a conservatory

flower · little moisture · moisture · wet

Trachelospermum

Star Jasmine

Readily available from nurseries in full flower, Trachelospermum is ideal for immediate effect. A courtyard garden will benefit from its abundant foliage, flowers and fragrance. It can also be grown as ground cover, so long as the upright shoots are cut off regularly. In temperate climates, for all year round enjoyment grow Trachelospermum in a conservatory.

Star Jasmine is a popular and widespread climber that is grown in a lot in gardens for its pure white and scented flowers. A well established plant will produce an abundance of flowers and plenty of scent, though the plant can take a while to get to this point. It has star-like flowers borne in little clusters, and its tough and slightly glossy leaves are evergreen and ovate shaped. There is a rare variegated leaf form called *T. jasminoides* 'Variegatum'. The best place to grow these is in full sun, with some shade in hottest climates, as they live native in the warmer parts of the Far East. Plant in fertile, well-drained soil and make sure that the plant is well watered. However, water sparingly during the winter months.

Trachelospermum jasminoides

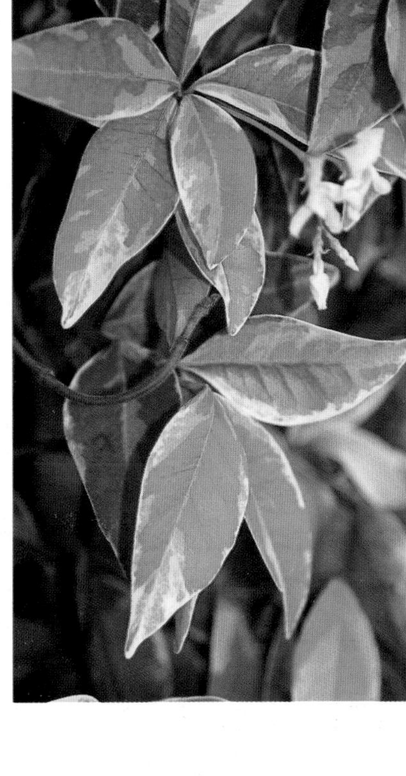

Trachelospermum jasminoides 'Variegatum'

	SPRING	SUMMER	AUTUMN	WINTER	height (cm)	spread (cm)	min temp (°C)	moisture	sun/shade	colours	
Trachelospermum asiaticum					610	90	-5°				Fragrant flowers
T. jasminoides 'Variegatum'					850	120	-5°				Yellow edges to leaves

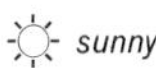  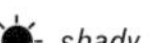

Tropaeolum

Nasturtiums

The common name of Tropaeolum – nasturtium – should not be confused with watercress, which is called by its Latin name of Nasturtium. In this case, Tropaeolum is the Latin name of plants that are confusingly called nasturtiums, and bear no relation to watercress. The best way to get started with nasturtiums is to grow them from seed. Cuttings can also be made from stem tips of favoured varieties and these can be grown on. There are many varieties from which to choose. Grow them as annuals.

Along with the thunbergias, nasturtiums are among some of the most easily manageable climbers for most gardeners. Nasturtiums are also some of the most exciting climbers to grow because they produce results very quickly when grown from seed. Within a few weeks from sowing the seed in a patio pot, they can be up and away on trellises, or if planted in the ground, sprawling as ground cover with thick stems over 2.5m (8ft) long. There is a great range of species from which to choose, though the most widespread is *T. majus*. Two of the most popular varieties are 'Hermine Grashoff' and 'Peaches and Cream'.

Tropaeolum can be grown over an arch or pergola, or grown as ground cover. A much smaller decorative species is *T. speciosum*, that has bright red flowers, and one of the best places to show this off is against a dark hedge such as yew. Many of the tropaeolums have small and fragile stems that often need support, and among these are *T. tuberosum*, with small orange flowers, and *T. peregrinum*, the yellow nasturtium. It can be grown around the base of a potted shrub so that its delicate flowers can intermingle. The variety of colour is so great in nasturtiums that they are useful in enlivening gardens and giving points of single colour or kaleidoscopic colour. They can be used as cascades down steps, around figures, used in hanging

Tropaeolum tuberosum var. *lineamaculatum* 'Ken Aslet'

Tropaeolum speciosum

TIP

During growth, although you have to make sure that the plants are kept well watered, reduce the amount of water once the leaves start to wither, and when the plant is dormant, keep barely moist.

 *flower*
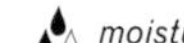 *little moisture* *moisture*
 *wet*

baskets and pedestalled vases, and intermingled among the climbing beans in a kitchen garden. Readily self-sown, they will reliably spring up all over the place the following year, instantly adding colour and form.

The best site in which to grow Tropaeolum is

Tropaeolum perigrinum

Tropaeolum majus

Tropaeolum majus 'Variegatum'

well-drained, moderately fertile soil in the full sun, but with some shade available. Keep them well watered. Watch out for white caterpillars that like to eat the foliage.

	SPRING			SUMMER			AUTUMN			WINTER			height (cm)	spread (cm)	min temp (°C)	moisture	sun/shade	colours	
Tropaeolum majus				●	●	●	●	●	●				300	460	5°				Popular choice to start off growing
T. majus 'Hermine Grashoff'				●	●	●	●	●	●				300	460	5°				Double bright red flowers
T. majus 'Peaches and Cream'				●	●	●	●	●	●				300	460	5°				Interesting pastel shades
T. majus 'Variegatum'				●	●	●	●	●	●				300	460	5°				Variegated leaves
T. peregrinum				●	●	●	●	●	●				370	90	5°				A delicate yellow climber
T. speciosum				●	●	●	●	●	●				300	30	-5°				An excellent mixer for contrast
T. tuberosum					●	●	●	●	●				370	60	0°				Interesting leaf shapes
T. t. var. *lineamaculatum* 'Ken Aslet'					●	●	●	●	●				370	60	0°				Small orange coloured flowers

 *sunny*  *semi-shady* *shady*

Vicia

***Vicia cracca* is a good example of this family of plants which includes the familiar broad bean, a truly upwardly mobile genus that needs a lot of support when it is grown as a climber. *V. cracca* is a familiar sight in the hedgerows and meadows where it climbs through other vegetation. Grown in the more natural or wild garden, Vicia is rampant and gives a strong purple colour to whatever it is grown through.**

As a member of the pea family, Vicia has a natural ability to climb, and it produces its typical leguminous flowers all along one stem. Its fruits are produced in a pod, and can be collected for propagation.

Grow Vicia as an annual. Any type of moist, well-drained garden soil will suffice. Seeds can be sown in compost and grown on in a propagator. Allow space for the plant to develop, and provide plenty of support to help it become established. It is best to grow it through a low shrub in a sunny position.

This plant is ideal for high summer, and the hotter the situation the better, but keep it well watered. Watch out for moth larvae, which delight in chomping through the leaves.

Vicia cracca

Vicia cracca

V

Climbers

 *flower* 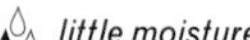 *little moisture* 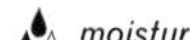 *moisture*  *wet*

Vinca

Periwinkle

Grown as perennials, vincas are an interesting group to have on show in the garden. They are suitable for those wishing to create a natural-looking garden. They are also good for small colourful detail up against a wall, or even in a pot where their stems will overflow the container.

Vincas are smart plants. They have glossy green and evergreen leaves, and are so loaded with poisons that nothing eats them – not even goats! Fortunately, they will only cause minor stomach upsets in humans if they are ingested.

These plants are useful in the garden as they are perennial and produce lots of purple flowers. Vincas perform well in any garden soil type, as well as tolerating both full sun and shade. Plants only need watering before they are well established; after that they generally tend to take care of themselves. If grown at the base of the hedgerow they will climb through and put out their flowers in various quarters. There are a few varieties with different shaped petals and a white periwinkle. Once established, they are hard to eradicate. They can be strimmed and clipped and will still come back with new growth. These climbers are very reliable, very predictable and have extremely pretty flowers.

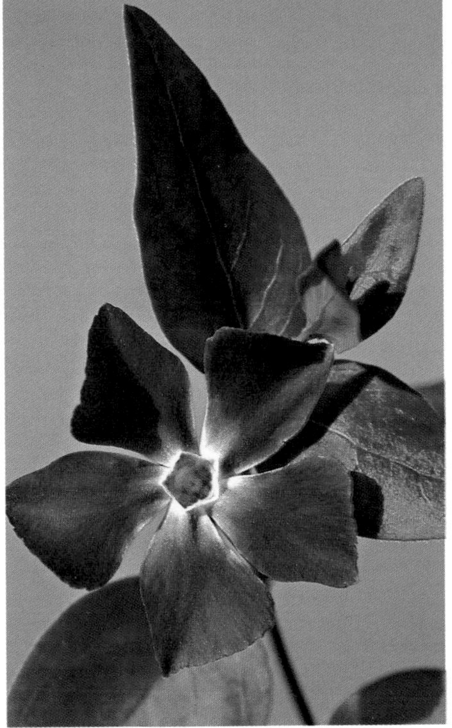
Vinca major

Vinca major 'Variegata' with 7-spot ladybird

V

Climbers

	SPRING			SUMMER			AUTUMN			WINTER			height (cm)	spread (cm)	min temp (°C)	moisture	sun/shade	colours	
Vinca difformis	●											●	30	300	-5°		semi-shady		Lance-shaped dark green leaves
V. major		●	●	●	●	●	●	●					45	300	-15°		semi-shady		Very long flowering season
V. major 'Reticulata'		●	●	●	●	●	●	●					45	300	-15°		semi-shady		Leaves veined with yellow or cream
V. major 'Variegata'		●	●	●	●	●	●	●					45	300	-15°		semi-shady		Attractive cream-edged leaves
V. minor 'Alba Variegata'		●	●	●	●	●	●	●					20	300	-15°		semi-shady		Also known as white periwinkle

 *sunny* 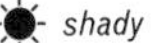 *semi-shady* *shady*

Vitis

Vines

Vines, in their true sense, are reliably good in the garden. They can be grown up walls or alternatively there are forms that are compact and suited to container growth. They can be propagated without too much difficulty from cuttings made from hard wood, or from grafting. They can even be grown from seed.

Grape vines really epitomize the whole world of climbers, being ancient plants that were part of man's early staple diet and vigorous growers to boot. The gardening interest with vines lies not only in festooning conservatories with garlands of grapes, or decorating a pergola with fruit, but also in dark leaved varieties such as *V. vinifera* 'Purpurea', that offer different effects. There are other Vitis species available that are decorative and not edible.

The most popular species of vine is the deciduous *V. coignetiae* that has large green leaves that turn to maroon in the autumn, providing plenty of colourful foliage whenever it is needed during summer and autumn.

Vitis coignetiae

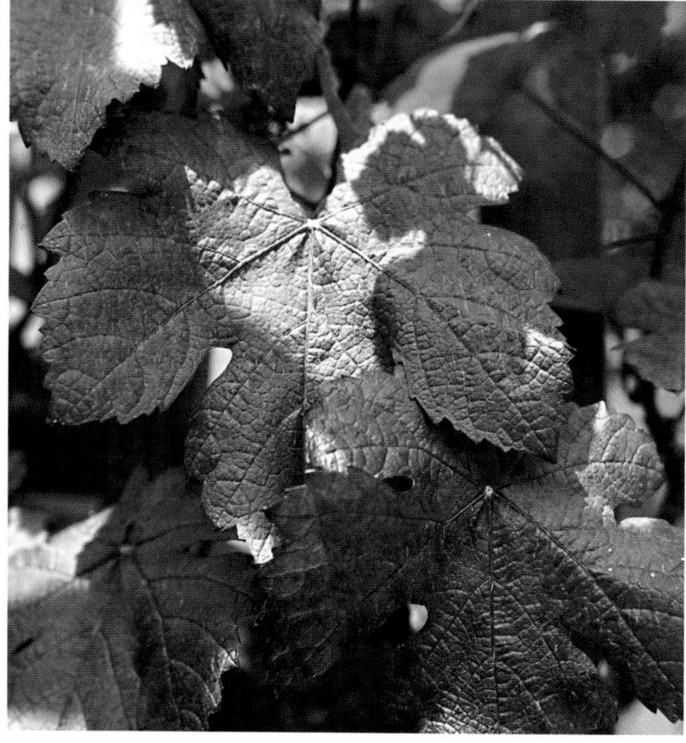

Vitis vinifera 'Purpurea'

Grape vines demand well-drained, preferably neutral to alkaline, humus-rich soil in the full sun or partial shade. Keep this plant well watered to start off with. Prune it back to restrict the growth, particularly if more formal training up a pergola is required.

	SPRING	SUMMER	AUTUMN	WINTER	height (cm)	spread (cm)	min temp (°C)	moisture	sun/shade	colours	
Vitis coignetiae		flower flower flower			1,520	300	-15°	little moisture	sun		Best for autumn colours
V. vinifera 'Purpurea'		flower flower flower			600	180	15°	little moisture	sun		Try the weeping form

flower · little moisture · moisture · wet

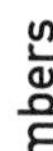

Wisteria

Wisterias are springtime wonders, being so vigorous that they often burst forth in full flower before their leaves have opened. Such is their rush to benefit from spring's early insects for pollination that they seize the chance to flower early on, much to the benefit of gardeners.

Belonging to the pea family, wisterias produce long trusses of flowers in blue and white, depending on the species and the cultivar, and are much visited by bees. Masses of leaves are produced later on and the plant is good for foliage that also changes colour in the autumn to make a spectacular golden glow. Wisteria can grow in most garden soil types, in a combination of sun and shade. Give it plenty of water to start off with, then leave it more or less to its own devices. The plant needs support, if not growing into a tree shape, but check that the stems do not grow into any supporting wires.

The long pods of wisteria are not produced that often, but when they do appear they contain spherical brown seeds. These can be collected and sown. Cuttings can also be taken for propagation. Wisterias are very vigorous and need pruning. They can be pruned back hard and this will produce strong growth the following year. Although generally trouble-free, some butterfly larvae will eat the leaves.

Wisteria floribunda 'Issai'

Wisteria in autumn colours

W

Climbers

	SPRING	SUMMER	AUTUMN	WINTER	height (cm)	spread (cm)	min temp (°C)	moisture	sun/shade	colours	
Wisteria floribunda 'Issai'	✿ ✿ ✿				760	300	-15°		semi-shady		Very vigorous, twining climber
W. sinensis	✿ ✿ ✿				760	300	-15°		semi-shady		Fragrant flowers

 *sunny*  *semi-shady*  *shady*

Troubleshooting

Growing a varied range of plants attracts an equally varied selection of pests, diseases and other problems. The following diagram is designed to help you diagnose problems with your plants from the symptoms you can observe. Starting with the part of the plant that appears to be most affected – flowers, leaves, stems or roots – and by answering successive questions 'yes' [✓] or 'no' [✗], you will quickly arrive at a probable cause. Once you have identified the cause, turn to the relevant entry in the directory of pests and diseases for details of how to treat the problem.

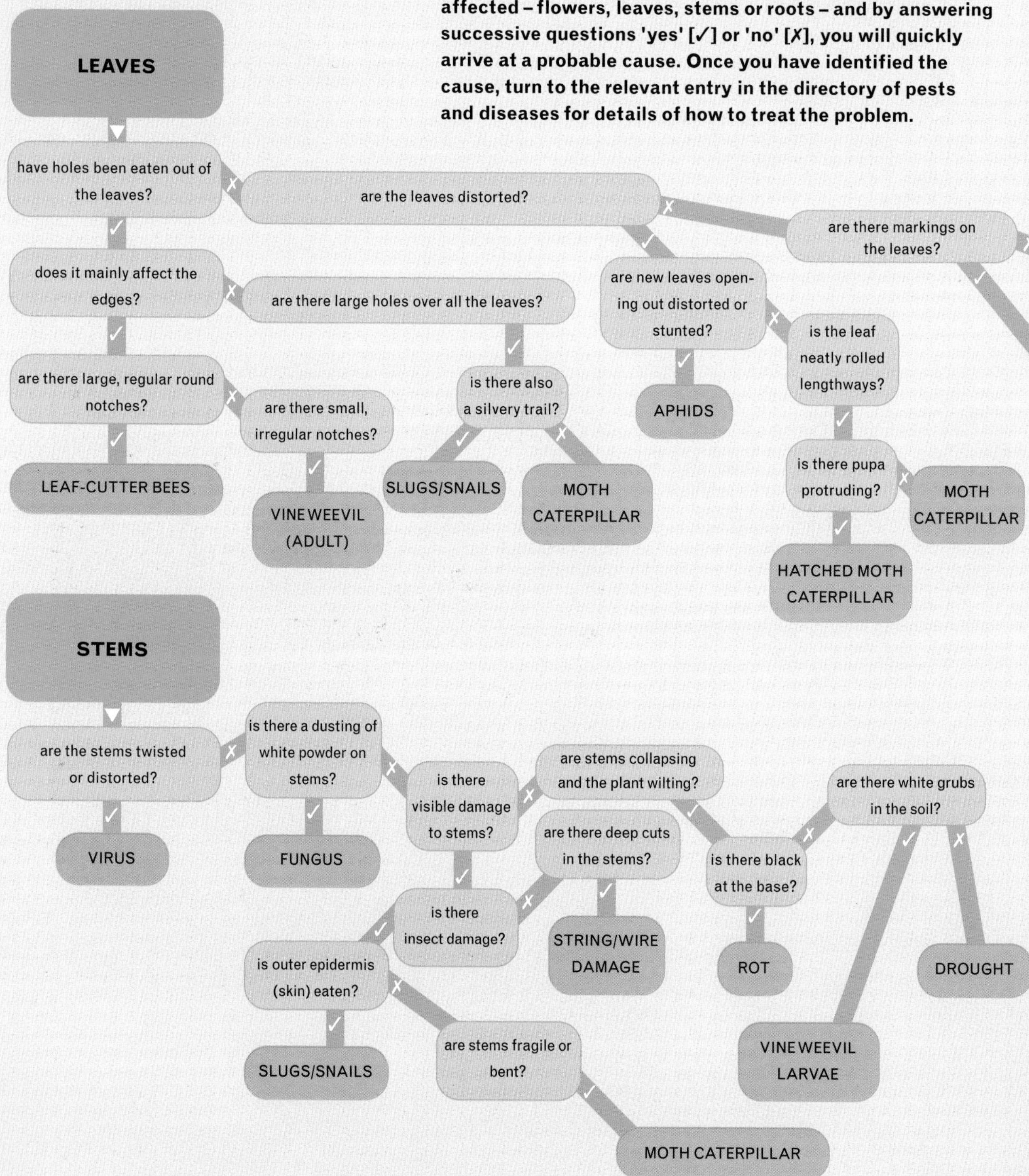

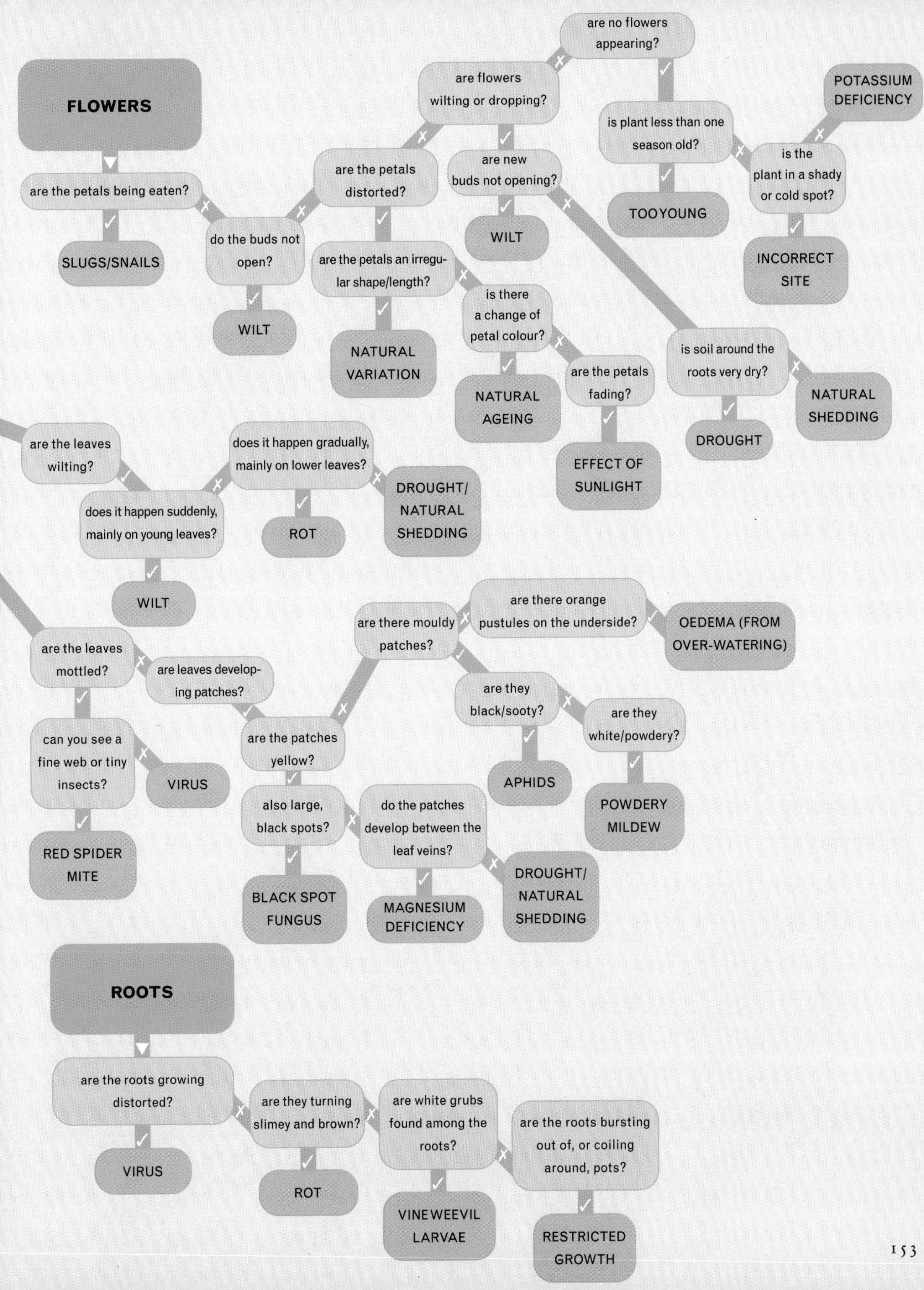

FLOWERS
are the petals being eaten?
SLUGS/SNAILS
do the buds not open?
WILT
are the petals distorted?
are the petals an irregular shape/length?
NATURAL VARIATION
is there a change of petal colour?
NATURAL AGEING
are the petals fading?
EFFECT OF SUNLIGHT
are flowers wilting or dropping?
are new buds not opening?
WILT
are no flowers appearing?
is plant less than one season old?
TOO YOUNG
is the plant in a shady or cold spot?
POTASSIUM DEFICIENCY
INCORRECT SITE
is soil around the roots very dry?
DROUGHT
NATURAL SHEDDING
are the leaves wilting?
does it happen suddenly, mainly on young leaves?
WILT
does it happen gradually, mainly on lower leaves?
ROT
DROUGHT/ NATURAL SHEDDING
are the leaves mottled?
can you see a fine web or tiny insects?
RED SPIDER MITE
VIRUS
are leaves developing patches?
are the patches yellow?
also large, black spots?
BLACK SPOT FUNGUS
do the patches develop between the leaf veins?
MAGNESIUM DEFICIENCY
DROUGHT/ NATURAL SHEDDING
are there mouldy patches?
are there orange pustules on the underside?
OEDEMA (FROM OVER-WATERING)
are they black/sooty?
APHIDS
are they white/powdery?
POWDERY MILDEW
ROOTS
are the roots growing distorted?
VIRUS
are they turning slimey and brown?
ROT
are white grubs found among the roots?
VINE WEEVIL LARVAE
are the roots bursting out of, or coiling around, pots?
RESTRICTED GROWTH

Pests & Diseases

Clematis and climbers are susceptible to a great multitude of diseases and pests; they have tasty leaves and stems, and juicy sap that the pests will seek. The growing parts of the plant – lead shoots, side branches and roots – are often attacked first since the plant has not yet toughened up its cells to beat off predators. The lead shoots of some climbers are differently coloured from the other parts to confuse leaf-eaters where the tastiest bits are. Some plants lay down poisons in their cells as active feeding deterrents (eg. Aristolochia, Solanum), and some have such tough leaves that small insects have no chance eating them (Mandevilla, Monstera).

Vigour is often the key to beating off attacks from pests and diseases. A plant, completely set back by a severe attack from a pest, will send another shoot out of the stem further back, totally disregarding the other stem that has been affected. The potential vigour of a plant switches into play and rescues it. However tasty the leaves, if the plant has enough strength it can overcome these temporary set backs.

Unfortunately, the way so many plants have been cultivated has weakened the stock of many climbing species, especially clematis. Many have completely lost the ability to bounce back and are highly susceptible to disease. This makes it an even greater priority to attend to cultural instructions – not overwatering, for instance, especially in shady areas where fungi will have a tendency to prosper. Wilt is the plague of many a plant, and the clematis hybrids can struggle. If you have a choice between a species plant and a hybrid, go for the species for vigour, and a hybrid for prettiness.

The foliage of climbers is a defoliator's paradise. Aphids succeed in numbers and if knocked out in one place will survive somewhere else. Vine weevils, slugs and snails are all part of the biodiverse field of wildlife awaiting anyone wishing to cultivate a particular genus of climbers. The more vigorous the climber, the better able it is to cope with insect attack.

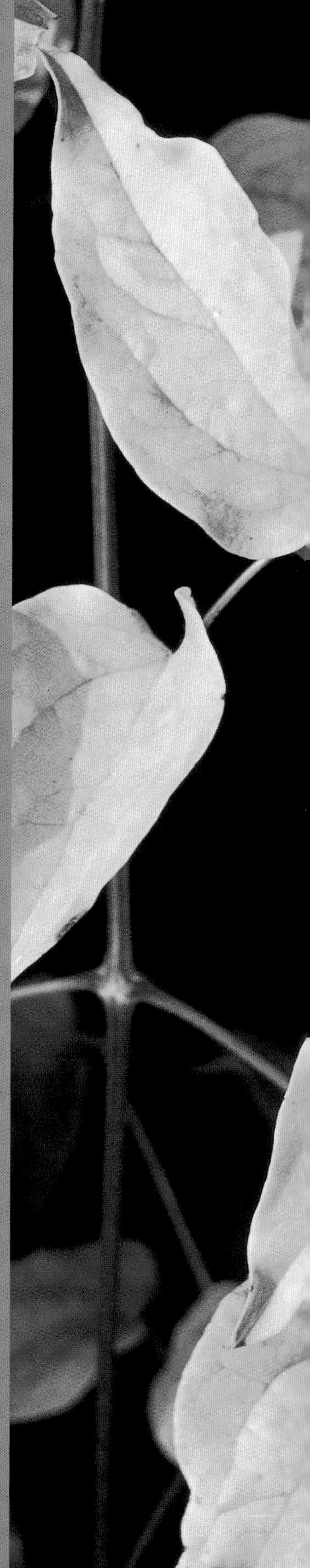

Pests

Moth larvae

There are hundreds of moths whose larvae will eat the foliage of climbers such as roses. Eggs are laid on the underside of the leaf at night, and the larvae will often curl up the sides of the leaf and hide from bird predators while they feed. Such leaves are easy to spot. They can be removed. Mature caterpillars will eat more than one leaf a day and spoil the looks of a lead shoot.

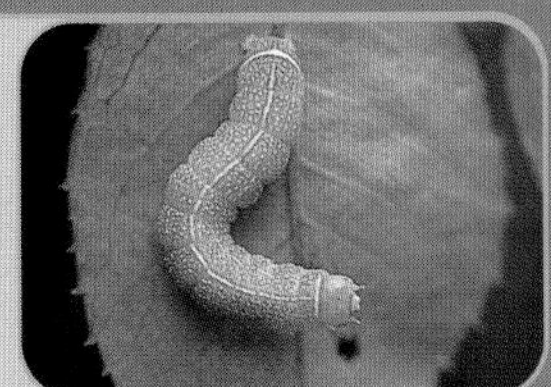

Bee: leaf cutter

There is a large group of bees that cut holes in leaves of plants, and they are called leaf-cutting bees. They are not honeybees and are generally harmless. They fly the cut-off section of the plant back to their nests. The effect on a specimen plant can be major, especially if the plant is for display. If, however, the plant is in an herbaceous border then the effect is neglible and it will not affect the vigour of the plant. Leaf-cutting bees can be more obvious in some areas than others. It is very difficult to prevent their chomping.

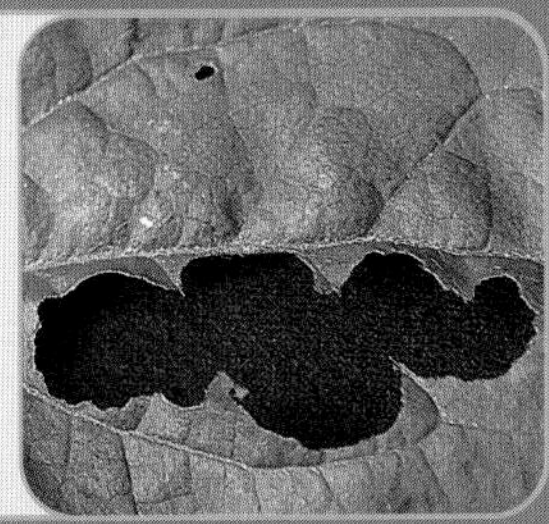

Snails

At night, slugs and snails attack many a climber and clematis, eating their way through flowers, buds, foliage and stems. The traces of their slime trails and faeces taint leaves, and their nibbling on leaves makes the foliage look unsightly with newly created holes and windows. Perennially difficult to control there are many methods to try, including putting down crushed up egg shells, slug pellets, slug pubs and removing them during a night patrol.

Slug damage

The tell-tale presence of a slug's nightly foraging over the flower beds is shown here with the tasty outer epidermis of the clematis stem neatly eaten off and holes in the leaves. There is little to do after the damage has been found. It will weaken the plant and open it up to infection from fungal spores. Best to leave the plant as it is to see whether it is affected. If it is, then that shoot should be pruned out. The problem may have arisen from not weeding the base of the plant and allowing too many weeds or too much mulch to harbour slugs.

Aphids & ants

Aphids are the big problem when growing clematis and other climbers; ants rarely are. There may be colonies of ants in the soil, especially against a brick wall, but they are actually beneficial rather than being a nuisance, as they feed on the aphids. Ants will often be found scurrying around the foliage of plants, as they seek out small prey to eat. Roses are particularly prone to attack from aphids, and ants will help reduce their numbers, thus protecting the plant.

Butterfly larvae

Nasturtium leaves are especially sought after by the Large White butterfly, *Pieris brassicae*, and the Small White butterfly, *Pieris rapae*. *P. brassicae* lay their eggs in clusters, *P. rapae* as single eggs on the leaves. Large White larvae are brightly coloured, unlike those of the Small White that are camouflaged green, matching the leaf colour. Both pest species can be removed from the leaf, or even better is to remove the eggs before they hatch.

Vine weevil

Vine weevil larvae live underground and cause plenty of damage to roots. They are white and about 1cm (½in) long, and they eat the roots of clematis and grape vines, as well as plenty of other garden plants including camellias and rhododendrons. When a young plant wilts and dies it may be because it has lost all its roots to vine weevils. The adults eat as well. They nibble notches out of petals and their presence is often suspected first, before they are found wandering around looking for more plants to attack.

Fungi and Viruses

Multi-headed rose

Certain climbing roses are susceptible to the virus that causes the flowerhead to become double. This is referred to as a multi-headed rose, which is not to be confused with those roses that are either double or have similar sorts of heads. It is impossible to know where this virus will strike and on which variety, but some roses will suffer from this and others will escape. Thankfully it is not a frequent event. There are two main options: simply do nothing and keep the plant (it does not look too bad the way it is) or, more drastically, dig up the whole plant and burn it.

Black spot

Black spot on roses is caused by a fungus. It is very common and is sometimes impossible to avoid. Nursery stock still comes with black spot, though it is always sound advice to ask if there are any fungus-resistant strains that have been developed. Though unsightly it does not always affect the flowering of the plant. Leaves should be removed and burnt. Some areas are more particularly prone to black spot than others.

Leaf virus

There are hundreds of known viruses that can attack the leaves of climbers, and they have different forms and patterns of attack. There is very little preventative action that you can take to avoid a viral attack, since the virus is spread through the air. It is worth asking your local nursery or garden centre for virus resistant stock if available.

Wilt

Wilt is caused by a fungus. It is an insidious disease that affects clematis, especially hybrids. These are less hardy than species clematis and do not have their natural resistance, having become weakened through breeding. Wilt can show itself overnight. The leaves or flowers, or both, will suddenly wilt, go brown and eventually die. Remove all affected parts and burn. Sometimes the plant will continue to grow from the base, some way back from the infection; sometimes the whole plant will die. Either way the plant has an inability to cope with fungus attack and may repeat the process of dying off later in the year, or year after year. If it does that, it needs to be removed. Note the humidity – if it is shady with high humidity, then that area will harbour fungal spores in the air, rather than a sunny, partially shady spot. Give the plant a chance, read the label.

Mineral Deficiencies

Yellowing leaves

Yellowing of leaves is caused by a number of different factors. Firstly, it could be that the leaf is being lost by the plant, and as it dies its colours will fade. Secondly, it may just be its natural autumnal colours. Thirdly, if the plant is starved of water, the green pigments break down showing the underlying yellow to orange pigments. Finally, it could be a mineral deficiency. Magnesium is sometimes to blame for loss of pigmentation as it is the mineral used in pigment manufacture.

Oedema

Oedema or dropsy, as illustrated here, is a condition, not a pest or disease. It reflects a problem with watering. It occurs when the plant has taken on too much water than it needs. This may have happened when the plant was pruned but still kept on its normal watering cycle. It manifests itself by producing unsightly orange blisters on the undersides of the leaves. Keep an eye on how you are watering a houseplant – for it is here that it is more likely to strike – and reduce accordingly. If the problem affects a single leaf, then remove the leaf.

Decreasing Invertebrate Pests

Insect refuge

You will never defeat insect pests, but you can at least help to reduce their numbers and effectiveness. One way is to encourage beneficial insects such as the many species of solitary bees and wasps that like to breed and shelter in tubes. In nature they might choose the old tubes of umbeliferous plants, but you can provide card and plastic tubes cut up and fitted into a plastic tube. This can then be suspended in a tree or wedged in a hedge, choosing a reasonably dry place. The insects are also useful for pollination.

Earwig trap

Trapping for earwigs can be quite effective by placing an upturned pot filled with straw on a stake and locating this near the climbers that are affected. Earwigs are nocturnal pests that crawl around (a few fly) and eat flower petals, thus disfiguring the plant. During the day they gather in dark places with plenty of thin spaces, and by packing the pot tightly with straw it makes an ideal daytime resting place. At regular intervals the pot can be emptied of its contents and the earwigs can then be disposed of.

Natural remedies

It is always a good idea to grow colourful wild flowers right next to your climbing plants. This also applies when you are growing crops and do not want their harvest to be devoured. In the picture, runner beans are grown alongside the African marigold (Tagetes). Many flying insect pests are drawn to the bright yellow colour of the marigold and feed on the flowering plant instead of the crop. Other wild flowering varieties to try next to your clematis or climber include Calendula marigolds, Zinnia and Cosmos, which also provide colourful lures.

Index of Plants

This index lists the plants mentioned in this book by their common names where applicable and their Latin names in all other instances

General Index

Acknowledgements

The author would like to thank the following people for their assistance with the preparation of this book: Dame Miriam Rothschild of Ashton Wold; Hopleys of Much Hadham; Joyce and Brian Hargreaves of Playden; Mary and Peter Griffiths of Hooe; and Vera and Tony Orsbourne of Sellinge, and all those who have allowed access to their gardens.

Photographs for this book were taken in the UK, Germany, Holland, the Mediterranean littoral, Florida, California and America's deep south, Brazil, Costa Rica and Mexico.

Many climbers of garden merit are described in this book, and the author acknowledges The Royal Horticultural Society for its contribution to highlighting horticultural quality, and for its inspirational gardens and books.

The publishers would like to thank Coolings Nurseries for their cooperation and assistance with the photography in this book, including the loan of tools and much specialist equipment. Special thanks go to: Sandra Gratwick; Garry Norris; Ian Hazon; and Brian Archibald. Coolings Nurseries Ltd., Rushmore Hill, Knockholt, Kent, TN14 7NN.
Tel: 01959 532269; Email: coolings@coolings.co.uk; Website: www.coolings.co.uk